Salford. He was a founder member of Joy Division and New Order and now DJs throughout the world as himself and also with the revived Haçienda. He lives in Cheshire with his wife Rebecca and has three children, Heather, Jack and Jess.

www.fac51thehacienda.com
www.peterhook.co.uk

Further praise for *The Haçienda*

'The Hacienda was, as Hook says, in many ways the perfect example of how not to run a club – if you view a night-club as a money-making business. But if, like the baggy trousered philanthropists Factory, you see it as a altruistic gift to your hometown and a breeding ground for the next generation of youth culture, it was, accidentally, purposefully, shambolically, anarchically, thrillingly, scarily, inspirationally perfect'
Observer

'Hook himself is revealed as a born anecdotalist, firing off quips, pithy asides and self-lacerating *mea culpas* like a scatter-gun. The sections that interweave his narrative – DJ playlists, club nights, minutes of board meetings, pie-in-the-sky company accounts, a roll call of artists, including Madonna, who appeared at the club – are often revealing or evocative, but it is the author's own voice that makes the book such a compelling read'
Sunday Times

'A testosterone-scented transcript of ripping yarns . . . There's much fun to be hand within – much like the Hacienda itself'
Q Magazine

'Peter Hook's book lifts the lid on the true story behind the legendary Manchester club that brought acid-house music to the north and changed the face of UK clubbing forever . . . Hooky's memoir offers a real insight into what actually happened'
Independent

'A delightfully pungent, occasionally depressing, generally very funny insider's account'
Metro

'Chiming perfectly with the nation's twin fears of urban violence and monetary collapse, this book should become a cautionary tale of modern times'
Mojo, 5 stars

'A worthy addition to the archives of glorious rock follies, recounted with candour, humour and gob-smacking detail'
Scotland on Sunday

'It's to Hook's admirable credit that he can reflect on the fifteen years when the Hacienda lurched from disaster to disaster, via calamity and catastrophe, with only modest rancour and a great deal of gallows humour'
Uncut

'It was the party to end all parties – fourteen years of hedonism and debauchery which revolutionised nightlife in Britain forever, created acid house and the concept of clubbing as we know it. The Hacienda not only transformed Manchester but had a phenomenal impact on the UK as a whole, an impact which continues to shape our lives today'
Scottish Daily Record

'A hugely candid work'
Word

THE HAÇIENDA
HOW NOT TO RUN A CLUB

PETER HOOK

POCKET BOOKS

LONDON • SYDNEY • NEW YORK • TORONTO

First published in Great Britain by Simon & Schuster UK Ltd, 2009
This edition published by Pocket Books, 2010
An imprint of Simon & Schuster UK Ltd
A CBS COMPANY

1 3 5 7 9 10 8 6 4 2

Simon & Schuster UK Ltd
1st Floor
222 Gray's Inn Road
London WC1X 8HB

www.simonandschuster.co.uk

Simon & Schuster Australia
Sydney

A CIP catalogue record for this book is available
from the British Library.

ISBN: 978-1-84739-177-3

Typeset by M Rules
Printed in the UK by CPI Cox & Wyman, Reading, Berkshire RG1 8EX

Dedicated, with love, to my mother, Irene Hook

Rest in Peace:
Ian Curtis, Martin Hannett, Rob Gretton, Tony Wilson and Ruth Polsky,
without whom the Haçienda would not have been built

Contents

The Guilty Parties

It was always going to be a problem.

In fact, when it was suggested by Claude Flowers that I write my Haçienda memoirs in 2003, the first thing that came to mind was that famous quote about the sixties. How if you remember them then you weren't really there. That's how I felt about the Hac.

So, I was going to need a bit of help, and putting this book together has been a lot of a combined effort. It was Claude who got the ball rolling and prompted me to remember a lot of stuff I thought I'd forgotten, while Andrew Holmes provided those very important 'in between bits' and sorted out all the paperwork.

Anything you like, I'll take the credit for. Anything you don't, blame them.

Hooky

Foreword

What a fuck up we made of it.

Or did we? Sitting here now, I wonder. It's 2009 and the Haçienda has never been more well known. Still doesn't make any money, though; no change there then. This year we celebrate twenty-one years of acid house; we are holding Haçienda nights all across the UK and now have merchandise deals for CDs, T-shirts, shoes, postcards, posters, a bespoke bike frame, even a fine-art project with Ben Kelly, for God's sake. Where will it end?

It looks as though our manager Rob Gretton was right about the Haçienda, just as he was at Ian Curtis's wake when he told us, 'Joy Division will be huge in ten years' time.' It wasn't much solace at that particular moment but he was spot on: Joy Division *were* huge in ten years; also in twenty and thirty years. Still are. A great testament to the music.

Then, when the Haçienda was going bankrupt – voluntarily, I might add – he said we needed to buy all the names from the receiver.

'Why?' I said.

'They'll be worth something in the future.'

'No chance,' I thought. 'Who cares?' I was sick of it.

He cared. No one else was interested so I gave him the money to buy them. Since then it's been a long, hard process of tying up the loose ends. A never-ending stream of registrations and legal fees. Battles with bootleggers. But we got there in the end. Now, hopefully, we can enjoy the fruit of our labours . . .

But I need to tell you the story first, don't I? I need to tell you how the Haçienda changed the shape of clubbing in England. Where it all went wrong, and how what should have been a dream come true became a cautionary tale.

And what a story it is. Because while there's a lot about the Haçienda that shouldn't be glorified – the gangsters, the drugs, the violence, the cops – there's also the stuff of legend: the fact that it was a superclub before the term had even been invented; that it was the birthplace of acid house in the north and the home of Madchester, two musical movements that went round the world; that it was the scene of too many great nights and gigs to recall – not that you were in any state to do so.

When the Haçienda opened, Factory and New Order had no experience running a commercial enterprise; we just invested our money and trusted the staff, mostly our friends, to sort everything out. Bad idea. Your friends are your friends not because they're good at business. But we learned that the hard way. We learned everything the hard way.

At first the band didn't have much to do with it; in fact, for the first few years, I didn't even use my connection with the Haçienda on a social level let alone get involved in the business side of things. I never felt involved with it, to be honest. I got free entry and that was about it (some members of the band couldn't even manage that sometimes); so even though I had this club – this huge club costing me a fortune – I was reluctant to go, and certainly didn't feel like it was mine any more than a punter would. None of us did. But, as the problems mounted, we had to get more and more involved, until by 1988 I was helping to run it. By that time the mess was too big for anyone to fix.

And I was into it too far to get out.

As my accountant likes to tell me, I won't appreciate how much cash the Haçienda lost until I stop earning money.

'Then,' he says, 'it'll hit you like a juggernaut.'

We once worked out that, from the time it opened in 1982 to when it closed in 1997, each punter through the door cost us £10. We wasted *that much* through bad management and sheer stupidity. As far as we were concerned it was history we were making, not money. But if I'm ever skint I'll walk around Manchester asking everyone to give me my tenner back.

I'll split it with the rest of them, honest.

Beyond that, though, I'll never truly know how much money we lost on the Haçienda because our record label, Factory, New Order's partner in the club, never accounted to the band, ever: no one has ever told us how many records we sold in England or around the world.

So Tony Wilson, who owned Factory, wouldn't say, 'New Order just sold 100,000 albums in China, here's your cut of the profits.' Instead, the way it worked was that Rob would collect royalties by walking in and demanding cash off him. If Tony had money, he'd give it to him; if he didn't, he'd tell Rob to fuck off. That was how they ran it. With our approval, I should add. It was chaos, punk, anarchy and we loved it.

Well, back then we did. Now, of course, it just seems like a good old-fashioned mess. Because not only were we never told how much we'd earned, but also we weren't told how much we'd invested in the club, either, so we can't know for certain how much of our earnings were used to keep the Haçienda afloat. It was clearly a huge fuck-up, but one we'll never be able to gauge the true scale of.

As my mother Irene used to say, God rest her soul, 'You'll never get into trouble if you tell the truth, our Peter.' Let's see if she's right. This book is the truth, the whole truth, and nothing but the truth.

As I remember it.

Hooky, 2009

Prologue: One Night at the Haçienda, 1991

It's eleven o'clock Saturday morning and I'm well up for it. Tonight's going to be a big night for me. I'm doing the door in my own nightclub, the Haçienda: the biggest, wildest place in Manchester, in England and possibly the world. Where everything happens and anyone who's anyone goes to do it.

The reason I'm working the door? We've had a lot of trouble.

We always have trouble, of course, but complaints against the doormen have reached an all-time high. The management say they're on the take and that they're worse than the gangs. The police say they're worse than the gangs. Even the gangs are saying they're worse than the gangs . . .

Meanwhile, the punters are unhappy, too, and there's been a growing number of complaints from women. Violence against male punters isn't exactly unheard of, but now they're saying that girls are on the receiving end as well. A couple have been slapped, one punched, one beaten up, and we've had a few women alleging that what started as a 'drug search' ended with a bouncer's hand down their knickers.

I guess that's really what's made me take action and why it's different from all the previous moaning about the doormen: these complaints have come from girls.

Talking about it to our head doorman, Paul Carroll, he brushed it off: 'You can just as easily be stabbed or shot by a woman as a man, Hooky. And anyway, if you're so fucking clever, why don't you come and do the door?'

'Right, right,' I said, 'I will. Saturday. You're on. You can rest easy now, Paul. I'll be in charge!'

Fucking hell. Me and my big mouth.

I get the kids ready to take back to their mam's house. One of the only good things about being a single parent, you always have a babysitter for your nights out. It's unusual for me to go on a Saturday, though. I'm more of a Friday person myself: I prefer the music. Saturdays at the

Haçienda tend to be a bit too dressed-up for me, both sartorially and musically. But tonight I'll make an exception.

I phone my mate Twinny and arrange to meet him in the Swan in Salford about one p.m. 'Get stocked up,' he says, 'and I'll bring the little fellas.'

Dutifully I phone my friend in Chorlton and arrange a couple of Gs of Colombia's finest for later.

Now, what does one wear to do the door? Hmm.

Black?

Too formal.

Something casual?

No authority.

I know, the linen look: Armani suit, white shirt, brown loafers – my summer 1991 outfit. Sorted.

God, I'm excited. Scared, mainly. It's amazing how fucking dangerous the door can be, from roaming hordes of Leeds stag-nighters to gangsters demanding respect by not paying and scores being settled both on the way in and on the way out. It all happens on the door.

I get ready, shower and dress. My mate Rex brings me a glass of milk. He's an old Joy Division follower, from when he was fourteen. It was he who tested our flight cases, by which I mean we'd lock him in one and roll it down five flights of stairs. He's ended up homeless for a while, so he's living with me and engineering in my studio for me too.

'Best to line your stomach for later,' he says in his strong Blackburn/Chorley accent.

He's a good lad.

So, at last I'm ready. Phone the cab, do a cheeky line of speed and off I go. Man, these Withington cabs stink; I'm worried about my suit already. I stop off at my friend Wendy's house to collect. God bless her, nice to see her. She's a lovely lady. We chat for a while, she does me a sample and I'm off again.

Salford, here I come. Home sweet home. The Swan is an old pub on Eccles New Road opposite Weaste bus depot, an area I've hung around my whole life. I was born in Ordsall and grew up there; when we formed the band in 1976 we used to practise upstairs at the Swan – it cost us 50p each, as long as we bought a pie and a pint. That was just before we got our drummer, Steve. Then Ian moved back to Macclesfield and we mainly practised there.

That room above the Swan is still there, exactly the same. The pictures on the wall have been taken but the fag smoke has framed them perfectly forever. It's very weird seeing it. I go up every now and then – if I'm melancholic about how Joy Division ended up, or pissed off with New Order. Reduces me to tears sometimes.

But not today. Today I'm buzzing.

I walk into the pub. Twinny's already here and he's with Cormac, Beckett and Jim Beswick, who gets the first pint. A nice tradition: you never pay for your first drink. Well, it's only fair as I'll be paying for them all in the club later.

There's an electricity about the place. It's just a normal, shitty, working-man's pub but it seems too alive today. What's going on? I look around to see what's happening. There's a crowd in the snug – unusual for one in the afternoon.

'Ah,' Twinny laughs. 'It's the Salford lot . . .'

Turns out a bunch of the younger gang members had recognized two 'dealers' as undercover cops – a man and a woman posing as a couple – and arranged to meet them here, away from prying eyes, to quietly do a 'deal'. Then a team of armed gangsters had turned up and hemmed the coppers in.

I go over and have a look. Trapped like mice tormented by a cat, the poor bastards are pinned in the corner being made to smoke a joint while someone else chops out a line of whizz for them, insisting that they take one each. Fuck, what a joke. Seems they'd been recognized from court and there you go: some light entertainment for the afternoon. Fuckin' hell. Half an hour later the coppers are being sent on their way, stoned, whizzing, with a kick up the arse. See you.

We settle down to an afternoon's hard drinking. Two more pints and I'm feeling very brave about later.

'There are problems at the Haçienda,' I tell the lads. 'I'll get to the bottom of it, sort it out.'

The lads are laughing. The afternoon passes in a haze of dope smoke, beer and prawns from the market. 'Rhythm is a Dancer' on repeat. Beckett almost sells a car he's got outside but ends up having a fight with a prospective customer who's over-revving the engine. He even gets in the guy's car and screws that, too. Hilarious. As daylight fades, I'm offered everything from racing bikes to CDs, washing machines, fags, sweets and holidays in Turkey . . . Fuck, it's endless. And before you know it it's nine p.m. Time for work. The lads go home to get changed while I head for the Haç.

Manchester's buzzing now. Loads of people everywhere. God, I love this city. I'm so proud to be part of its heritage. As I round Deansgate and head up Whitworth Street I can hear the bass drum from our sound system, the one I helped to build. I love the way it makes the Haçienda's windows rattle. Who'd have windows in a nightclub? Us. Yes, fucking twelve of them, all rattling away like a manic mullah calling us to worship.

I step out of the car. What, no red carpet?

'Where have you been, cunt?' asks Paul Carroll.

Charming. I walk inside, towards the bar, get in the corner. I work out an arrangement with Anton, the bar manager, where he'll bring me a treble vodka and orange every twenty minutes. A Special. I neck the first one. Then go to the door. Right, bring it on.

I check the regular doormen: Damien Noonan, Pete Hay, Stav, several others I know to nod to. Good lads. They're smiling. Why are they smiling?

Because *fuck* this is boring. I'm whizzing me tits off. It's very slow between nine and eleven p.m., just a few trying to get the cheap 'before ten thirty' admission, but we're sold out – always are. We've sold 2000 tickets in advance at our bar, Dry, earning us a £2 premium on each. (Don't tell the licensing, ha ha: we're only meant to hold 1400.)

Then, as we near eleven p.m., there's a definite change of atmosphere. It becomes more intense, hectic, like things are about to spin out of control. Suddenly everyone's rushing, shouting, wide-eyed. The pubs are closing and they all want to get in before the queues form. Our bouncers are good, working well, recognizing a few teams as small-time gang members and refusing them entry, no trouble. A couple of drunks are sent on their way with a slap.

'This is going well,' I think sipping my third drink, watching someone arguing about the guest-list. He's claiming to be Barney's brother; there'll be maybe five or six brothers and sisters for each member of New Order coming every night. This one gets knocked back and slinks off with his tail between his legs.

Then it happens.

One of the doormen is talking to a mate. I'm watching, and suddenly his mate disappears. He's collapsed. It goes off like the Wild West: he's been poleaxed, stabbed in the head. The guilty little fucker's run off down Whitworth Street before our lads can do anything. The door-man cradles his mate's bleeding head in his hands.

'John. John . . .'

Fucking hell. But then he's up and OK. Shit.

Another Special comes my way. I grab Anton and say, 'Better change that to every ten minutes, mate.'

My heart's pounding. Then it goes off again. One of the older Salford lot is arguing about paying the £2 guest-list that we have to charge in order to keep the licence. He's got one of the very well-known Salford girls with him and it's going off royal. Damien is shouting, then they're all shouting. Fuck me. Suddenly two lads from a rival gang take the hump at being refused and kick off. They're turfed out but retaliate by throw-ing bottles at the door. Our doormen give chase and catch them on the pool-hall steps, unfortunately for them. It took me a while to realize that there are two sorts of bouncers: the big, muscly ones we all know and love; and the little ones built entirely for speed, like cheetahs and lions.

But fuck me. I've had enough of this.

I check my watch. It's ten forty-five. Paul Carroll and Damien are laughing their bollocks off as I skulk away, tail between my legs.

Welcome to the Haçienda.

I slide in through the famous doors, with their number 51 cut into them, wipe my feet on the '51' mats. The place is packed now. Throbbing. Nearly full. Do I know everyone in here? Suppose I do.

I make my way towards the bar. Seems to take forever. I'm fucked. I need another drink. I meander to my corner at the bottom of the stairs where Ang Matthews and Leroy Richardson, the co-managers, hang out. I take in the club and watch the shenanigans. The bouncers are all laughing now about my evening as a failed doorman. Bastards. Stav comes by – to 'watch over' me, he says. But I know that the true reason is that he loves to share my drugs. He's always getting a bol-locking off Paul for it, but we have a laugh.

I settle in. This is a good night, a constant parade of people: friends, acquaintances, drug dealers, load of girls. I'm single but never can quite seem to make it with the women here. It's more like they come for the occasion, not to cop off. Either that or I'm too fucked to get it together.

It's really busy, so I go up to the DJ box. I bang on the door for what seems like an hour and finally Graeme Park lets me in.

'Oh Hooky, here's a tape for you,' he says, handing it to me.

'Great, a Saturday-night tape from last weekend,' I think. 'That's nice of him.' (Not realizing that he's been selling them on the quiet for £10 each and making anywhere from £500 to a grand extra per night. Good lad; wish we'd thought of that.)

Where were we? Right, lines. I bring out the charlie, chop them out and survey the madness: a sea of hands, flashing lights, all moving to the *bang, bang, bang* of the bass drum. God, it's good to be alive and owner of the Haçienda. What happened earlier? Can't quite recall.

Later I rejoin the lads. My mate Travis is in.

'Go and get us a couple of little fellas from the Salford lot,' I say, and he departs to the back corner of the alcove. The alcoves are famous. Each contains a different gang, but we call this particular one Hell. This is gang-member territory. If you wander in without approval you get a slap and you're shoved back out if you're lucky. Even I won't go in there without Cormac or Twinny. My lot are in the second alcove; they're the older Salford lot. Travis takes ages, comes back with a bloody nose, says they've fucked him right off.

I'm angry now, so I storm off to the door to get hold of Paul or Damien, shouting, 'How long do we have to put up with this . . . ?'

Nah, nah, nah. I sound just like a baby, screaming, 'These little fuckers . . .'

'All right,' they say, 'don't be a twat all your life.' Laughing again.

'Right,' I say, and storm back in to see Suzanne, who runs the kitchen.

'Your bucket's over there,' she says.

This is one of the perks of management: because we didn't put in enough toilets when we built the bloody place, you can never get a piss. Plus I always get hassle in the bogs anyway. So I'm the proud user of a Hellmann's mayonnaise bucket with my name on it, which stays in the kitchen. It's a source of great hilarity to everyone (until they want a piss too). Suzanne actually has a great trick of getting people to hold it for a while. Then, when they ask 'What's this for?' she tells them. Ah well, little things please little minds.

However: 'No, I don't want a piss, love,' I tell her. 'Just a breather.'

Refreshed, I come out and spot a line of bouncers wielding baseball bats, all of them heading for the back corner. They go in and beat the shit out of some gangsters.

Turns out that they'd twatted a pot collector. Damien is very protective of the staff.

So far tonight there have been four fights, one gun pulled, two bar staff assaulted, rough justice in the corner, drug dealing and drug taking on a normal scale (well, normal for us).

I leg it back to the DJ box to lie low. That ploy is soon forgotten, though, as I join everyone else in being too wasted to notice anything. We're 'avin' it LARGE. The police come in to look for bail-jumpers, or spot drug use, and to generally give us grief. They're escorted around by the bouncers, who protect them from the crowd. The cops depart, covered in spit and beer but they don't retaliate. (Why do it at all? I wonder. Call that a show of force?).

Next the licensing authorities are in and they're hassling Ang. At one forty-five a.m. you're supposed to stop serving, then you have fifteen minutes to collect all the open drinks. This, of course, causes the most trouble because no one wants to hand over their drink – especially the gangsters, who openly defy the rule. So the licensing go mad and threaten us.

After what seems like a few minutes – too soon – it's two a.m. and it's all over. The music is switched off, the crowd are screaming: 'ONE MORE TUNE. ONE MORE TUNE.'

I tell Graeme, 'Go on, put another one on.'

He asks, 'Are you sure? Does Ang know?'

As licence-holder, Ang is responsible for making certain we close at the proper time, or the authorities will bust us for operating after hours.

'Of course. She said it's fine,' I lie. 'Anyway, I'm the boss, ha ha.'

He puts it on Candi Stanton: 'You Got the Love'. I throw my hands up in the air (just like Candi does in the lyrics) and sing, 'I know I can count on you.' What a twat.

The place erupts.

'Yeah,' I'm screaming. '*Yeah, yeah, yeah.*'

The moment quickly ends. Ang bursts into the DJ box and cuffs me. Graeme ducks and Ang flicks the needle off the record.

'The licensing are in,' she shouts. '*Fuckin' pack it in.*'

Oops, I've done it again. I may be co-owner of the Haçienda, but I'm not the one who runs it. Thank God. I step out of the booth feeling rather sheepish and follow her downstairs.

'Can we have a lock-in, Ang?'

She presses something heavy into my chest. 'No. Here's a bag of beer, now fuck off,' she says.

Charming.

I rally my mates and we head for the door, me clutching the bag. We're all in a Ford Escort, two doors, heading to an after-party in Salford. We set off. The driver's tripping.

'Don't worry,' Twinny tells me, 'he's not had a drink.'

We break out the cans, pop a cassette into the stereo, turn the volume up and settle in. We stop at the lights on Regent Road. Oops, there's a cop car behind.

A cop car. Christ, we've got more drugs on us than Hope Hospital. I'm trolleyed.

'Keep calm, it's OK,' says the driver, but when the lights change he doesn't pull forward; he's tripping so much he's gone colour blind.

Suddenly the cops are on us and it's all over. We're kicked out of the car and our driver is carted off. How are we going to get home?

Just then a copper turns to me. 'Are you Peter Hook from New Order?'

'Oh, fuckin' excellent,' I think, 'he's a fan.'

I smile, look him in the eye, and say, 'Yeah, that's me. Can you drop me off in Salford please, occifer?'

'Fuck off,' he says. 'I always preferred the Smiths.'

We set off to walk home. Coming down, I'll stay at Twinny's tonight, get back in the Swan for the first pint at eleven. Drown my sorrows.

Top night.

1980

'If you like Deep Purple you'll love these lads'

I started going to pubs and clubs when I was fifteen, in 1971. They didn't check ID back then, so if you looked tall enough – as in over five feet – you could get in and they'd serve you. My first time, I went to a pub on The Precinct, Salford called the Church with my old schoolmate Terry Mason, who I've known since I was eight (and who later became Joy Division's manager for a while).

We were suedeheads, post-skinheads. I walked up to the bar and ordered a pint. I was shaking. 'Can I have a beer?'

Bartender: 'Do you want mild or bitter?'

Me: 'No, beer.'

Fuck knows what he gave me, but I was pissed as a fart on one pint. When I came out I slipped and fell in some dog shit, which was a great start to my drinking. Quite prophetic, really: you start drinking, you end up in the shit, ha ha.

I'd met Bernard Sumner at school. Back then we were best friends and would be for years. When we left school I worked in the Manchester Town Hall, which was where I first DJed: I played records at the Town Hall Conveyancing Department's 1975 Christmas party, would you believe.

Barney and I used to go to all the regular clubs in Manchester, where the traditional crowd was girls in high heels and boys in white shirts and jackets, a pretty formal dress code and not really what we were about. By 1977 punk had happened but the shows were isolated events and once the concert was over it was back to normal. People like us still didn't have anywhere to go dressed how we wanted – nowhere regular, anyway. Even back then, all those years ago, the need for the Haçienda was there. The seeds were being sown.

After seeing the Sex Pistols perform at the Lesser Free Trade Hall in 1976, Barney and I formed a band. First we were called Warsaw, then

Joy Division. When the line-up settled, it was me on bass, him on guitar and Ian Curtis as our lead singer. After one or two drumming turkeys had been and gone, we found Steve Morris; he'd answered the advertisement for a drummer that Ian had put in a record shop in Macclesfield.

Now, because we were in a group, we were able to go to a lot of places and perform for fun, which was great for us, of course, but still the Manchester club scene stayed unhealthy. My favourite spot back then was Rafters. Barney, Terry and I used to go there to see gigs promoted by Music Force, which was run by Martin Hannett, who played bass in a band called Greasy Bear. He shared a booking agency in Manchester with another guy named Alan Wise (who had an undeserved reputation in those days as the fastest promoter in the north, because of his habit of legging it with the money, ha ha). Together with Alan Erasmus (a local actor and band manager) they put shows on all over the city. That's how Martin started his career, before he began producing records for Joy Division.

Next, Alan Erasmus, along with the Granada TV presenter Tony Wilson, began hosting club nights they called the Factory, where Joy Division also performed.

The Factory club night was held at the 800-capacity Russell Club, Hulme, or 'The Russell Club, Royce Road, Moss Side' according to designer Peter Saville's now-legendary mis-spelt poster. The first, on 19 May 1978, featured performances from the Durutti Column and Jilted John. Joy Division first played on 9 June that year, while Iggy Pop and UB40 would appear at subsequent events, their presence testifying to the night's growing kudos and popularity. Later that year, Factory Records was formed to release A Factory Sampler, a four-track EP mainly produced by Martin Hannett, who had made his name producing the Buzzcock's seminal Spiral Scratch EP. It featured contributions from Joy Division, the Durutti Column, John Dowie and Cabaret Voltaire, and was catalogue number FAC 02. (The poster was retrospectively awarded the FAC 01 number at Saville's insistence, kicking off an idiosyncratic cataloguing system.) Run from a first-floor flat at number 86 Palatine Road, Manchester — the home of Alan Erasmus — Factory Records was at first made up of Erasmus, Tony Wilson and Saville, with Gretton and in-house producer Martin Hannett joining as partners during the first year.

It was the two Alans, along with Tony, John Brierley (owner of Cargo Studios in Rochdale) and the designer Peter Saville who launched Factory (although John bowed out early, opting for a one-time pay cheque rather than a share of the company), while Rob Gretton, who DJed at Rafters on most nights, became our manager. It was a very small, insular community.

I'd been aware of Tony's family since childhood, way before I actually met him. His father was a tobacconist with a shop on Regent Road in Salford where my mum used to take me to buy her cigarettes. I would have been about three, but even at that age I could see how outlandish Mr Wilson looked compared to everyone else. He wore really loud dicky bows and a suit, completely out of place for Salford in the 1950s. I later had the shock of my life when I realized that Tony was his son.

Tony stood out as a maverick among television personalities of the time. He looked scruffy, had long hair and seemed at odds with the rest of the TV industry, which was very square. He got away with it because of his flamboyance. He was very much like Martin Hannett. Similar demeanour and appearance. Both of them dressed strangely, like an early Dr Who.

Tony was quite religious, which seemed at odds with his character. He was slightly older than us and it felt like he belonged to a different generation. We viewed him as the boss, not as a peer, and he was very much the man in charge. Every so often he'd check on the band to see how we were doing and I suppose we felt a bit in awe of him because of his success on television: he was a star, a very important mover and shaker, whereas we were just working-class tossers from Salford. There were many times when his passion gave us the drive to carry on. He was very enthusiastic and always worked hard for things he believed in. Ideas were his thing but, as in time I came to realize, he glossed over details. They slowed him down, bored him and stopped him from moving on to the next project, which he had this compulsion to do. It meant he'd put things in motion then leave others to implement them without always ensuring that the lieutenants he put into place were qualified. The day-to-day running of Factory he'd leave to Alan, but Alan (unlike Tony) wasn't very good with people – I suppose they comple-mented each other's weaknesses in that respect.

Our manager Rob was one of the most important people in my career. At the time he began working with us, Rob lived in a one-room bedsit in Chorlton and had no money. He was a working-class Wythenshawe boy from a big family with a sister and two brothers. Relationships mattered a lot to him. Throughout his life he needed to be surrounded by people he felt close to. Loyalty defined him, as did his love for Manchester: promoting anything to do with the city was his passion.

Rob hated his previous job, working for Eagle Star Insurance in Manchester. Getting rich didn't motivate him as much as freedom and enjoying himself. He disliked being told what to do, so he looked at ways of making his own opportunities. First he promoted events at the Oaks in Chorlton (I went to see Siouxsie and the Banshees there, and still have the ticket), then he started his own record label to release a single by the Panik – funnily enough stealing our then drummer, Steve Brotherdale, from us – plus he worked as a roadie for the band Slaughter and the Dogs, as well as producing and creating a fanzine for them.

Rob and Joy Division ran parallel to one another for some time before he decided to ally himself with us. If anything, we came into his scene, rather than him into ours, because by the time we started playing Rob was very involved locally. Like I say, it was a real community back then. There were no fortunes to be made or lost so financial concerns never came into our minds. We played for a sense of achievement and in the hope of one day educating and changing the world. It felt like us against the establishment. We were rebels.

Rob – like virtually everyone associated with Factory – was raised Catholic (Bernard and I were the only two Protestants on the label, which became the source of some amusement). Rob didn't talk much about his spiritual life, although he and his girlfriend Lesley Gilbert once worked together at a kibbutz in Israel. He'd decided to take a year off for it, but got pissed off because of the scary, oppressive atmosphere and the fact that he had to carry a rifle. He never did well with mechanical things and he disliked guns – I'm surprised he didn't accidentally shoot Lesley, or himself.

The band didn't have much to do with Lesley. Perhaps it's because Rob did his level best to keep our professional and personal lives separate. He didn't like girlfriends (or, as in Ian's case, even wives) coming to shows. To him, what happened backstage stayed there – and a lot of what went on wasn't particularly compatible with family life. Rob structured things so that we could be different people on the road; it became a bit Jekyll and Hyde.

I remember we were forever looking for places to play. At the Factory Records' New Year's Eve concert in 1979, Joy Division performed, along with the Distractions and another Factory band, Section 25.

Earlier that afternoon Tony told Rob, 'Buy some cans of beer and we'll sell them to everybody for 50p each.'

And so during the sets Rob stood behind the bar, hoping to earn some cash on this scheme. Of course, nobody had exact change in their pockets and he didn't think to set up a till. In the end he muttered, 'Fuck it, let's just give it away.' Which is exactly what he did.

We often used to go the Ranch, which was owned by Foo Foo Lammar – Frank, to his friends. A nice guy, he was a female impersonator, a forerunner to Lily Savage, and with the Ranch and Metz he was one of the club owners who paved the way for the Gay Village. Every Thursday night was punk night: members of the Buzzcocks, Slaughter and the Dogs, the Drones, Manicured Noise and everybody else who played punk music in Manchester congregated there. You did have to be careful, though: right-wing Teddy Boys from God knows where would sometimes come down and lie in wait for us. Pub-and-clubland was still a dangerous place to be, wherever your allegiances lay.

Joy Division used to play at the Ranch, too. On one such occasion we'd already tried our luck at a talent night at the Stocks in Walkden near where I lived in Little Hulton. It was one of those nights where acts who wanted to be signed up performed in front of 'judges' (the bloke who ran the agency and his mate), who then decided whether or not they had potential. Before we went on Ian got a treat when he accidentally walked into the dressing room where the singer before us was getting changed and he saw her tits. He was made up about that.

The guy who introduced us, a proper old-school compere, said, 'How do you want to be introduced, lads?'

We said, 'Um . . .' and looked at one another.

He said, 'Well, what are you like?'

We said, 'Uh . . .'

With no articulate answer from us he introduced us with the immortal words: 'If you like Deep Purple you'll love these lads.'

We trudged on and did two songs. The power kept cutting off

because we were tripping the limiter. A coach-load of old ladies from Farnworth all had their hands over their ears. We absolutely bombed. Needless to say we weren't seen as 'having potential' and weren't signed by the agency. We were so wound up by the whole thing. Once we'd we thrown our gear in the back of my old Jag Ian said, 'Come on. The Ranch is open. Let's go and play there.'

So we did. They let us set up and play and we went down a storm. Those were the days.

Despite the Electric Circus closing in October 1977, by 1978 the Punk scene had really grown and there were gigs all the time. The only thing that stopped us going out every night was cash: one or two shows a week was our limit. When we could afford to go out, though, we were spoilt for choice: Rafters, the Ranch, the Factory nights at the Russell. There were gigs all over the city. One venue, called the Squat, had been taken over by hippies and all the punks used to go there; any passing group could set up and play. It was great for a time, a really good scene, but by the following year it had splintered with both the Ranch and Rafters closing to punk.

Out of ambition and necessity we expanded our territory. Joy Division pretty quickly became quite successful, so we performed not only around Britain but also in Europe. We felt so happy to be liked for what we did as musicians, we played anywhere that asked us; then, as the money came in and bigger concert promoters hired us to play, we earned enough to quit our day jobs. Everything seemed to be moving forward in the best possible way: Rob was running our careers, Martin Hannett was producing our records, Pete Saville designed the covers (convinced in his own mind that people bought our stuff because they loved his art rather than the music), Factory released it all, and we felt like we were really on our way.

By early 1980 plans were afoot for us to tour the United States. By now we'd released one album, *Unknown Pleasures*, with another one, *Closer*, already recorded.

All that came to an end when Ian killed himself, right before we were to fly to America. Personally, of course, we were heartbroken. Professionally, we were back to square one. As you can imagine, it was a tough time – but that's a story for another day.

Anyway, we picked ourselves up and Barney, Steve and I decided to keep going. We called ourselves New Order. Barney became lead singer; we toured as a three-piece, with the songs from the album that would become *Movement*, and after a while Steve's girlfriend, Gillian Gilbert, became supplementary guitarist and keyboardist.

If you liked alternative, underground and non-mainstream music in 1980, you read the weekly music papers and listened to John Peel. Indeed it was Peel, a huge Joy Division supporter, who first announced the death of Ian Curtis to a nationwide audience. Weeklies Melody Maker and the NME were on strike (the NME would return from its six-week break on 14 June with an Ian Curtis cover), so it was left to Dave McCullough in Sounds to provide the music papers' sole contemporaneous obituary, almost a fortnight after his death. In purple prose somewhat derided at the time, he ended by saying, 'That man cared for you, that man died for you', reflecting the impact Joy Division had made in a relatively short space of time. Already beloved of the NME and Peel, their appeal was to go mainstream with the release of 'Love Will Tear Us Apart' shortly after Curtis' death. With the singer's suicide lending an already jawdropping song extra poignancy, it propelled Joy Division up the singles charts and on to daytime radio, pulling Unknown Pleasures back into the mainstream album charts (it was already a permanent fixture on the fledgling independent charts, which had been introduced in January 1980), where it reached a high of number 71 in August that year – sales having been further boosted by the release of Closer, a number-6 album, in July.

Interest in both albums was of course generated by Curtis's death but also by a mini-controversy surrounding Peter Saville's sleeve for Closer, which showed a photograph of the Appiani family tomb and was thought to be a tasteless reference to the suicide. A bemused Saville pointed out that the design had been finalized prior to Curtis's death.

As the year closed, the profile of Joy Division was at a high from which the band has never truly descended, and sales were giving Factory the financial health it would need to even consider projects on the scale of the Haçienda.

It was the year of the Iranian Embassy siege, of the continued reign of the Yorkshire Ripper, the ever-present threat of nuclear war and the assassination of John Lennon. A dark, moribund year.

MANCHESTER CLUBS THAT INSPIRED THE HAÇIENDA

The Oasis Club

On Lloyd Street, the Oasis was 'the north's largest coffee bar and rhythm club' and ran during the early 1960s when it hosted all of the era's big bands, including, of course, the Beatles. Towards the end of the decade it fell out of favour and its audience drifted towards the Twisted Wheel. After that it became Sloopy's, then Yer Father's Moustache.

The Twisted Wheel

The original Twisted Wheel opened in Brazennose Street in 1963 playing R&B and chart music before moving to Whitworth Street in 1966, where it gained a reputation as one of the country's best soul clubs, staging all-nighters and hosting soul stars of the day, including Edwin Starr and Ben E. King. It was in a feature about the club that the term 'Northern Soul' was coined. However, after problems with drugs the club closed in 1971. It reopened on Whitworth Street in 1999.

Pips

Based on Fennel Street, Pips had six dance floors during its heyday in the late 1970s, and was a hangout for many of those would go on become the big names in the Manchester music scene. You could expect to see Peter Hook, Barney Sumner, Ian Curtis, Morrissey, Peter Saville and Johnny Marr among the David Bowie and Bryan Ferry clones and for this clientele the big draw was the Roxy Room, where they could hear DJ Dave Booth of Garlands fame playing David Bowie, Lou Reed, Iggy Pop and Kraftwerk. Later, in January 1978, Joy Division's first concert as Joy Division was at Pips. Bryan Ferry, after a Roxy Music gig at Belle Vue, was famously refused entry on the grounds that he was wearing jeans. The club closed at the beginning of the 1980s but later reopened as the infamous Konspiracy.

The Reno

The Haçienda's first resident DJ, Hewan Clarke, cut his teeth playing jazz-funk at the Reno on Princess Road in the late 1970s. It was situated below the Nile, which played reggae, and together the two clubs had a fearsome reputation – as opposed to Rafters and Rufus in town, where the sounds were more commercial. A mainly black crowd would pack Renos until five or six in the morning, the air heavy with weed smoke, the dancing serious. Clarke later moved to Fevers, where he came to the attention of A Certain Ratio and Tony Wilson . . .

Legends

Based on Princess Street, Legends took over from Pips as Manchester's main alternative hangout, especially on Thursdays. Wednesday nights, however, were presided over by DJ Greg Wilson, who, later, would also play a major part in shaping the Haçienda's musical direction, educating audiences in a new, streetwise sound that was set to drag dance music out of the cul-de-sac offered by disco: electro. More on him later.

Electric Circus

Along with the Ranch and Rafters, the Electric Circus was one of the main Manchester venues to cater for the interest in punk after the Sex Pistols played the Lesser Free Trade Hall in June and July 1976; indeed, the Pistols would play this Collyhurst Road venue twice, further inspiring the home-grown bands. Around these venues, and with the Buzzcocks at its core, grew what we know today as the city's post-punk scene (though everybody simply called it punk at the time), championed by journalists such as Jon Savage, Paul Morley and Mick Middles and spawning labels Rabid, Factory and New Hormones. Rob Gretton was part of the same scene. As DJ at Rafters, he had first seen Warsaw there, then later saw them again as Joy Division at the Electric Circus; he subsequently approached Barney at a Manchester phone box with an offer of management and got the job. The Electric Circus closed in October 1977, though Rafters, the Ranch and the Oaks in Chorlton remained popular punk venues.

The Factory

Wilson and Erasmus hosted the Factory nights at the Russell Club/PSV in Hulme between May 1978 and April 1980, before the idea of the

Haçienda was mooted. As host of Granada TV's *So It Goes*, Wilson was able to entice those who appeared on the show to play the Factory: thus the night hosted performances by a mouthwatering who's-who of big names, including Public Image Limited, Pere Ubu, Magazine, Suicide, Iggy Pop, Stiff Little Fingers, the Pop Group, the Specials and Dexys Midnight Runners. Those who attended speak fondly of the Red Stripe, the goat pasties and the reggae played by the in-house DJ between bands. There was, they say, a very palpable sense of a scene developing.

It's fair to say that many of those involved in the early stages of planning for the Haçienda expected it to be like the PSV, which was quite dark and stuffy, had low ceilings and complied with most people's expectations of a music venue. The Haçienda was to overturn all of those expectations — indeed, it would be instrumental in creating many new ones.

1981

'Double bubble'

It took a long time for New Order to recapture the ground we lost when Ian died, not to mention the emotional fall-out, which still gets me now. There isn't a day that goes by when I don't think of him and what we achieved. But by 1981 we were climbing the ladder again. We were touring and visiting great clubs in amazing cities. We liked the sleaziness of the places we discovered in New York, places like Hurrah, Danceteria, Tier 3 and Eden. In Manhattan at the time you'd find these steamy, sweaty, dark, low-end clubs, like the Fun House, a black-painted box that just felt vibey, and then you'd go into ritzy places with art installations, like Studio 54 and Area.

But whenever we returned it was to a Manchester scene that was still pretty stagnant. So it was, then, that Tony and Rob came up with the idea of opening their own place – they'd been impressed by what they'd seen in New York, and promoting the Factory nights at the Russell Club had gone well.

At first New Order didn't really listen. We were concentrating on making music. Eventually we were forced to pay attention because whenever we'd get into conversations with Rob the club would always be his main subject. It got so it was all he'd talk about. His pitch centred around the notion that people like us deserved somewhere to social-ize; and this club would serve that need. He insisted that, as Manchester treated us well, we should give something back. (All very altruistic, of course, but we didn't realize that he meant to give the city *everything* we had, financially and emotionally.)

He told us the club would cost around £70,000. Being a small label with limited overheads, Factory possessed some capital, which could be invested – money from the sale of Joy Division records, presumably – so the label would pay half. The other half would be paid by New Order and would be tax-deductible as an investment.

What? We couldn't believe it. £35,000. We were musicians living on £20 per week. Where the hell was this fortune going to come from?

'We'll use our profits from the sale of *Unknown Pleasures*,' he replied. He had this habit of pushing his glasses up his nose when he spoke. 'We'll put that in. It'll be a great investment – and on top of that we'll finally have somewhere to go to. Double bubble.'

Mind you, if the money really was to come from the sales of Joy Division records, then Debbie Curtis – Ian's widow, who received his share of band revenue – needed to be declared a partner in the club. But she never was. Rob left Debbie out of it by naming New Order, not Joy Division, as partners and stating that the money came from the sales of New Order's records. However, I'd imagine revenue from both bands was used to pay for the club: if you think about it, Joy Division had at the time sold more records than New Order, so it's only logical to assume that they served as the primary income.

Either way, we'd agreed to fund a club.

A new face had joined the Factory team by then. He was Howard 'Ginger' Jones, a local promoter who had impressed Rob by promoting a successful New Order gig at the Manchester Students Union. In conversation with Rob Gretton he'd said that one day he hoped to run a nightclub in the city that would provide an alternative to the Manchester raincoat-brigade scene. Gretton, who recognized a kindred spirit when he saw one, hired him virtually on the spot. Ginger's task: to find a venue. One of those initially considered, then dropped, was the Tatler Cinema Club, but it was too small. They settled on a carpet warehouse on Oldham Street (near what would eventually be Dry), which was perfect. The purchase fell through, but the team were suitably fired up about the club and rushed into looking for another place. They found the International Marine Centre – a huge open space which was part of a building on the corner of Whitworth Street, not far from the Russell Club. Little more than a disused warehouse, it nevertheless fired the imaginations of Jones, Wilson, Gretton and Erasmus. Factory took the lease. Notably they didn't buy the building, just took the lease. A mistake that would come back to haunt them.

As plans began to move forward, Mike Pickering came aboard. He was a friend of Gretton, having met him years ago, aged sixteen, when the two Manchester City fans were being chased by Nottingham Forest fans at an away game. 'I just jumped in a garden and hid behind a hedge and he did the same thing,' said Pickering. 'That was it then. We were best mates.'

In 1979 Pickering had relocated to Rotterdam, where he lived with Gonnie Rietveld. Together they formed the band Quando Quango and hosted nights at a squat in a disused water works. There he began DJing ('Chic and Stacey Lattislaw'), as well as inviting Factory bands to play, having stayed in touch with Gretton.

Those who made the trip included A Certain Ratio, the Durutti Column, Section 25 and New Order – the latter's second performance after the death of Ian Curtis. It was there that Gretton told Pickering about the Haçienda.

Gretton had legendary powers of persuasion. It is said that he was able to talk people into performing pranks on his behalf: pushing people into swimming pools, or trashing bars. So he had no problem talking Pickering into returning to the UK to take care of booking acts for the Haçienda. With the site still 'a pile of rubble', according to Pickering, he was back in Manchester preparing to launch a club that had yet to be built.

Rob and Tony wanted it run like a seven-days-a-week members' club. They imagined that if someone popped into town they could stop by and get something to eat, have a cup of coffee or a beer. Furthermore, it could be somewhere you could go wearing whatever you liked. No dress code. Before it accomplished anything else, our place changed the face of clubbing in Manchester on that level because other clubs soon realized they needed to adapt.

Now all we needed was a name, which came from Tony. He'd got it from *Leaving the 20th Century: The Incomplete Work of the Situationist International*, a book published in 1974 as a limited edition that became something of an underground classic. It featured essays from a magazine called *Internationale Situationniste* that said society had become boring, and that the only way to put everyone back on track was to create jarring 'situations' by combining all types of art, including architecture. Rob and Tony saw the club as a means of doing so. Situationism was their thing, not mine, although some of the concepts stuck with me and the people around us.

And you, forgotten, your memories ravaged by all the consternations of two hemispheres, stranded in the Red Cellars of Pali-Kao, without music and without geography, no longer setting out for the hacienda where the roots think of the child and where the wine is finished off with fables from an old almanac. That's all over. You'll never see the hacienda. It doesn't exist. The hacienda must be built.

Ivan Chtcheglov, 1953

Tony picked up on that last phrase, 'The hacienda must be built', which became his call to action and gave us 'hacienda'. To that was added a cedilla – so legend has it, in order that together the c and the i looked more like the number 51, which was to be the club's catalogue number – and we had our name: the Haçienda.

'Punk had levelled the ground,' said Peter Saville. 'It had burned for about eighteen months and all of us involved in that moment were wondering what you then build. There was a strong feeling that it was a post-revolutionary moment and that you had to then build the future. The Haçienda must be built was a great statement for that moment in time.'

However, Saville didn't feel able to design the club. He was shown around the yacht showroom by Gretton and Wilson and was stunned by the space and flattered by the offer, but ultimately thought it a job more suited to Ben Kelly, of Ben Kelly Design.

London-based Kelly was a veteran of the punk years, having been at its epicentre: he was one of those arrested during the Pistols' infamous Jubilee riverboat escapade; he spent the night in the cells and was later given a two-year suspended sentence. He had designed the shop front for Malcom McLaren and Vivienne Westwood's legendary Seditionaries clothes shop on Kings Road, where anarchy shirts, bondage suits and parachute tops were available to London's punks – a more fashion-conscious bunch than their Manchester contemporaries. He'd also designed the Glitterbest office, HQ for McLaren and the Pistols, then was asked to make their Denmark Street rehearsal rooms habitable. (Upon arriving there for the first time, he found himself being chased down the street by the Pistols' drummer, Paul Cook, who was wearing just a pair of underpants.) Next he was asked by Steve Jones to do some work on his West Hampstead flat. The brief: 'I don't care what you do, as long as it impresses the birds.' It worked – Kelly recalled seeing most of Hot Gossip leaving Jones's bedroom one morning. So, for Factory, his punk-rock credentials were impeccable.

Kelly and Saville had already collaborated on the sleeve for a single by Orchestral Manoeuvres in the Dark (an ex-Factory band who have since moved to Virgin, where Saville had links), plus a Section 25 release for Factory. Work on the Haçienda would be an altogether more complex and three-dimensional task.

'I got on a train and went to Manchester to be met by Howard 'Ginger' Jones in a red sports car,' Kelly told journalist Miranda Sawyer. 'We went to this place and Mr Wilson was there, Mr Erasmus was there, we walked round it and Tony Wilson said to me, "Do you want the job?" And I said, "Of course I want the fucking job."'

His first task was to deal with the often conflicting desires of the Factory people, with their imaginations sparked by trips to New York nightclubs: the Fun House, Hurrah, Danceteria, and Paradise Garage. Gretton and Wilson had returned from these trips full of adjectives like 'dark', 'intense', 'sleazy', while the New Order contingent had been seduced by the half-lit corners and sense of mystery they'd encountered.

Yet, as Gretton was also keen to stress, the club had to be much more than a disco. It needed to be a venue and a club, an idea taken from the huge three-storey set-ups they'd discovered on their travels, where fans of both dance music and rock music were catered for on different floors or in different rooms. The trouble – as would later become painfully clear – was that this just wasn't a concept that existed in the UK at the time, despite the good work and forward motion of New Order.

Meanwhile, Wilson and Gretton each had opposing ideas about where the stage should be situated. Gretton proposed it be located at the far end, where the bar went; Wilson wanted it along the side, where it eventually ended up. Gretton and Pickering were alive to the possibilities of dance music, of DJs and discos; Wilson more comfortable with live music. Then there was the fact that the Haçienda needed to act as a meeting place, so would be open during the day. Gretton said later that he'd wanted the club to be a place in which to 'ogle birds', and in this respect it was a brief not dissimilar to that provided by Steve Jones – the difference being that Gretton was half-joking and, as journalist John McReady wrote, 'in truth it had more to do with his secret artiness, and the need of a shop to talk shop in.'

So, at the last count, it needed to be a disco, a venue, a bar, a café, a restaurant, somewhere to ogle birds and a place in which to trade ideas and inspiration . . .

The truth was that nobody really knew what the Haçienda was or what it should be, though in typical fashion Wilson would later spin this fact, *calling it a 'community service', 'a space where things can happen, a place where people can meet.'*

One thing that was certain and propaganda-free was the collective desire to give something to Manchester, to inject something into the city – whatever that something might turn out to be. All were horrified by the Beatles model: you make it, go to London and spend your money there. The Beatles' Apple HQ on Savile Row was the antithesis of the Factory way.

'The difference is Manchester,' said Wilson. '10CC, for example, made a load of cash and built Strawberry Studios in the early 1970s, so when Factory came on stream we had an international recording facility just around the corner from us. Similarly, New Order make a pile of money and together with a load of other people they're able to build the Haçienda . . .'

This isn't to suggest that Rob and Tony stood on equal footing. From early on, everybody recognized the club as being Rob's baby. As Tony put it, 'The Haçienda was Rob's idea because nowhere else in Manchester would let him DJ, so he had to open his own club to do it.' (Actually, Rob never DJed there; he preferred to watch the girls and get drunk.)

I don't think Tony would have even tried it without Rob's backing. Rob was intimidating, a huge physical presence in the early days. He was what you'd call a bit bullish, to be frank, and he took advantage of our smaller natures to railroad us into going along with lots of things.

They incorporated the business as FAC 51 Limited. Ironically it was also then that I realized what a rip-off lawyers' fees could be. Our solicitor charged us £5,000 for registering the company, when in fact the fee to do it yourself was £175. FAC 51 was the Factory Records catalogue number that Tony assigned to the club. It was a limited-liability company, which gave us as shareholders a degree of personal protection because it meant that creditors couldn't come after us personally and seize our assets. There was a legal barrier between our personal lives and our lives as the directors of the Haçienda. This was good because one of the most important conditions of having a limited company is the filing of annual accounts. If the company fails to do this, the directors of the company will be prosecuted, the company itself can be dissolved, and assets can become property of the Crown. Even if an accountant is used, the ultimate responsibility of filing the accounts lies with the directors.

Try to remember this. It'll all come back to haunt us, believe me.

Now, talking of accountants, we had a right one.

Prior to 1981 Rob had an accountant for the band who'd been chosen because he had experience with other groups. But things didn't work out so, around the time we were going to open the club, we moved to another accountant: Keith Taylor.

He didn't have any other clients like us; I think his other clients were two newsagents in Cheetham Hill. But for some reason Rob and Tony decided that Keith was the man to run the accounts not only for the Haçienda but for Joy Division, New Order and Factory too. Keith was Jewish and I think Rob and Tony liked the fact that we had a Jewish accountant while at the same time were being accused of being fascists because of the names Joy Division and New Order (which some people incorrectly said we used in reference to fascism) and the fact that another Factory band, A Certain Ratio, had used Nazi imagery on one of their sleeves. Keith always used to drive up to meetings playing the German national anthem, 'Deutschland, Deutschland Uber Alles', in his car, laughing. Maybe he was thinking of the fees?

Keith did stand up and say that he believed the Haçienda was being run badly – he insisted that it was overstaffed and not profitable, and that the staff were overpaid (which was all true) – yet we came to regret hiring him. He didn't seem to have the skill or experience for the job and I felt he caused us loads of problems and made lots of mistakes.

Gradually, the affairs of New Order, the Haçienda and Factory became entwined with each other on every conceivable level and this happened without any of us in New Order noticing. We stayed on the periphery of it all – which was odd, not to mention foolhardy, considering the amount of money we had at stake. We were only consulted about what went on at the club when it slipped into dire financial straits. The rest of the time we were allowed (or encouraged, more like) to keep our noses out, which was fine by us. We were too busy getting pissed and travelling. We were never even interested in what we made from record and gigs, when that's the first thing we should have asked. Even Barney, who could be notoriously 'careful', didn't bother about how much money was at stake. It was *boring* and we wanted to leave it to Rob. That head-in-the-sand attitude is the only reason we all agreed to go along with it. The only people we have to blame are ourselves.

It still all seemed so surreal. The first time Rob took me to see the building that became the Haçienda it still had yachts in it. I walked around the interior with him going, 'This is where the bar is gonna be . . . This is where the stage is going to be . . .' and me saying, 'Yeah!' as if I shared his passion. But deep down I wasn't interested.

I should have been.

NEW YORK CLUBS THAT INSPIRED THE HAÇIENDA

Area
Open from 1983 to 1987, Area was famous for its 'themes': 'Night', 'Surrealism' and 'Gnarly', for example. The themes changed every six weeks or so and were created by well-known artists of the era so attracted a significant celebrity following.

The Loft
David Mancuso is often credited with giving birth to modern dance-music culture at parties held at his Broadway apartment. Begun in 1970, they were invitation-only and held for a love of the music, creating a scene – mainly gay, black and Hispanic – that also included clubs such as the Gallery, Salvation and Sanctuary. Insiders included legendary DJs Frankie Knuckles and Larry Levan, who were introduced to the art of mixing. Knuckles relocated to Chicago where his residency at the Warehouse was to give the world house music. Levan stayed in New York and opened the Paradise Garage.

The Paradise Garage
Like the Loft, the Paradise Garage was not open to the general public and did not serve food or drink. Instead the hedonistic scene was fuelled by amphetamines, quaaludes and LSD. Music was paramount, and Levan played an eclectic selection with the emphasis on dance-ability: you'd be just as likely to hear the Clash's 'Magnificent Seven' as Sylvester, while performers included Grace Jones and Madonna. The club inspired many a visiting Brit – including Paul Oakenfold, who would help kick-start acid house in the south of England, and the Factory crew, who would do the same in the north.

Danceteria
Based on 21st Street, Danceteria was *the* New York club between 1980 and 1986 and was equally influential on the Haçienda. DJ Mark

Kamins was the main draw, and it was seeing him at work that would eventually inspire Mike Pickering to shake up the Haçienda's musical policy (more of that later). Another favoured hangout of Madonna, the Danceteria was used for the nightclub scene in *Desperately Seeking Susan* and featured four floors playing hip hop, post-punk, disco and chill-out in a wild, Bacchanalian environment.

Hurrah

A focal point for the city's punk and post-punk scenes in the early 1980s, Hurrah was the base for Ruth Polsky, who was talent buyer there before moving to Danceteria. Polsky was crucial when it came to breaking UK post-punk bands in the US and was a major figure in creating the Manchester–New York connection; therefore she was important in the birth of the Haçienda. She had booked the May 1980 Joy Division tour and had also booked A Certain Ratio. They, along with Tony Wilson, spent about six weeks in the city in 1980, recording ACR's debut album and absorbing the nightlife. There they came into contact with ESG, hip, young stalwarts of the club scene, who opened for ACR then recorded with Martin Hannett, forging yet another lasting link between Factory and the Big Apple. 'That was us taking a bit of New York back to the UK,' said ACR's Martin Moscrop. 'and it's the same with New Order. When they came to New York, they were still sort of in the rocky phase. But they started getting more dance-orientated. We were both taking New York back to Manchester.'

Fun House

Fun House at 526 West 26th Street reached its height in the early 1980s and was where John 'Jellybean' Benitez – later the boyfriend and producer of Madonna – made his name as a DJ. It was to Fun House in 1983 that producer Arthur Baker took an early version of New Order's 'Confusion' for Benitez to test on the crowd – to an overwhelmingly positive response.

Roxy

Based at 515 West 18th Street, the Roxy was open from 1978 to 2008 and was initially the main competitor to the legendary Studio 54. At one point it had the world's most expensive dance floor in the Floating Floor, a roller-skating rink that had cost the club $500,000.

WBLS and Kiss FM

Visiting bands were as impressed by the pre-club warm-up mixes offered by the city's radio stations as they were by the clubs themselves. Tony Wilson had become fond of the DJ Frankie Crocker on WBLS, while New Order loved Shep Pettibone's famous mastermixes.

1982

'It felt like somebody else's money'

Work on the Haçienda continued, with Kelly managing the expectations of the Factory bosses while enjoying the freedom allowed by the brief he'd been given: 'Big bar, small bar, food, stage, dance floor, balcony, and a cocktail bar in the basement.'

Kelly said he took his inspiration from the building itself and 'my arrogance in thinking I knew what a club designed for Factory and New Order should look like'.

Saville, meanwhile, agreed; the idea was for it to be a three-dimensional manifestation of Factory Records, he said. As a result, the Haçienda was to boast the same commitment to arty functionality, the same attention to detail.

All of which cost loads of money – which came from . . . ?

New Order's first album, Movement, their last to be produced by Hannett, had been released at the end of 1981 and standalone singles 'Ceremony', 'Everything's Gone Green' and 'Temptation' were mainstays of the indie chart. Yet the individual members of the band were seeing few fruits of their labour. Instead the money was disappearing down what Hannett would later describe as 'a hole in the ground called the Haçienda'.

And it was a big hole. Though the initial budget was naively estimated at around £70,000, the eventual cost would be over £340,000. This was split between Whitbread Breweries, which parted with £140,000, New Order/Joy Division, who were initially asked for £35,000 but actually provided more than £100,000, and Factory, which came up with the rest.

Howard Jones, tasked with finding the cash to meet the cost of Ben Kelly's vision, remembered having 'raging rows' with Wilson over money – though they would always end with Wilson handing over another cheque.

'What Tony liked to express was did I know how much pressure I was putting Factory Records as a company under, to make FAC 51 happen,' he said.

Before we knew it, they started remodelling the interior and the budget had escalated to £155,000. It was around that time that Rob stopped consulting us about money.

As if Ben's ambitious design wasn't enough, they also appeared not to follow the local building regulations. They submitted plans featuring the existing wooden balcony, which unto itself wasn't a bad idea – saving us the money on building a new one. Trouble was, we were told it didn't meet fire regulations. So they had to rebuild it, which added something like £45,000 to the bill.

Think about it: the Haçienda cost £344,000 to build in 1981. That's equivalent to about three million now. If you spent three million on a club today people would think you were potty.

In New Order we'd sit there laughing about cock-ups and cost overruns. Otherwise we didn't get involved. It would have been a bit mind-blowing to watch someone squander that much money when each of us lived on £20 a week. As it was, it felt like someone else's money.

The only time we were asked for our opinions was when we got involved with the argument over the placement of the stage: whether to put it at the end of the main bar or in the middle. We all wanted it at the end, and guess where they put it? The middle. I'm sure Tony asked for that, if only to be contrary.

My most significant input was the decision of where to put the stage and the dance floor. I didn't want the stage at the end because it would dominate the space and make it a performance space, as opposed to the basic idea, which was that it was a discotheque. It was me who said the dance floor should go in the middle and the stage where it is. It doesn't dominate the club but groups that have large lighting rigs just can't play there, so I've had a lot of stick in the past for that choice.'

Tony Wilson, quoted in *The Haçienda Must be Built*,
edited by Jon Savage

Then, as building work neared completion, it became obvious there was going to be a shortfall, so we borrowed the money from Whitbread to finish it off. That's quite a common thing to do in the UK. You borrow the money but have to sign an exclusive contract with the brewery; and once you take that loan you lose all bargaining power over the wholesale price of any beer you purchase. That was the deal. As far as the brewery was concerned: you can borrow the money from us, but you forfeit any discount on what you buy until the loan's repaid. We didn't realize the significance of that until we opened.

That contract locked us into a money-draining situation from which we'd never recover. Eventually we were among those selling the highest volume of beer in the northwest of England but we never made any profit on it thanks to that deal. Some little pub in Levenshulme may have been paying Whitbread 10p a pint, yet the Haçienda, which should have received a quantity discount, was paying £1 a pint.

We weren't making any money on the draught or the brewery bottles and after a while the manager took to sneaking off to Makro to buy beer cheap to sell behind the bar for cash to keep the club going. (We weren't actually the biggest beer-seller in Manchester; that honour went to the Old Monkey on Portland Street, a Holt's pub that sells it at a pound a pint. Consistently the champion.)

Another big mistake made – again, because of inexperience – was the lease. The owners of the building, who would turn out to be a proper bunch of bastards, demanded a twenty-five-year lease. We settled on that. They even did the oldest trick in the book, the 'we've got somebody else very interested, you better hurry up' ploy. Guess what? We fell for it. And became the proud owners of a very expensive club with a quarter-century lease.

Next the band made a mistake. Looking back, perhaps the biggest mistake possible.

We were persuaded to sign personal guarantees for the bank, the lessees, the brewery and to all intents and purposes the devil, which made us personally liable for all debts. Before, we had been shareholders in a limited company with our personal assets protected by that status. Now, if the club went bust before we repaid the debts, we would all be liable/fucked: the bank would be free to take our homes, cars, first-born – anything we had to our name – and sell them to recoup its losses. To Rob, an inveterate gambler, this amounted to an acceptable risk.

Once they became clear to us we were terrified of the potential consequences, and for years they hung over our heads like Damocles's sword. At least Rob was in it with us. He'd signed a personal guarantee, too, and on more than one occasion over the years to come nearly lost his own house because of it.

Of course, the money drain had started as soon as we employed our architect.

Somebody once asked me who I thought was responsible for the ultimate demise of the Haçienda. The answer at the time was Ben Kelly.

I know different these days, of course, I realize that none of us were blameless. But it was Ben who – appropriately for an architect – laid the foundations.

Everything he did for us – starting with the Haçienda then later our bar, Dry; the Factory Records office building; and even Tony Wilson's own flat – came in massively over budget. The people in charge gave Ben complete freedom to do whatever he wanted to do and actively encouraged him to go totally over the top. He's a nice guy, but he'd never worked on a club before and admitted as much. By the time it was finished, the Haçienda was 5000 per cent over-designed for its audience. On walking in, the initial impression was always 'Wow', but at the end of the day concert-goers don't care about the architectural style of venues, they just want to see bands play without fucking gird-ers in the way and shit sound. Later, during the acid-house era, people enjoyed themselves just as much dancing in shitholes that cost nothing as they did inside the Haçienda, which cost a fortune. So it's debatable how much of the Haçienda's success was down to Ben.

That said, he certainly came up with a unique, iconic design that has stood the test of time. You've got to give him that. It is still a landmark, a classic.

When finished the club would be described as 'neither a venue nor a disco, a real-life stage-set built with the most mundane materials used to maximum effect.'

Walls were painted in shades of cool, airy blue-grey. Pigeon Blue BS409, to be exact. The structural elements of the building were emphasized rather than hidden. Supports and girders boasted black and yellow safety stripes, echoing Peter Saville's graphic design and harking back to the early days of the Factory nights and the famous 'wear hearing protection' poster.

Kelly has described the design as boasting 'visual puns'. The line of steel columns was colour coded to warn you: take care – you never know who you might bump into on the dance floor. A formal disco environment was out of the question, he said, and sure enough he'd backed Wilson when it came to the placement of the stage, wanting to emphasize the function of the place as club not venue. Additionally, fly bars with theatrical lights were introduced so the management could tailor the lighting to the event, rather than have the event dictated by the lighting.

Overall, Kelly brought to it what's been described as 'an inside/outside tension', a city within a city, a place of walkways, plazas and bars, complete with bollards and cats eyes, supports and stripes suggesting certain journeys through the building. The materials were hard-wearing. The dance floor was made of sprung maple, the material used in professional dance-rehearsal spaces and thus built to last; bar tops were made of concrete and granite. It's a tribute to both the design and the materials that in fifteen years of the club being open the look remained the same, and refurbishment was mainly limited to extra coats of Pigeon Blue BS409.

Still the schizophrenia over its purpose persisted. Packed in was a café/restaurant, stage, dance floor, three bars – the Gay Traitor, the Kim Philby and Hicks – on three levels. It meant you could dance, drink, dine, see a band – all, according to the Ben Kelly book Plans and Elevations, in 'an environment which was visually stimulating . . . Adaptable to a variety of activities, have flexibility within its framework to change with changing ideas and attitudes, and initiate change within an environment which questions the language and values of the established disco/club format.'

'But there's no back room,' said Richard Boon, Buzzcocks manager and a promoter in the Manchester scene who supported us as Joy Division.

He was right. Unlike other clubs, the Haçienda didn't have a VIP area. At the time, of course, that felt like a mistake, but during our heyday it was part of the club's appeal. No VIP area meant that celebrities had to mix with the regular punters instead of hiding behind a velvet rope. You could go into the Haçienda and stand at the bar next to Shaun Ryder, find yourself dancing alongside Ian Brown.

Like I say, though, when it first opened it just felt like another cock-up to go along with the DJ booth, which initially was in an amp room by the side of the stage. It had a tiny window, which meant DJs couldn't see the dance floor unless they stood on a crate. Plus, the decks were at the back of the booth, opposite the window, so DJs would have to turn their back on the window to put records on. Absolutely useless. We ended up having to move it to the balcony.

The glass roof was never painted out. Why? I don't know. Ben's decision? I must ask him. I suppose he must have liked the look of it. But in the summer the club stayed light until late at night because of it. It was airy, though. A normal designer would have put in a low ceiling to give it atmosphere but Ben Kelly approached it from an architect's point of view, not that of a clubber.

Everyone thought it was fucking mad, but on the other hand that's also why they loved it so much. It looked great . . . for an art gallery. For a club, it was too bright, so un-club like – especially with only a few people in it. It was as though Rob and Tony had deliberately picked the building least favourable for creating a club in, a huge, empty shell, instead of getting some place purpose-made. That was very typical of Rob. He was always so stubborn. It was if he had looked at this yacht showroom and decided, 'Right! You're going to be a club.'

You could spend forever arguing whether or not there was a need to be so arty, but a less artistic club wouldn't have pleased Rob or Tony and maybe not us, either. Then, we'd be just one more club owner among thousands. We wanted something extraordinary.

Apparently they didn't consider how great their reputation was among music fans. The Factory tie-in alone would have earned them a fortune and an audience, whatever kind of place they'd opened, or perhaps their egos required more. No one ever changed the world by being normal. Everything comes down to leaving a great legacy. That's why we ended up with the most avant-garde club in the whole world.

Aesthetically the Haçienda established its graphic style very early on. The black and yellow stripes are iconic. One look and you instantly know it's the Haçienda. Rob commissioned Saville to design all of the club's posters and advertisements, again giving him the freedom to do as he wished. The old joke about him being late on all of his projects stayed true, though, and over the years Rob and Saville fell out often; they were always at each other's throats. Later, a Manchester-based designer named Trevor Johnson took over and handled a lot of the advertising, often using Peter's work as a starting point. Eventually we employed an in-house design team to do the work.

As for the Haçienda, a lot of other clubs have since copied many aspects of its style, and I'd like to think that their designers didn't come in on time or on budget either.

'About a week before we opened,' said Tony Wilson, 'I was showing some-body around and they said, "Who the hell are you building this for?" And we said, "Well, the kids." And they said, "When was the last time you saw the kids? It was in Rafters, wasn't it, nine months ago, and they were all wear-ing raincoats and long drab clothes, watching a band in the corner of the room. So why are you building a glossy New York discotheque?" I was rather stumped. I couldn't answer that question.'

Martin Hannett remained deeply unhappy about the enterprise, loudly making his frustration clear to visiting bands in the studio. He had wanted to plough the cash back into what he considered to be the label's core product: music. At best he wanted a studio, at the very least a new syn-thesizer: a Fairlight CMI Series II, which was being used by the likes of Kate Bush, Jean Michel Jarre and Hannett's great rival, Trevor Horn.

Sure enough, shortly before the club was due to launch, Factory's musi-cal magician filed a lawsuit against the label he'd helped create, attempting to prevent the opening and claim more money from his stake in the label. It was the beginning of the end of his relationship with Factory . . .

Amazingly, the club only took up a fraction of the space available to us in the building. There were three floors above the Haçienda, as well as the entire left-hand side of the building, which we called the Round House (an area with its own, separate entrance), and they went mainly unused. There was always talk of renting those bits out, but nothing much came of that idea. Bands would use them for rehearsing (the Stone Roses for a while, the Doves and the Happy Mondays) but only for short periods. The only business willing to take a longer lease turned out to be a brothel – which Tony felt was a stop too far, even for us.

The basement was especially complicated. Down there we had the famous Gay Traitor bar. In that was a set of double doors. People were forever trying to go through but they stayed locked. If they had got through, they would have found a huge storage area full of posters and junk. Cross the floor and there was a set of doors with a ramp leading to them. Outside those: the canal bank. To the right, another door, another area. This was slightly less scruffy and would later become

Swing, our hairdressing salon, which doubled as a dressing room for visiting bands. Having got changed (and done whatever else it is that bands do in dressing rooms before a gig) it was then a case of going up a set of narrow stairs to get to the stage.

So, it seemed like we had everything we needed in the club. Even so, not long before opening night, Terry Mason, who provided a lot of the hands-on labour, and our roadie Corky Caulfield were in the building, helping Alan Erasmus with some last details. Corky, who'd worked in clubs before, looked around the building and asked, 'Where's the cloakroom? I've not seen it yet.'

'Cloakroom? Oh, fuck.'

They'd forgotten to put one in. With no time left to build one, they took a tiny utility area by the door – a storage space – and decided to use that instead.

One great testament I thought to Factory's popularity was the membership debacle. The licensing committee had worked their magic and decided that we would be limited to having a member's-only licence. So we had to put a Plan B in place.

Only we didn't have one; the thought of membership hadn't crossed our minds. Once we put it onto operation, though, the response was fantastic.

Which reminds me: not long ago, a girl approached me and asked me to sign her Haçienda membership card. It was number 6724. First of all, I was flabbergasted because I thought we'd only issued 2000 memberships. Yet it turns out the figure is closer to 7000. At £5.25 each (and while we're on the subject, why not £5.10? Think about it. FAC 51 – £5.10. How Tony missed that I don't know), that should have earned more than £35,000 for the club. Later I asked Mike Pickering why it never appeared in the accounts. He had no idea.

People applied from all over the world, knowing they'd probably never make an appearance in the building, just wanting to be in on what we were doing. A great compliment. Many people still treasure their membership cards to this day.

Membership cards were designed by Saville and arrived late. Because of that, Factory had to issue temporary cards for the opening night – at great expense. While the standard membership cards are indeed collectors' items, these temporary versions are even more sought after. Saville was also responsible for the invitations to the opening, which were also late, but had been intended for the musicians, journalists, movers and shakers in the Manchester music scene – who turned up anyway. The kids for whom the club was supposedly built could come the next night to see Cabaret Voltaire, said Wilson.

For the night, on 21 May 1982, comedian Bernard Manning performed – to boos, abuse and feedback through a sound system that all agreed had room for improvement. DJ for the evening was Hewan Clarke and live music came courtesy of ESG, who, either by accident or design, perfectly articulated the ideals of the Haçienda. A trio of very young (they were chaperoned by their mother) sisters from New York, ESG played a bass-heavy, spare funk that has since been credited with inspiring new-wave, punk and hip-hop artists. At the time they were mainstays of the New York club scene from which the Haçienda drew so much inspiration, and had opened for Public Image Limited and A Certain Ratio, the latter performance bringing them to the attention of Tony Wilson. He then brought them to Factory in 1981 for an EP, You're No Good, which had been produced by Hannett and featured the much-sampled 'UFO', one of the hippest and most influential tunes of the era.

'We were kids at the time,' said singer Renee Scroggins of the band's Haçienda appearance. 'We were excited to be in a new place – out of the Bronx. When people ask me what it was like being the first band to open the club . . . The place was full of sawdust. They were still building the club. My memory is plenty of sawdust and coffee – wasn't exactly a pleasant memory. They were still testing the sound system. It was crazy.'

The club was packed on the night. ('It was the next five years that were empty,' said Wilson later.) Guests struggled with a take-a-ticket system at the bar, similar to that used in supermarkets and based on what the team had seen in action at Danceteria. The system didn't cross the ocean, however, and was dropped after some months. Those who were there recall the smell of paint, planks on the floor, the fact that it was so light and airy – and very cold.

I went to the opening with Iris, my girlfriend at the time. We got an invite in the post like everybody else.

As for the night's entertainment, Hewan Clarke – a lovely bloke who had a trademark lisp – was the DJ. Because of his speech impediment, we teased him by saying, 'The Hathienda mutht be built.' He'd stick with us for years. He was a nice, quiet guy. I don't remember much about his musical tastes, but my memories of him are all good. The cult of the DJ hadn't yet begun. On the opening night he DJed between acts but nobody paid any attention to what records he was playing.

Bernard Manning was the compère for the evening. Manning was a comedian who owned the World Famous Embassy Club on Rochdale Road in Manchester (which has outlasted even him and us), near where I used to live in Moston. Rob and Tony thought it was ironic, having him do a spot on the opening night. To them he represented the sort of old-school, working-men's club environment the Haçienda meant to replace. The crowd were bemused, quite rightly. As for Manning, he took one look at the Haçienda and sussed out it was run by idiots. He laughed his balls off as we tried to pay him. He turned to Rob, Tony and me and said, 'Keep it. You've never run a club before, have you?'

We stared at him, puzzled. What did he mean?

'Fucking stick to your day jobs, lads, 'cause you're not cut out for clubs. Give up now while you've got the chance.' Then he walked off.

We chuckled, thinking, 'We'll show him.'

From what he'd seen that night, Manning thought it was doomed. Nobody in the audience could hear what he said over the PA because the sound system and acoustics were so terrible. It confused people. That's probably another reason I don't remember Hewan's set: the dreadful sound. It was bloody awful. I might have felt a bit detached from the place at first but I ended up being so embarrassed about the sound – especially later, on club nights – that I got involved just to sort it out. And thank God I did. A few months later, when Chris Hewitt from Tractor Music took down the original sound system, he discovered that of the twenty speakers only two worked; the other eighteen had blown out immediately. (Another great bargain. This time by Court Acoustics, who'd charged us £30,000 for what we'd been told was a top-of-the-range system.)

It turned out that the Haçienda, one of the biggest clubs of its time, had been running on what amounted to a public address system.

In short, the night was a bit of a mess. And people never expected that from a club associated with Factory, which had a reputation for quality.

The night after the opening, Cabaret Voltaire did indeed play, as Wilson had said – attracting an audience of around seventy-five. It marked the beginning of the lean years for the Haçienda, a time when the club was quite simply too far ahead of its time – ahead of trends in fashion and music and ahead of its target audience. Mike Pickering would often say, 'If only we could move this place brick by brick to New York.'

Meanwhile, the resident DJ charged with shaping the sound of the Haçienda was Clarke, who played at the club every night it was open right up until 1984. Given that this was a venue associated with Factory Records, one of the archetypal indie labels, it speaks volumes of the club's open-mindedness (or sheer bloody mindedness) that the first resident was a Jamaican-born jazz-funk and soul DJ, a veteran of the Reno, then Fevers, where the groove of choice was jazz-funk.

How did it happen? Playing at Fevers, Hewan had begun to notice two polite-looking white kids who'd come and sit in the corner. One night they came over: 'We're Martin and Simon and we're in a band called A Certain Ratio.' They were always asking Hewan for names of this stuff he was playing: Latin, Brazilian, Samba and jazz-Latin vocal. A Certain Ratio were, of course, signed to Factory, where they were managed by Tony Wilson. They were then going through a 'transitional' phase that would later be satirized in the 24 Hour Party People film but did in fact see the band operating way ahead of the curve. About to embark on a UK tour, they'd decided not to have a support band, to have a DJ instead, and would Hewan do it? He would and he did, and in doing so formed a bond with ACR's manager, the two sharing a favourite DJ, Frankie Crocker, who worked on WBLS in New York.

During their conversations Wilson said that he planned to open a club in two years' time, and that he wanted to Clarke to be the DJ. 'Yeah, yeah,' thought Clarke. But when the Haçienda happened Wilson came good on his promise and hired him.

And so it was that the Haçienda's first resident wasn't spinning Joy Division, New Order and the Smiths; he wasn't playing bands on Factory and Rough Trade and Cherry Red. He was playing Sugarhill, Roy Ayers, Gil Scott Heron and Herbie Hancock, mixing it up with the more commercial hits of the day when he needed to fill the floor. A typical month's top five might read:

1. *Yazoo – 'Situation' (Francois Kevorkian's Dub Mix)*
2. *Sharon Redd – 'Can You Handle It?'*
3. *Q – 'The Voice of Q'*

4. *D Train – 'You're the One for Me'*
5. *The Peech Boys –'Don't Make Me Wait' (Original 12" Dub Mix)*

The Thompson Twins, Heaven 17 and ABC also featured; plus, some of the emerging electro hits would find their way into his set: 'Buffalo Girls' by Malcolm McLaren, impLOG's 'Don't Make Me Wait' and 'Walking on Sunshine' by Rockers Revenge.

It was a musical policy encouraged by Wilson; indeed, Clarke recalls Wilson telling him that black music was going to be the next commercial dance music, even as the newly opened Haçienda began to fill with curious punks and Goths who were expecting a continuation of the Factory nights at the PSV. 'Mohicans and everything,' remembers Clarke, who became paranoid when none of the punks would dance to the usual funky black tunes guaranteed to fill the floor at the Reno. 'Tony would come into the DJ box saying, "Wonderful, keep it up, darling," and I'm thinking, 'but nobody's dancing.'

They would, though. Given time.

For the moment, the Haçienda would be best known as a live venue, hosting some legendary shows.

The difficulties we had getting the place open only worsened from that point on. Yes, the premiere night was packed (the booze and entrance was free – what do you expect?), but after that you could literally count on your fingers the punters who turned up each night.

Even so, Tony and Rob went full tilt, keeping the club open seven nights a week, plus lunchtime on Saturday and Sunday, the ethos being we always offered the members somewhere to go. Now, if you ever saw the Haçienda, you'd know it was hardly the most convivial venue for an afternoon club. The glass roof made it too bright during daytime, and the size of the place made it cold and uncomfortable. It was like trying to relax in a museum café, and nobody really wanted that kind of atmosphere.

We also employed a chef. I ate there because he was really good. He concocted these wonderful stuffed-chicken pancakes with a creamy sauce that I thought were amazing. Of course, as a co-owner I didn't have to pay to eat at the Haçienda, so I thought I was getting a bargain. Little did I know I was actually paying a fortune for them. He didn't last that long – just a matter of weeks – because he didn't cook for anyone apart from me. Shame. He was a great chef.

The hopes for the place were ridiculous, really, because no club is open seven nights a week. Common sense should have told us that after the first month – when we hadn't made any money at all during the daytime because nobody came and the place was fully staffed for a non-existent clientele – we should have changed things immediately. Yet we stayed open that way for what felt like two years before anybody had the brains to ask, 'What the fuck are we doing?' Bizarre.

And what the fuck were we doing? Probably Rob gambled on people having a change of heart and coming in again in record numbers. He was compulsive that way. I once saw him on a ferry going to France, placing bets till he was the last one standing. He turned his pockets out, doing his elephant impression, and when his money was all gone he went to bed.

Initially, entry to the Haçienda was free between Monday and Thursday (for members this was; the club had a members-only licence for the first two years). Those who came through the door tended to congregate in the Gay Traitor bar. 'We'd have fifty or sixty people just sitting round having a drink, and those people loved it,' said manager Howard Jones. Big gig nights – New Order, Culture Club, Bow Wow Wow – could do well, attracting up to 1400 people, and weekend club nights were also attracting 'never less than 1000 people', according to Jones. 'What caused the financial problem was that club was open seven nights a week, for six months from the opening night.'

I remember it being more like two or three hundred on even the weekend club nights, but everyone's memory is different.

The best thing about the early days of the Haçienda was that each night revolved around the club itself, not any one DJ or concept. It offered an overall aesthetic experience. We hired Claude Bessy to produce the video installations, which became very important in setting the tone. The first thing many people noticed were the film collages – cutups – that he projected on the screens. Steve Morris got involved with that too for a little while in the early eighties. We got in trouble over it with the Jewish community in Manchester because Bessy utilized a lot of Nazi stuff, intercutting Hitler speeches – in a very punky way – with all kinds of footage, creating a sort of editorial comment on events of the day.

Someone picked up on it, imagining all sorts of pro-Nazi messages, similar to what had happened with A Certain Ratio and New Order, and the *Jewish Chronicle* held Tony to blame. It never went anywhere once everybody understood the context, but Tony was pleased to end up in the *Jewish Chronicle* – it was his first front cover.

To a degree, we tried to turn it into a hip-hop sort of place, like the clubs in New York, with different rooms and events: fashion shows, gigs, things like that, but for years we couldn't establish it as anything but a concert venue. Nothing else really took root.

The New York influence came through Ruth Polsky. Ruth – one of the unsung heroines of the era – had been the first US promoter to dive into the British punk and post-punk scene, bringing a lot of the bands over for their first tours of America.

The thing that most impressed us about the American clubs was that we got in for free. Everyone was so in awe of groups: 'Oh, man, you are New Order? Come on in.'

If we went to a club in London, we'd say, 'Hi, we're in a group,' and they'd go, 'Yeah? Fuck off.'

America dazzled us. For a young guy from England, it seemed like somebody giving me the keys to a sweet shop, saying, 'Take what you want.' And the girls in America were very easily impressed, whereas in England they couldn't give a fuck if you were in a group. Americans were much more friendly, much more open about sex. In England you just about had to be married before you slept with a girl. In America, if you carried a guitar or had an English accent, somebody'd shag you. We had a wild time over there.

That's why New Order toured the USA so much during the 1980s: the weather was great, and we could go everywhere for free. Europe was shit in comparison. For years, we concentrated on America with great success, and did tour after tour there. Unfortunately, we later discovered that nearly all of the money we'd earn from playing over in the states got sucked up by the Haçienda's black hole. Our shows became benefit concerts to keep the club open.

New Order first played the club on 26 June 1982.

The first time we played in the Haçienda Rob told our sound guy Ozzie to fit a huge PA. We were setting the club off, I suppose, by being the loudest thing yet. We sound-checked OK but, when we came to play, on the stroke of the first chord the power for the stage blew out straight away. Seems they were trying to save money (for the first time) by putting in a thirteen-amp stage supply instead of a fifteen-amp as it should have been. Ozzie put silver paper around the fuse so we could carry on, while a roadie was fanning it to keep it up cool. Great gig, though. A total sell-out. The money earned, the same with all our gigs there, disappeared into the club's coffers.

What often happened with New Order, gig-wise, was that whenever the Haçienda really needed money we would play there and the club would take the profits – much to Bernard's annoyance; it drove him fucking mad.

Plus, while we were living hand-to-mouth, we were pretty generous to other bands who played the club. Right from the start, Rob paid groups who played the Haçienda a flat fee, rather than a door deal based on how many tickets they sold. That's unusual: in the days of Joy Division promoters would tell us something like, 'We'll give you £100 up front, plus 50 per cent of what we make at the door up to 400 people, then 90 per cent of what we make at the door from 400 to 600 people. Blah blah blah . . .'

It was a sliding scale that rewarded you for bringing in larger crowds, and protected the club owners in the event that nobody attended.

Easy enough system? Well, Rob hated it. He thought it was too complicated and boring. His ultimate aim was to spare other bands the pain that Joy Division went through when we toured: promoters who'd offer a generous deal, only to later come up after the gig and say, 'Oh, you put loads of friends on the guest-list. I can't pay you.' He wanted to do things even more simply by telling musicians, 'Come play at the Haç. We'll give you a thousand quid regardless of how many people come in.'

He wanted it to be a musicians' co-op, which made it a very popu- lar spot. Even if the acoustics inside were shite, the money was great so the response was fantastic.

A fine example was Teardrop Explodes in May 1982. They were

massive at the time and Rob paid them £3000 to do a 'secret' gig (nudge-nudge, wink-wink, but you're supposed to let the word out so everyone will come).

We kept it so secret only eight people turned up.

WHAT'S ON AT THE HAÇIENDA IN 1982

MAY

Friday 21st	OPENING NIGHT Bernard Manning; ESG
Saturday 22nd	Cabaret Voltaire
Thursday 27th	Teardrop Explodes
Saturday 29th	23 Skidoo

JUNE

Tuesday 1st	Vic Goddard; Subway Sect
Tuesday 8th	John Cooper Clarke
Friday 11th	James King & the Lone Wolves
Tuesday 15th	Orange Juice
Saturday 19th	Culture Club
Tuesday 22nd	Defunkt; the Higsons; the Kray Brothers
Wednesday 23rd	The Durutti Column
Saturday 26th	New Order *(The first of the band's many shows to serve as* de facto *fundraisers for the club)*

Set-list: 'Dreams Never End', '586', 'Procession', 'Chosen Time', 'Truth', 'Senses', 'Ultraviolence', 'Everything's Gone Green', 'Temptation', 'In a Lonely Place'

Tuesday 29th	Swamp Children; 52nd Street

JULY

Saturday 3rd	Funkapolitan
Wednesday 7th	Liaisons Dangereuses
Friday 9th	A Certain Ratio

Set-list: 'Kether Hot Knives', 'Back to the Start', 'Showcase', 'I'd Like to See You Again', 'Tumba Rumba', 'Skip Skada', 'Axis', 'Sommadub', 'Who's to Say', 'Hot Nights', 'Guess Who', 'Touch', 'Knife Slits Water'

Wednesday 14th	Echo & the Bunnymen
Saturday 17th	Simple Minds

Monday 19th	Blancmange

Set-list: 'Can't Explain', 'I Would', 'I've Seen the Word', 'Kind (Save Me)', 'Running Thin', 'Feel Me', 'Cruel', 'Wasted', 'Waves', 'God's Kitchen', 'Living on the Ceiling', 'Sad Day', 'Kind (Save Me)'

Thursday 22nd	The Birthday Party
Wednesday 28th	Buzzz
Friday 30th	J. Walter Negro & the Loose Jointz

AUGUST

Wednesday 11th	Allez Allez
Friday 13th	Delta 5; Secret Seven
Saturday 14th	Bauhaus
Tuesday 17th	Rip, Rag & Panic
Thursday 19th	Bow Wow Wow
Saturday 21st	The Jazz Defektors
Wednesday 25th	The Associates

SEPTEMBER

Thursday 2nd	Tik & Tok
Monday 6th	W.B.
Thursday 9th	The Pale Fountains
Monday 13th	Annette Peacock
Monday 20th	Yazoo
Tuesday 21st	Mark Stewart's Mafia
Thursday 23rd	The Durutti Column
Monday 27th	The Appollinaires
Wednesday 29th	Maximum Joy

OCTOBER

Monday 4th	William S. Burroughs; Psychic TV *(The audience all sat down)*
Tuesday 5th	Jah Wobble
Wednesday 6th	Palais Schaumburg
Thursday 7th	The Psychedelic Furs; Sisters of Mercy
Tuesday 12th	Blue Zoo
Wednesday 13th	Brilliant
Friday 15th	Pulsallama
Sunday 17th	Blancmange; Fiat Lux

THE HAÇIENDA

Monday 18th	Gaspar Lawall
Friday 22nd	Eddie and Sunshine
Monday 25th	David Thomas
Tuesday 26th	Cabaret Voltaire *(video screening)*
Wednesday 27th	J. Walter & Members
Thursday 28th	Buzzz
Friday 29th	The Thompson Twins; Tears for Fears

NOVEMBER

Friday 5th	Ludus
Tuesday 9th	Swans Way
Thursday 11th	The Higsons
Friday 12th	The Honeymoon Killers
Wednesday 17th	Big Country
Friday 19th	Hey Elastica
Monday 22nd	Gregory Isaacs; Michael Smith
Wednesday 24th	Orange Juice; Strawberry Switchblade
Friday 26th	Sandi & the Sunsetz
Monday 29th	Palais Schaumburg

DECEMBER

Monday 6th	Dillinger
Friday 10th	Grandmaster Flash
Monday 13th	Thomas Dolby
Friday 17th	Blancmange
Wednesday 22nd	A Certain Ratio

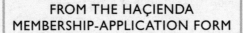

FROM THE HAÇIENDA
MEMBERSHIP-APPLICATION FORM

FAC 51 The Haçienda
11/13 Whitworth Street West
Manchester M3 3AL

Function: club, disco, videotek, venue, club
Telephone: 061-236-5051
Opening: 21 May 1982
Facilities: 3 levels, 3 bars, dance floor (136m²), stage (72.25m²), restaurant, balconies, basement
Capacity: 1650
Dance-Floor Sound and Light: control equipment by Gamma, 15,000 watts of lighting, 43km of 1.5mm hard wire
Video: 2 × 2540mm low-gain screens, 2 × Sony VPK 720PS video-projection units and power packs
Colours: Pigeon Blue, Poppy, RAF Blue Aztec Gold, Salmon Red, Black, Aluminium, Pale Gold, Goose Grey, Signal Red & Light Orange
Approach: industrial fantasy
General Manager: Howard Jones
Booker: Mike Pickering
Design: Ben Kelly/Peter Saville (graphics)
Lights, Sound, Video: Martin Disney
Admission: members only
Membership: £5.25 per annum
Age Limit: over 18
Application: Passport photograph, SAE, and cheque made payable to FAC 51Ltd., and sent to The Haçienda, 11/13 Whitworth Street West, Manchester, M3 3AL.
Intention: To restore a sense of place. 'The Haçienda must be built.'

Licensing regulations attendant on the building of the Haçienda mean that admission to the club is restricted to members only. We will endeavour to keep our door and drink prices as low as possible. Membership will be £5.25 per annum. We believe that this is a small price to pay for a higher state of awareness.

'Well, you've blown it now. You'll never see The Hacienda. It doesn't exist anywhere. THE HACIENDA MUST BE BUILT.'

FAC 51 the Haçienda: application for membership
Name:
Address:
Date of Birth:
What You Want from the Haçienda:

I am over 18 years of age
I agree to be bound by the rules of the club

Signature:

Admission to members only
For official use only
N:
A:
DOB:
O. Stamp

THE HAÇIENDA TOP TWENTY FOR 1982
Published in the End-of-Year Newsletter

1. Marvin Gaye – 'Sexual Healing'
2. Grandmaster Flash and the Furious Five – 'The Message'
3. ABC – 'Poison Arrow'
4. D Train – 'You're the One for Me'
5. Soft Cell – 'Torch'
6. Rockers Revenge – 'Walking On Sunshine'
7. Junior – 'Mama Used to Say'
8. The Associates – 'Party Fears Two'
9. New Order – 'Temptation'
10. Yazoo – 'Only You/Situation'
11. Dazz Band – 'Let It Whip'
12. Kid Creole and the Coconuts – 'I'm a Wonderful Thing Baby'
13. The Peech Boys – 'Don't Make Me Wait'
14. Roxy Music – 'Avalon'
15. Alton Edwards – 'I Just Wanna'
16. Patrice Rushen – 'Forget Me Nots'
17. Kool and the Gang – 'Get Down On It'
18. Spandau Ballet – 'Instinction'
19. A Certain Ratio – 'Knife Slits Water'
20. Soul Sonic Force – 'Planet Rock'

MISCELLANEOUS QUOTES AND FACTS

'Jon Savage's letters page [includes] the following gems: Legitimate gripes. [Member numbers] 04408 and 01510 note that the price of a pint of lager at the Philby Bar has increased from 66p to 70p, and that "£3 for Bauhaus is unreasonable", a request for better chips, a public telephone and a playing list, and [member number] 00419 a.k.a. [local promoter] Alan Wise sends "a letter of protest that is so boring that I will not say any more".'

From 'FAC 51 the Haçienda Newsletter 6'

'It's very fitting that [the colour] International Orange was used in the Haçienda as it's an active, creative and exuberant colour, between the passion of red and the mental stimulation of yellow. Orange is full of energy and will always be used to promote vibrant optimism.'

Inner Spaces documentary, BBC2, 2004

'Opening night: Tony Wilson complained about the acoustics. They were crap, he said. They were blah and blah. Six years later he wouldn't be complaining any more. Six years later he'd be talking breathlessly about the high roof, about Gothic cathedrals – about hymns to the Gods.'

Peter Saville

'It cost £5.25 to become a member of the Haçienda and for that you would get a pound discount on everything. Which meant you got in free half the time. Drink was alehouse cheap at this stage. Many people came simply to get slotted and found themselves sitting on the floor listening to William Burroughs reading aloud from his mucky books.'

John McReady

1983

'What a bunch of dickheads we were'

In January a press ad promised that: 'Over the next two months the Haçienda will be returning to what we consider to be the best of the Manchester bands rather than place these acts in support slots at the mercy of main groups' sound engineers. We offer the opportunity to display their wares in a proper manner.'

But times were hard for the club, partly because it remained ahead of the pack. Booker Mike Pickering had a reputation for booking bands months before they made it big, and it became a standing joke that other promoters could benefit simply by booking the same bands six months later and reaping the financial rewards.

While others profited from its foresight, the Haçienda gained a name as a worthy, arty place, full of good intentions but not of customers. The suicidal cavalier opening policy meant that the club was often catering for fewer customers than staff; bands were being paid more than the going rate, no matter what size audience they attracted; pilfering was rife and overheads were vast. For the owners, keeping the club going was already a hands-on task . . .

At that time, the only thing keeping the Haçienda going was the success of Joy Division and New Order. We were earning so much for Factory that they could afford to be complacent, at least for a while.

Meanwhile, the club was losing an average of £10,000 a month, much of that in wages. There was this guiding principle that if we paid our staff well they would be loyal and work hard. That was the principle, but in reality it was bollocks: some of the employees just got paid more to rip us off. They must have thought it was fucking Christmas. The whole thing functioned on misplaced trust, and we got shafted.

One spring day my mate Andy Fisher (who had done well for himself as a promoter) rang me; as we chatted he said to me, 'I can always tell the Haçienda bar staff when they're walking home from the club.'

He laughed. I laughed, too. It was a joke, right?

'No, it's true,' he said. 'I can always tell the Haçienda bar staff when they're walking down Oxford Road on their way home at night.'

'How?' I was puzzled. They looked just like any other bar staff. It wasn't like we had a dress code.

He said, 'You want me to tell you?'

'Go on, smartarse.'

'They're always carrying a crate of beer.'

It was true: at the end of a shift they'd each grab a crate and leave. Suddenly it all made sense. Whenever there was a stock-take everything was missing and nobody could figure out what happened to the beer. Seems some of the staff certainly knew.

It even got to the stage where I was sick of asking, 'Where's everything going?'; 'Where have all the lights gone?' The trusses, the dimmer racks, the par cans, the slide projectors – some or all had disappeared and we were left with a right cheap, tatty-looking set-up. It turned out that one of the lighting guys, a disgraced ex-roadie, had somehow wormed his way in with Rob – was now running his own lighting company out of his South Manchester flat: renting out our bleeding lights. He only got caught when he'd tried to hire them to a tour manager I knew. Apparently he'd smuggled everything out bit by bit during the day, stored it all in his flat and eventually went into business for himself. If a band phoned up saying, 'We need twenty lights, some racking, couple of dimmers and a lighting desk,' he'd hire out the Haçienda's stuff to them. When we found out, the lads went over and got it all back off him and sent him packing with a good clip round the ear.

Years later he came back to the club and spoke to our receptionist, who was then Fiona Allen (who went on to find fame in *Smack the Pony*): 'You all right? Can I come in?'

She looked at him, gobsmacked – couldn't believe the sheer nerve of the bloke.

'Damien,' she called to the head doorman, 'throw this fucker in the canal.'

'Right,' he said.

So he did. Picked him up and chucked him in the canal. Damien came back, sat back down, and – I loved this – didn't even ask her why.

Back then theft on this scale was an everyday occurrence. The security in the early 1980s was so lax that video players, turntables, lights, speakers, tills, etc., etc., disappeared every week. Everything that could be stolen got stolen. Because of the size of the building, you needed to police it really well or else whenever some twat wanted something they'd just go down to the Haçienda and take it! It would even happen when we were open. The sheer scale of the place made it easy to miss what was going on.

On any given night one of the employees would invariably come by and go, 'Oh, somebody's just nicked the video out of the video booth and run off with it.' We were being eaten from within and without.

I remember Andy Liddle, New Order's lighting guy, putting the rig together for our American tour in 1993 – the Technique tour – and taking great delight in showing Rob the two slide projectors he had hired from a Birmingham lighting company. They still had 'FAC 51' scratched on the side. They had been stolen, sold on, then rented back to us. Rob had paid for them out of his own money to jazz up the club.

On top of all this, costly mistakes were still being made. It turned out that D.G., a drinking buddy of ours who looked after the sound, was making a fundamental error that only came to light when Chris Hewitt kept telling me – laughing about it, actually – how much he was making by replacing speakers in our system. Five hundred quid a month. I couldn't figure it out. Why did the speakers need replacing so often? I'd go in screaming at the DJs, who'd assure me it wasn't anything to do with them. I was completely mystified. Then one night I was in the club, plastered, biding my time in the DJ box, and D.G. came in and started turning off the decks, etc., *before he'd turned off the amplifiers*. The bloody popping of the speakers exploding was deafening. Ah well another mystery solved. D.G. thought it was normal . . .

So, our employees were either nicking from us or making a balls-up of their job; the club was always empty and our opening policy was mis-guided and costly. At least we were using the club to promote Factory's bands, right?

Wrong. The Haçienda was rarely used as a platform for Factory bands. The groups' managers would ask Tony for a night at the Haçienda, but it seemed like neither he nor Rob were ever that inter-ested. Tony used it as a bigger and better version of the original Factory club in Hulme, booking arty bands. Unfortunately, the bands (for the most part) tended to be small while the venue was huge. When you consider how much it cost to run the place, the folly of it looks worse and worse. We'd need a nearly full house just to cover expenses yet put on acts who could only attract 400 people. That kind of reckless-ness shows how little planning went into it, but the idea was to champion groups that we loved, which – at the time – tended to be proper indie British post-punk bands.

There was a small army of regulars: arty, delicate types who might not go to a place like Fagin's or the other normal clubs in town (because they were full of lager louts), but who came to the Haçienda because they felt safe. But actual ticket sales remained a serious issue. We struggled to expand our clientele. The building itself put off a lot of people, the crappy sound kept proper music fans away, and when we did get people through the door, they'd come in find the place empty and lacking any atmosphere. As a result, groups started talking about not coming back, despite the generous fees.

It was the year 'Blue Monday' was released. It came out on 7 March and charted twice – the second time as a result of having been a massive hit with holidaymakers, who'd heard it abroad during the summer, returned to the UK and bought it (often going into shops and asking for 'New Order' by Blue Monday).

As a result it went on to become the biggest-selling 12" of all time, spending a total of thirty-four weeks in the chart.

Thanks in no small part to the 24 Hour Party People film, enduring myth has it that each copy of 'Blue Monday' lost Factory Records money because of Peter Saville's intricate die-cut sleeve. This isn't completely true. It was, indeed, die-cut by hand three times (the most expensive thing on the sleeve were the pieces people didn't actually get, according to Steven Morris) – meaning that the design lost Factory 10p on each copy sold during the initial run of more than two million.. On the subsequent 'holiday hit' pressing, however, printing costs decreased when a less expensive sleeve was used, 'the problem' having been spotted.

'Blue Monday' wasn't the only Factory product losing money thanks to over-ambitiousness. So too was the Haçienda.

Visiting bands spoke in glowing terms of the club's dressing-room hospi-tality, for example. How the rooms were filled with flowers and booze, how it was far more comfortable than other venues and how at the end of their performance they were given a video by the video-maker Malcolm Whitehead. Where other clubs might have attempted to profit from the footage, Haçienda simply gave it away.

That year, Frankie Goes to Hollywood played and Rob Gretton insisted that the Haçienda's hospitality should match that of the Paradise Garage in New York. The dressing room was even more beautifully decorated than ever, piled high with fruit and flowers, while the main hall played host to more grand flower arrangements.

Bar manager Leroy Richardson recalls the club being over-generous with drinks given out to staff, and the stock-take revealing a huge shortfall. Staff weren't 'stealing' the drinks, Richardson maintains; it was just that nobody was keeping a tally of what was taken. There was an unusual system for serving customers, too: one member of staff took the order then passed it to another to complete – so it took two members of staff to serve one customer. This was yet another somewhat ill-advised and costly idea transplanted from New York.

You'd think that being 3000 quid down on the too-secret secret Teardrop Explodes gig would have taught us a valuable business lesson. But no. We carried on doing business the same way – like it was a badge of honour.

So, our promotion continued to be haphazard (remember: the poster timings could be variable), plus we were treating visiting bands like they were kings. Rob's attitude was, 'If somebody plays in my club, I treat them like I'd expect to be treated' – which unfortunately meant that we'd lose money each time we booked a gig and the bands would be thinking, 'It's great playing here, isn't it?' (Credit where it's due, though: Tears for Fears played for the £150 they'd arranged before they'd got to number 1 – then played to a sold-out house. Very honourable, well done, lads.

We frittered cash away each day. On special days we threw it away – 'like a man with ten arms', as Barney liked to say.

I remember going to the Haçienda's first birthday party in May, walking into the dressing rooms and being delighted to see them full of beer and booze – all free. It felt like we'd died and gone to heaven; because we were still living on the breadline, yet here at the Haç was everything we wanted – which, back then, amounted to beer and food – laid out for us.

Only years later did it occur to me that New Order had paid for it all anyway. What a bunch of dickheads. We just got stuck in, like pigs at a trough. It's easy to divert a musician: just show him free booze and he'll forget (or forgive) just about anything.

I made so many wrong assumptions. I never associated what I saw at the Haçienda with our money. I believed that everyone who worked there had the same objective in mind as me: to make it a success. I assumed that everyone knew what they were doing. I was wrong on all counts.

For his review of the club for the Local Times that year, correspondent Robert King interviewed Rob Gretton in the downstairs Gay Traitor bar.

'What sort of people are you aiming to attract?' he asked.

'The kind with two arms and two legs,' sighed Gretton in reply.

The sort of people actually turning up, wrote King, were 'a hairstyle exhibition'. 'There can't be too many clubs where men wear dark overcoats well into June,' he added.

At least they were coming in. A gig by Culture Club in 1982 had kick-started a successful Saturday night, ushering in a trendy crowd who danced to Heaven 17, ABC and Soul Sonic Force. Even so, the numbers still weren't enough. Plus, it wasn't quite the sort of clientele Factory had been hoping to attract.

'There is nobody on Earth who loathes Simple Minds as much as me,' moaned Tony Wilson to the writer Mick Middles following a gig by the band. 'I'm offended by this crap, by the fact that it is taking place in our club, and that this is our fullest night to date. If this is really what the Manchester public want, then we have been completely wasting our time. Still, I'm happy to let this night subsidize a few more important evenings . . .'

The truth was, however, that the gig had still only been half-full. Simple Minds hadn't done much subsidizing at all.

Which meant that not only was the club failing to deliver financially, but also that it wasn't satisfying the aim of being more about the music than the fashion, of being somewhere for Factory and their friends to hang out, wearing what they wanted. Instead, it was a bit 'trendy', in inverted commas. Plus the Friday night still hadn't sufficiently made its mark.

All that was about to change thanks to Pickering. That year he'd visited New York with his band, Quando Quango. The DJ and then-boyfriend of Madonna Mark Kamins had remixed their 'Love Tempo', which had in turn been played by legendary Paradise Garage DJ Larry Levan. As a result, Quando Quango were asked to play a live PA at the Garage. Enjoying the New York nightlife, Pickering also visited Danceteria, Fun House and the Loft. Like New Order, he experienced a musical epiphany.

At the Danceteria Pickering saw Kamins mix electro such as Man Parrish with indie records. Back home this just wasn't done. Meanwhile, at the Paradise Garage, a place Pickering later described as 'heaven', Rob Gretton told him, 'This is it. This is what we've got to do. This is what our club should be like.'

Here was a club where the emphasis was very much on music and people – alcohol wasn't even served – and in contrast to DJs back home, there was no use of the microphone. In fact, the DJs were mixing. This was just the vibe Pickering wanted. To help create it he wanted to attract the black audience who were attending Legends back home. The white trendies in long dark overcoats would just have to get used to it, he reasoned.

To achieve his aim, he first called on DJ Greg Wilson, who was then a mainstay at Legends. There Wilson was famous for having introduced Manchester to electro.

A New York-based movement spearheaded by Afrika Bambaataa, electro was to provide the building blocks of techno and house on which the Haçienda's name would be made. It was inspired by the emerging hip-hop movement, by the sleek, robotic rhythms of Giorgio Moroder and Kraftwerk, and by the distinctive noises produced by the Roland TR-808 drum machine. A cold, yet undeniably funky sound, its Mancunian appeal was obvious.

And it was making Greg Wilson's name at Legends. He'd done away with DJ banter and introduced mixing, packing the club out in the process. In the same month as the Haçienda opened in 1982, he appeared on Mike Shaft's legendary Piccadilly Radio show, TCOB, playing electro and ushering in an era of mixes that inspired a generation of the city's musicians and DJs (not least Gerald Simpson, a.k.a. A Guy Called Gerald, who fondly remembers rushing out to buy C90 cassettes in anticipation of their broadcast).

Wilson had also appeared on Channel Four's The Tube that February, demonstrating this new art of mixing to presenter Jools Holland. As a result of his appearance, the traditional white Factory crowd had begun tuning into his shows on Piccadilly. This fact caught the attention of Pickering, who had returned from the States inspired by what he'd seen at Danceteria and

Paradise Garage and determined to push the musical envelope at the Haçienda. He secretly resented the fact that the club had to put bands on and wanted it to operate more like these New York clubs: with a great sound system, packed with a mixed crowd dancing to a wide variety of music.

Thus he set about shaking up the Haçienda's music policy, hiring not only Greg Wilson but John Tracey and Chad Jackson too. Wilson was given the responsibility of shaking up Friday nights with an electro-based sound, 'bringing what I was doing at Legends to a new audience'.

The night was called Fridays Go Truly Transatlantic, promising 'DJ Greg Wilson with the newest in Funk and Dance' and it debuted on Friday 19 August. From then on, Friday nights would be a largely black-music night (though the club still struggled to attract the black crowd it wanted), while Saturday nights catered more for the traditionally white Factory audience, with the odd slot from a moonlighting Greg Wilson in an attempt to familiarize the crowd with the sound of Fridays.

So, on Friday night you could expect to hear Wilson play 'White Lines' by Grandmaster Flash and Melle Mel (which he'd received on import that September) among the new sounds of hip hop and electro, while on Saturday night John Tracey played a mix that included Simple Minds, Willie Hutch, Iggy Pop and Sharon Redd. His top tune was 'Shout' by Lulu and he often ended the evening with the Thunderbirds themetune.

In addition to his Saturday-night slot Tracey took over Tuesday nights, hosting The End: A No-Funk Night. It went on to become the club's most popular night until mid-1984. Again Greg Wilson was asked to play a slot during the evening, the club being absolutely determined to open its audience to new sounds – despite opposition from customers, some of whom even wrote to complain about the proliferation of 'jazz, funk, disco, whatever it's called'. Nevertheless, while this policy of playing different styles of music may have bewildered the audience at the time, it was to pay dividends in the future. The Haçienda was educating its customers, priming them for the genre-mashing rave and Madchester years ahead.

What's more, Wilson's legendary tenure at Piccadilly was doing the same thing. After Wilson came Stu Allan, widely credited with being the first radio DJ to champion Chicago house music in the mid-1980s, and switching on a generation of DJs in the process; names like Laurent Garnier and (once again) Gerald Simpson, who was inspired to make and send his own house tracks into the show. Allan gave the latter's cassette its first-ever *airplay, introducing it as being 'by a Guy called Gerald from Hulme'. The name stuck, and the destinies of the Haçienda and 'a guy called Gerald' were soon intertwined.*

Greg hosted black and funk nights aimed at white men. I remember him coming up to me, asking if he could remix 'Blue Monday.' I told him to fuck off, thinking it was the most disgusting thing anyone had ever suggested – why should we let someone tamper with our work? How times change. Nowadays the remixes are often better than the originals.

I don't remember much of Greg beyond that episode, although I know he mixed 'Walking on Sunshine' by Rockers Revenge into New Order's 'Confusion', which was ingenious. The first mash-up.

Greg Wilson also managed the Broken Glass Crew, a troupe of break-dancers that included Paul 'Kermit' Leveridge, who would later form Black Grape with Shaun Ryder of the Happy Mondays.

The focus of a piece in the Observer *in November that year was the Broken Glass Crew, a ten-strong team of breakdancers who regularly performed at the Haçienda. Whether they encouraged the overcoat brigade to dance or simply terrified them further is not clear, but it was an impressive spectacle. Manager Howard Jones informed the* Observer *that having breakdancers was never part of any masterplan: 'All we're interested in is if something's happening, to make sure we give it a chance.' In the same piece Sue Smith, a club regular, admitted to being somewhat baffled by the club's musical policy, the 'American dance music'.*

'But I'm prepared to put up with the music for the dead-genuine people,' she enthused. 'I just love it so much.'

The club put the Broken Glass Crew on the road as part of a Haçienda-sponsored tour, along with Quando Quango and Greg himself: our attempt to bring the experience of being at the club to the rest of England. I've no idea how well it did, but I can imagine it didn't work. Change comes slowly; you have to seduce people. Look at the club nights during the early years – very few people attended because nobody knew the music.

As a money-making venture the club was still a failure, but little did we know that we were helping to create today's whole bloody DJ culture by paying the DJs to be exclusive to our club.

I myself have always been cynical about DJs. I thought they were overpaid, arrogant twats. So when I became one I fitted in perfectly. These days someone like Carl Cox can charge a fortune to appear. One New Year's Eve he earned a million for performing at one party, then flew over the dateline and headlined somewhere else for another million. That culture would never have occurred without the Haçienda. We're responsible for it. We got people into the mindset of appreciating DJs as stars /entertainers in their own right, which was mainly down to Rob, who was very forward-thinking that way. He always talked about opening a Haçienda DJ agency because very early on he realized the power that a good one could wield. 'DJs are the next big thing, the next superstars who we should nurture,' he'd say, and he was putting on house-music nights way before the dance-music explosion. He just couldn't get people into it at the time, was too far ahead of the curve. Along with Mike Pickering, he was always on to something new well before it went mainstream.

As a band our biggest education came from the record producer Arthur Baker. Michael Shamberg, who produced our videos and ran the Factory USA office in Manhattan, said to Rob, 'This Arthur Baker is great. Get New Order hooked up with him', so we flew to New York to record in his Shakedown Studios.

Arthur Baker was the *crème de la crème* of New York producers. He was like a cuddly, fun version of Martin Hannett. Through Arthur, we discovered hip hop and dance music: Freeze's 'A.E.I.O.U.', Grandmaster Flash, Afrika Bambaata. Arthur was right on it. He was an electronic punk and at first it was terrifying working with him. It was the first recording session we'd ever done without writing anything beforehand. But 'Confusion' turned out great. He taught me to love making electronic music.

This was the year in which the Happy Mondays first played at the Haçienda, in one of the regular Battle of the Bands competitions organized by Pickering. It was their second-ever performance, it was a complete shambles, and they came last in the competition. However, the bassist, Paul Ryder, was Peter Hook's postman, and according to Hooky, 'He always slipped demo tapes through my door. It was when I got a tape of 'The Egg' that I passed one along to Tony Wilson. The Mondays came from Little Hulton (like me), I was really up for giving them a chance so I was livid with Tony when he gave the job of producing them to Barney. They ended up being the only other successful act on Factory.'

This was the year the Smiths broke, and they played the Haçienda three times, the first supporting 52nd Street in February. They were back, headlining, in July, when the stage was strewn with flowers – the beginning of what would come to be a vital part of the Smiths' image and identity. 'They're symbolic for at least three reasons,' Morrissey told Sounds. 'We introduced them as an antidote to the Haçienda when we played there; it was so sterile and inhuman. We wanted some harmony with nature. Also, to show some kind of optimism in Manchester, which the flowers represent. Manchester is semi-paralysed still. The paralysis just zips through the whole of Factory.'

By the time the Smiths returned to the Haçienda in November the place was full of customers (this and the New Order gigs were the only times the Haçienda sold out during its first two years) and full of flowers, producing a memorable atmosphere for what would later be regarded as one of the club's best-ever gigs. Not least among those who considered it so was Tony Wilson, who told writer Johnny Rogan: 'It was one of the great moments in the Haçienda's history. I was proud. There have been certain great gigs in Manchester's history: the Eagles at the Palace, Lou Reed at the Free Trade Hall, Joy Division at the Derby Hall, Bury. These are concerts you always remember, and the Smiths at the Haçienda was one of the great gigs.'

It might have become part of music history but I didn't see the Smiths at the Haçienda, though I did catch them by accident when they supported Richard Hell at Rafters. I wasn't impressed, but I'm too competitive so I've always been very anti-Smiths right from the word go – probably because I thought that musically they sounded very twelve-bar rock 'n' roll, the antithesis of what I liked. For that reason I wouldn't go and see them. That said, if I'm honest, it was obvious how good they were, and how big they were going to be.

I like the Fall. Always have, and they played at the club loads of times. I think Mark E. Smith is a twat, though. A right obnoxious bastard. And he's proud of it. One of his ex-girlfriends told me that he sometimes has for breakfast Guinness and cornflakes with his favourite stimulant sprinkled on them. He denies this, which is quite funny. Must be why you've got such great teeth, Mark. We're great friends.

I remember when OMD played; they sounded great because they

had a huge PA and blasted the bad acoustics out of the place. Their lights were stunning, too. Must have cost a fortune, but it added up to a great show.

If the Haçienda filled up you'd get an excellent gig, despite the bad sound, because of the atmosphere; the crowd worked as a sound baffle, cutting down the echoes, improving the acoustics a lot. But at poorly attended shows you had few people and thus bad sound, one compounding the other. It was an awful predicament.

Some of the most interesting concerts were largely ignored by the Manchester population and turnouts for some gigs could be really bad.

John Cale comes to mind. One of my heroes. I love his work with the Velvet Underground and the record he produced for Nico, *Chelsea Girls*, and his solo stuff.

I got into his solo material before I discovered the Velvets, whereas for most people it's the other way around. It happened when I was working at the docks in the 1970s. I worked in the canteen part-time during dinner, selling meal tickets. I ate free because of it; I was skint at the time so this was a great incentive. Anyway, the guy who worked during the lunch hour loved John Cale, weirdly a massive fan. Through talking to him on our five-minute changeover between shifts, I ended up borrowing all his LPs. From then on I was a massive Cale fan too. That's why the evening at the Haçienda pissed me off so much: it was a fantastic performance, but just forty people turned up. *And* most of them talked all the way through the show. Cale played piano and acoustic guitar, and the music was very quiet. All the chatter drove me insane. Marc Riley from the Fall – a radio presenter now – was as incensed as I was and we walked through the crowd, poking them telling them to shut up.

Cale lived in Manchester with Nico for a while in the 1990s. I never met him but he'd been suggested to produce New Order a couple of times, though nothing came of it.

Nico herself played her last gig at the Haçienda, in 1986. Another Factory band, Stockholm Monsters, were on tour with her at the time. At this point she was living in Manchester with the promoter Alan Wise. She used to say – in her flat, German accent – 'Hello, Peter, how are you?'

'I'm fine. Are you all right, love?

'Yes. But I hate Alan. He's a cunt.'

She forever went on about how she despised Alan for always trying to fuck her up the arse. He loved her, but Nico was a long-term drug addict and addicts are just not interested in sex. The drugs rob you of your libido.

She was a very grumpy and miserable lady. Hardly surprising, really – she'd gone from Jim Morrison in LA to a bedsit in Prestwich.

Whenever New Order weren't in the studio or on the road I worked as a humper at the Haçienda – looking after the visiting band's gear and PA – for a tenner a night to supplement my income. Ironic, really, considering how much of my money the club was losing every night. Then I got put in charge of backstage security, aided by members of the Stockholm Monsters: Slim, Chop, Ged, Shan and Tony.

I did live sound for the Monsters – I toured with them for two or three years – and I produced their records, so it was easy for us to work together and we were a great team.

We had a right laugh. I enjoyed doing the shows and I liked lording it over the bands. Naughty, I know. Like the time I threw out Pete Murphy of Bauhaus for saying those six immortal words to Slim when he'd forgotten his backstage pass: 'Don't you know who I am?'

'Ha, ha, yeah, I do,' I said. 'You're out, arsehole.'

The tour manager begged us to let him back in, so we relented. Pete Murphy still remembers it – he mentioned it to me when I DJed for him at an aftershow in 2008. How embarrassing. The Bauhaus gig was a good one, though. After we let Pete back in, that is. I remember pissing myself laughing because the bass player left his shades on during the show to look cool. Then, pissed up, he played 'Bela Lugosi's Dead' on the wrong string on a fretless. I'm glad it wasn't just me that sort of thing happened to.

Working security was great because I got to watch the bands from the stage. The fact that I was part-owner of the club meant nothing to me – what I was really thrilled about was being on stage with the bands.

The Birthday Party, in particular, ranked among my favourite groups of all time. One of the few bands I wished I had been in. Tracy Pew was my hero. They had a great image and the music was wonderful. They were my type of musicians, to be honest.

When they split in 1984, Nick Cave went on to form Nick Cave & the Bad Seeds (although they were called Nick Cave and the Cavemen for a while). They played the Haçienda that year. I worked on that night, too. I'll always remember that somebody rolled a dimpled pint pot onstage, Nick Cave punched it and smashed it into pieces. I was well impressed. It must've hurt, but he didn't show it. Pure class.

Another favourite were Bow Wow Wow. Rob and I had seen them at the Red Parrot in New York in September 1980 (this was during New Order's first tour of America and was the night after our first gig at Maxwell's, New Jersey, where we had all our gear stolen) and liked them a lot. As a group, they were very, very impressive: the bassist, drummer and guitarist were fantastic, and everybody loved the singer, Annabella Lwin. But they had the most obnoxious road crew I have ever met, a right bunch of bigmouth cockney bastards, and I don't know how we kept our tempers that night. They kept stage manager Terry Mason very busy.

Those gigs were well attended, but other times it was patchy. We fell foul of the usual attitude promoters have, which is, 'If we put one band on tonight, we'll attract 400 punters. If we put three on, we'll get 1200.' But it never worked like that. The same 400 people liked all three bands so we could never pull a bigger crowd – it was always the same people. We lost a lot more on the less popular gigs than we made on the successful ones.

We had a few rap concerts; and, despite the reputation they've got, none of them were ever heavy. I don't recall every having trouble with rap shows – or any shows – at the Haçienda, except a shitty Jesus & Mary Chain gig in 1985 I'll tell you about later. By the mid-1980s, though, rap shows didn't work. We'd haemorrhage money on them, so Rob stopped booking them, and they'd find deals elsewhere.

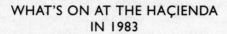

JANUARY

Friday 14th	The Kray Twins; Dog Musicians
Friday 21st	James; Discobolisk
Monday 24th	Kurtis Blow
Wednesday 26th	New Order

Set-list: 'Your Silent Face', 'Temptation', 'Ceremony', 'Leave Me Alone', 'Denial', '586', 'Age of Consent', 'Blue Monday'

Friday 28th	Chameleons; Foreign Press

FEBRUARY

Thursday 3rd	Section 25
Friday 4th	52nd Street; the Smiths

Set-list (the Smiths): 'These Things Take Time', 'What Difference Does it Make?', 'The Hand that Rocks the Cradle', 'Handsome Devil', 'Jeane', 'What Do You See in Him?', 'Hand in Glove', 'Miserable Lie'

Thursday 10th	Fad Gadget
Friday 11th	Jo Boxers
Wednesday 16th	Divine
Friday 18th	Animal Nightlife
Wednesday 23rd	Pigbag
Thursday 24th	The Birthday Party *(Most of this show, plus the show the previous year, was released on video as Pleasure Heads Must Burn.)*

MARCH

Wednesday 2nd	The Virgin Prunes
Thursday 3rd	Eurythmics
Wednesday 9th	The Pale Fountains
Thursday 10th	John Cale

Tuesday 15th	Spear of Destiny
Wednesday 23rd	The D Notes
Wednesday 30th	The Undertones

APRIL

Monday 4th	Orange Juice
Thursday 7th	Big Country
Wednesday 13th	Clock DVA
Thursday 14th	The Durutti Column
Wednesday 20th	The Gun Club; Sisters of Mercy
Thursday 21st	Klaus Schulze

MAY

Wednesday 4th	Little Steven & the Disciples of Soul
Thursday 5th	Vicious Pink
Wednesday 11th	The Box
Friday 13th	Prince Charles & the City Beat Band
Wednesday 18th	Secret Seven
Friday 20th	FIRST YEAR ANNIVERSARY PARTY
Saturday 21st	SURPRISE SATURDAY
Tuesday 24th	*Tales from the Newgate Calendar (play)*
Wednesday 25th	*Tales from the Newgate Calendar*
Thursday 26th	Robert Palmer

JUNE

Wednesday 1st	*Tales from the Newgate Calendar*
Thursday 2nd	The Bat Cave
Monday 6th	*Tales from the Newgate Calendar*
Wednesday 8th	Shriekback; Howard Devoto
Thursday 9th	Hey Elastica
Thursday 16th	Fun Boy Three
Friday 17th	Hunters and Collectors
Wednesday 22nd	Curtis Mayfield
Thursday 23rd	Set the Tone
Friday 24th	SAS
Wednesday 19th	A Certain Ratio; Quando Quango

JULY

Friday 1st	Matt Fretton; Porch Party
Wednesday 6th	The Smiths

Set-list: 'You've Got Everything Now', 'Handsome Devil',
'Reel Around the Fountain', 'What Difference Does it Make?',
'Wonderful Woman', 'These Things Take Time', 'Hand in Glove',
'I Don't Owe You Anything', 'Miserable Lie', 'Accept Yourself'

Friday 8th	FUNK Hewan Clarke; Colin Curtis
Tuesday 12th	Defunkt
Wednesday 13th	The Alarm
Thursday 14th	Howard Devoto; the Wake
Sunday 17th	Newgate 2
Wednesday 20th	New Order

Set-list: 'Blue Monday', 'Age of Consent', 'Lonesome Tonight',
'Your Silent Face', 'Leave Me Alone', '586', 'Denial', 'Confusion',
'Temptation', 'Thieves Like Us', 'In a Lonely Place', 'Everything's
Gone Green'

Friday 22nd	Jah Wobble
Wednesday 27th	The Fall
Thursday 28th	Animal Nightlife

AUGUST

Wednesday 3rd	Roman Holiday
Friday 5th	Lydia Lunch
Thursday 11th	Cabaret Voltaire
Friday 12th	The Peech Boys
Sunday 14th	SUNDAY BODEGA Andrew Berry
Wednesday 17th	Einstürzende Neubauten
Fri 19th	TRANSATLANTIC Greg Wilson
Saturday 20th	John Tracey; Greg Wilson
Thursday 25th	King; Gary Crowley
Sunday 28th	FUNK ALL-DAYER Mike Shaft; Colin Curtis; Greg Wilson; Jonathan; Clement Anderson; Paul Dixon; Carlos
Tuesday 30th	THE END: A NO-FUNK NIGHT John Tracey

SEPTEMBER

Thursday 1st	CLUB NIGHT Hewan Clarke
Friday 2nd	FUNK NIGHT Greg Wilson; Neutriment

THE HAÇIENDA

Sunday 4th   Marc Berry
Tuesday 6th   THE END: A NO-FUNK NIGHT John Tracey
Wednesday 7th   Violent Femmes
Friday 9th   Orchestral Manoeuvres in the Dark
Sunday 11th   Marc Berry
Tuesday 13th   THE END: A NO-FUNK NIGHT John Tracey
Wednesday 14th   Brilliant
Sunday 18th   Marc Berry
Tuesday 20th   THE END: A NO-FUNK NIGHT John Tracey
Thursday 22nd   Sisters of Mercy
Sunday 25th   Marc Berry
Wednesday 28th   Beast

OCTOBER

Thursday 6th   Eddie and Sunshine
Friday 7th   Elvis Costello
Wednesday 12th   The Respond Package
Thursday 13th   John Foxx
Wednesday 19th   Alan Vega
Thursday 20th   Fad Gadget
Wednesday 26th   S.P.K.
Friday 28th   FUNK NIGHT Greg Wilson

NOVEMBER

Wednesday 2nd   Test Department
Sunday 6th   Sheer Image
Wednesday 16th   S.P.K.
Thursday 17th   Icicle Works
Saturday 19th   Frankie Goes to Hollywood
Wednesday 23rd   Divine
Thursday 24th   The Smiths; James

Set-list (the Smiths): 'Handsome Devil', 'Still Ill', 'This Charming Man', 'Pretty Girls Make Graves', 'Reel Around the Fountain', 'Miserable Lie', 'This Night has Opened My Eyes', 'What Difference Does it Make?', 'Hand in Glove', 'You've Got Everything Now', 'These Things Take Time', 'This Charming Man', 'Accept Yourself', 'Hand in Glove'

Wednesday 30th   The Virgin Prunes

DECEMBER

Thursday 1st	China Crisis
Wednesday 7th	The Gun Club
Thursday 8th	Cocteau Twins

Set-list: 'When Mama was Moth', 'The Tinderbox', 'Glass Candle Grenades', 'In Our Angelhood', 'From the Flagstones', 'My Love Paramour', 'Sugar Hiccup', 'Hitherto', 'Musette and Drums'

Wednesday 14th	Killing Joke
Thursday 15th	Spear of Destiny
Friday 16th	The Fall
Tuesday 20th	THE END: A NO-FUNK NIGHT John Tracey
Friday 23rd	ALAN WISE PARTY
Wednesday 28th	The Durutti Column
Thursday 29th	The Durutti Column *(unconfirmed)*
Friday 30th	GINGER'S GOODBYE PARTY

EXCERPTS FROM COMPANY ACCOUNTS, 1983

FAC 51 Limited
Trading as: the Haçienda

REPORT OF THE DIRECTORS
The Directors submit their report and the audited accounts for the year ended 21 May 1983.

Principal activities
The principal activity of the Company is that of proprietors of a licensed club and recreation rooms.

Review of the business
In view of the fact that this is the Company's first year of trading, the Directors feel that the loss level is as expected. High priority is being given to the strict control of the Company's cash flow and a significant improvement in the results for 1984 is expected.

Tax losses currently available to the Company are in excess of £94,500.00 and these can be offset against future profits.

Results and dividends
The results of the Company are as shown on pages 3 to 8. No dividends are proposed or were paid.

Directors
The Directors who served during the year and their interests in the Company at the end of the year were as follows:

A. H. Wilson (held in trust for Factory Records)
R. L. Gretton (Communications) Limited
H. M. Jones
A. Erasmus

The following Directors are retiring by rotation and being eligible offer themselves for re-election:

A. Erasmus
R. L. Gretton

Taxation status
In the opinion of the Directors, the Company is a close Company within the meaning of the Income and Corporation Taxes Act 1970 (as amended).

Auditors
A resolution to reappoint the auditor Mr Keith Taylor FCA will be proposed, at the Annual General Meeting.

BY ORDER OF THE BOARD

[Signed by Alan Erasmus]

Secretary

FAC 51 Limited
Trading as: the Haçienda

PROFIT AND LOSS ACCOUNT (for the year ended 21 May 1983)

	(£)
Turnover	588,810.42
Cost of sales	377,707.99
Gross profit	211,102.43
Administrative expenses	207,757.33
Operating profit	3345.10
Interest payable and similar charges	12,212.97
Loss on ordinary activities before taxation	8867.87
Taxation	–
Loss on ordinary activities after taxation	8867.87
Retained loss for the year	8867.87

MISCELLANEOUS QUOTES
AND FACTS

In October 1983 a staff outing saw everybody pile on to a bus bound for Blackpool. Nathan McGough (later to become the Happy Mondays' manager) was dressed as a scout, members of staff were refused at pubs for having colourful hair and photographer Kevin Cummins was sick on a fair ride.

In November 1983 Dave Haslam launched his *Debris* fanzine, which dealt with the indie scene in Manchester. *Debris* hosted events at the Haçienda; and Haslam, of course, would later become one of the Haçienda's resident DJs.

'I was always going away with New Order and Quando Quango and I was always going away to New York. "Love Tempo" by Quando Quango was really big in the Paradise Garage. We actually did a PA there, when Larry Levan was DJing. I went to the Loft, and I was gob-smacked by it all, because I was just this little scally. So I went back to the Haçienda and I was, "This is what it's got to be like." So I ripped out the microphone; this is the future, you know.'

Mike Pickering, on djhistory.com

'It seemed like the BBC of nightclubs. It was like a subsidized, creative centre that didn't have to be that successful . . . that could explore and experiment. There were no grants, it seemed like it was all courtesy of New Order.'

Promoter Paul Cons

THE HAÇIENDA FRIDAY-NIGHT TOP TEN FOR 1983

1. The SOS Band – 'Just Be Good to Me'
2. The B Boys – 'Two, Three, Break'
3. Captain Rapp – 'Bad Times (I Can't Stand It)'
4. Cybotron – 'Clear'
5. Hashim – 'Al-Naafiysh (The Soul)'
6. Hot Streak – 'Body Work'
7. Shannon – 'Let the Music Pay'
8. Time Zone – 'The Wildstyle'
9. Two Sisters – 'High Noon'
10. Unique – 'What I Got is What You Need'

1984

'It was all down to us:
it was an inside job'

*A 1983 end-of-year review of Manchester's club scene in City Life maga-
zine said this of the Haçienda: 'Greg Wilson's faith in New York's
mind-hammering electro beat was confirmed with both growing crowds and
colour supplement coverage . . . interestingly, the sound flopped in the vast
chasms of the Haçienda.'*

*Greg Wilson didn't hang around to bathe in the City Life glory, however.
He retired from DJing altogether in January 1984, having decided to spend
more time managing the Broken Glass Crew and maybe to try his hand at
music production. (He has since come out of DJ retirement.) His departure
may well have suited Pickering, who hadn't been convinced about Wilson's
concentration on electro. Pickering liked electro; possibly he preferred it to the
diet of hairdresser and Goth music played on other nights. But he wanted it
as part of an overall music policy, not to the exclusion of everything else.*

*'I said that same thing to Greg as I said to Hewan,' he later told writer
Tim Lawrence. 'I said that I wanted this across-the-board mixture of music
I'd heard in New York. I wanted electro as part of a night, but I didn't want
electro on its own – or any music on its own.'*

*Having previously been edged out, Hewan Clarke now returned to Friday
nights, where the policy was a mix of electro, jazz and soul, enlivened by
jazz dancing from Foot Patrol and the Jazz Defektors.*

*So, as 1984 began, the Haçienda had an enviable line-up of DJ talent,
while still retaining its cutting-edge, stylish reputation and the enduring
kudos of its association with Factory. The perfect place, then, for Channel
Four to film a special episode of* The Tube *based around a rising New
York-based singer, the girlfriend of famous New York DJ Mark Kamins. You
know the one . . .*

I believe Madonna appeared as a personal favour to Mark Kamins, a
friend of ours who managed her.

He asked us if we could get her a gig, and because there was an episode of the *The Tube* being broadcast from the Haçienda Rob decided to put her on. You can see it on YouTube. Jools Holland and Paula Yates presented.

She lip-synced to two songs during the afternoon's filming. So there you go, Madonna's first appearance on British TV was all down to us: it was an inside job. And once again we were ahead of the trends. We already knew of her through her association with Kamins, Jellybean, and Arthur; she had no profile in the UK at all. That appearance at the Haçienda changed it all for her. The first step on her journey of world domination, God forgive us.

The Factory All-Stars also performed on *The Tube* that day, a band consisting of Barney, Donald Johnson, Vini Reilly and a few other people on the label. I didn't play – I don't know why. I'll play at every opportunity usually. Instead, I spent three days programming the DMX drum machine for a medley they intended to perform of New Order's 'Blue Monday', A Certain Ratio's 'Shack Up', and Joy Division's 'Love Will Tear Us Apart'.

The morning of the show, I had to take the wife to a furniture shop, then rush back home to finish programming the drum machine in time to get it to the All-Stars sound-check early enough for them to practise.

I got her to the shop, tore back home, finished programming the machine then jumped in the car and raced to the Haçienda. On the way, the coppers pulled me over and gave me a ticket for speeding. Bastards. Then, when I arrived at the club, Barney told me he'd changed the songs anyway. Why that surprised me I don't know. It was fucking typical.

Even so, the taping went well. Because this was an episode of *The Tube*, it attracted a different crowd to the one we normally drew; but by then we'd grown used to a bit of national exposure, so the historical significance of the day didn't dawn on us until much later.

Rob and I watched Madonna and were impressed.

'We should get her back here afterwards, to perform tonight,' he said, so we walked to the dressing room, where we found her with her backing dancers.

Rob said, 'Uh, hello. I'm Rob Gretton. I manage the club. Do you want to play later tonight? We'll give you fifty quid.'

She looked at him.

'Fuck off,' she drawled in her whiny Noo Yawk accent before turning away. That was it for the night. But there are two other stories that came out of her appearance.

The first was that somebody went into her bag in the dressing room and when she got back to her hotel room she found it had been completely cleaned out.

The other legend goes that she and Mark Kamins were staying at Mike Pickering's house in Chorlton, so, after they'd finished at the Haçienda, and they were both the worse for wear, they got a taxi back to Mike's place for the night. Now, English terrace houses tend to have a porch door and a front door, each of which opens with a key.

Mike had given the keys to Mark and Madonna so they could let themselves in, and they turned up, both completely drunk. They successfully unlocked the first door, stepped into the gap, and then the door slammed behind them with the key still in the lock.

At which point they were stuck. Mike woke up the next morning to hear that his missus had opened the door, causing Mark and Madonna to tumble into the house.

I don't know which story is true.

The other highlight of *The Tube* day was an interview with Morrissey and Rob. Now I don't know why, but Morrissey had always hated Joy Division. Maybe Rob got it right when after a lively debate as the cameras were turned off he turned to Morrissey and said, 'The trouble with you, Morrissey, is that you've never had the guts to kill yourself like Ian. You're fucking jealous.' You should have seen his face as he stormed off. I laughed me bollocks off.

Admission was free to those holding invitations, which had been given away.

The day included a performance by the Factory All-Stars, as we've heard, but also on the bill were the Jazz Defektors.

Managed by Ellie Gray, the Jazz Defektors were led by Salts, a club regular who recalls being one of the few black people to regularly visit the club during that era. Whenever possible the group would take over the club, gaining fame as much for their look as their music – the look being colour-co-ordinated 1950s suits, high-waisted trousers bought from second-hand clothes shops and charity stores. They'd been due to perform for a TV audience on The Tube *but when the day came Madonna's people insisted that she lip-sync to two songs, rather than one, meaning an act had to be cut for the running time. That act was the Jazz Defektors. 'She couldn't dance as well as us,' noted Salts ruefully.*

There's a postscript to the event. Years after, Tony Wilson found himself sitting opposite Madonna at dinner.

'I eventually plucked up the courage to look across the table to Madonna and ask, "Are you aware that the first place you appeared outside of New York was our club in Manchester?"

'She gave me an ice-cold stare and said, "My memory seems to have wiped that."'

Miaow.

Meanwhile, DJ Greg Wilson wasn't the only one to leave the Haçienda. Howard 'Ginger' Jones, a director and the club's manager, had left at the very end of 1983. His farewell party was held on 30 December.

He wanted something new, he said. Having heard the Stone Roses, he was thinking about a career in music management – and indeed went on to manage them briefly – so he handed in his notice during the club's Halloween party. As result 1984 began with nobody at the helm of the Haçienda, nor with anybody who was either qualified for or even wanted the job. So began the era of the infamous 'management committee', a co-operative including Mike Pickering, bar manager Penny Henry and Ellie Gray, plus input from Gretton and Wilson.

Gray had been receptionist since the club's opening, and was aware of financial problems from the very beginning. 'Debtors were always trying to get hold of Ginger and he was never available to them,' she told Jon Savage. When the management committee was formed it was up to her keep the bailiffs away. However, she remembers the committee working well at the beginning of its life, 'although no one knew what they were doing'.

By this time nearly everything that could have gone wrong had gone wrong. We should have brought in a professional club manager at this point or earlier, but we always employed our mates because we liked working with them, even if they knew fuck all about the job.

So when Ginger left in late December 1983 he was replaced by Penny. She lived at Alan Erasmus's house, which doubled as the original Factory office building on Palatine Road. I'd heard she had all the necessary credentials to be put in charge: she was an old friend. Or so I was told. As it turned out she had been recommended to and then headhunted by Ginger.

I thought it was Penny who came up with the idea to run the Haçienda as a collective, because suddenly, she, Ellie and Mike Pickering were putting everything to the vote. Price increases, for example. Obviously the staff didn't want the club to be expensive for their mates. They didn't care whether the Haçienda made a profit or not. So every time a price rise came up, they voted against it:

'Right, the wholesale cost of beer has gone up this week, we need to raise the price of a pint. Anybody in favour?'

Inevitably no one was. Prices stayed low, but at the same time nobody took action to bring expenses down, which meant that the club was losing even more money than before. Saying that, 'the people' loved us. Not only did we sell we the cheapest beer in Manchester but also we didn't put the prices up on Saturday. There's an unwritten law among pub and club owners that on Saturday night the price of every-thing goes up 10p. You charge extra simply because the market will bear it (i.e., everyone's pissed). The Haçienda never did that because the staff voted against it. They never missed an opportunity to miss an opportunity, as the saying goes. As long as money to fund the club came in from New Order and Joy Division and Factory, they didn't care how much cash flew out.

Penny Henny has since told me that she was never in charge of the bar or responsible for any financial decisions in the club, saying it was the directors' fault, so the mystery deepens.

To me, the decision to run the club as a co-operative was ridiculous because the members of the co-operative weren't risking anything. I think the staff decided, 'Oh, they're rock-star millionaires, fuck them, we'll keep it cheap for our mates.'

Rock-star millionaire? Where?

Seemed like everybody had that perception, though. One night I drove into town and parked my car outside the club. A brand-new Audi, it was, a company car – as in, a New Order car. When I came out later, it had been kicked to fuck. I mean, whoever had done it in had really done a number on it, lights, doors, roof, windscreen. I stormed back inside, steaming, only to bump into Tony Wilson on his way out.

'Hooky, darling, what's wrong?' he said. He called everyone darling, all the time.

I pointed back up the street to my mangled car, seething, 'A bunch of fucking twats have kicked my car in. Fucking car's trashed.'

'Well, darling,' he said, 'they paid for it,' and off he flounced, me lost for words in his wake.

Put it this way, Tony's words were no solace.

We continued to make mistakes. For example, the place would be repainted every week, which cost a fortune. But, rather than wash out the paint tray and rollers, staff would throw them in a pile then go to B&Q and buy new ones. I found that pile after we went bankrupt and it was like fucking Everest, had two Sherpas and a base camp on it. We were just spunking it up the wall, as we say in Madchester.

We got robbed literally, too, not just figuratively. One Monday morning the staff counted the weekend's revenue before taking it to the bank to deposit it all. The cleaners were in the club, too, tidying up. Standard procedure after a weekend.

Suddenly armed men burst in, held everyone at gunpoint, tied 'em all up, and took the money.

Police investigated but got nowhere, so we tried to put the experience behind us. About three weeks later, though, one of our staff said to a cleaner, 'That's a great tan, been on holiday?'

'Yes,' she replied. 'Want to see my piccies?'

'Sure.'

The cleaner took out her photos from Barbados or wherever, and uncovered a shot of her on the beach with an arm around one of the pricks who'd robbed us: her boyfriend.

Gotcha.

Whatever else was going on, though, the Haçienda was still a great place to hang out. Downstairs, Swing, the hairdressers, had advertised for female students with a 'models wanted' advert. Once there, the male hairdressers would work their mojo, promising them free entry into the club. Talk about grooming.

It primarily served as a place to hang out. It became a cult thing, certainly not a profit centre. All the Factory band members were there. Although I did get my first freebie there – a haircut, courtesy of Neil, Neil, Orange Peel. The only rent they ever paid. Swing eventually closed, though the basins remained – a weird reminder of what once had been.

1984

Hewan Clarke's notes complaining about the siting of the DJ box had become legendary and in 1984 it finally happened. Reluctantly – the one thing that the Haçienda didn't need was an extra cost – it was decided that the booth would be shifted from a room at one side of the stage (from where DJs couldn't see the crowd) to the balcony, where a wooden structure was built. Ben Kelly apparently objected, but it would turn out to be a smart move, paving the way for the era of the superstar DJ when one of the club's most enduring images would be of the smoke-shrouded DJ overseeing the carnage below, hands outstretched, in an almost Christ-like pose.

That was to come, though. In the meantime, the club continued to operate more like a venue. But still hosting some legendary concerts.

I was still watching groups all the time, whenever New Order were home. I'd occasionally see Barney there, although we'd never hang out together. We might nod and say, 'All right,' to one another, but he and I never socialized. We had different circles. If we went anywhere together, it was as New Order.

We were spoilt rotten by the number of big groups that came through during that time. Some I enjoyed, some I didn't. In either event, I never fraternized. I firmly believe in the maxim 'Don't meet your heroes'. What if they turned out to be horrible, or even ordinary? Ooooh! I got better at that as I got older.

I remember seeing Jonathan Richman, at his maddest, insisting on playing without a PA – just him and his acoustic guitar. Two hundred people came and nobody could hear him. They were either laughing at him – he looked like an escaped lunatic – or ignoring him. That night was a complete debacle, though, hilarious. And the funny thing was, I later saw him do the same set at Alan Wise's club, Six Six Six, on Fennel Street a couple of months later, and he was absolutely fantastic. In a small venue it worked, whereas in a big place it didn't. Some shows are like that. The setting makes all the difference.

Johnny Thunders (another hero of mine) played 'Chinese Rocks' three times during his set. He'd turned into a rock 'n' roll casualty to say the least. *(The ex-New York Dolls singer battled heroin addiction and died aged thirty-eight in mysterious circumstances.)* Shame, the Heartbreaker's were the first band we supported at Rafter's, but I enjoyed it. I love that extreme lifestyle. I love to witness it.

Likewise, I was a great fan of the Pogues, who headlined a few times and performed brilliantly. I'd see them perform elsewhere, too. New Order headlined Peter Gabriel's WOMAD Festival with them at the Isle of Wight. Our dressing rooms/tents were next to one another, and we walked into theirs by mistake; they had drinks and a huge buffet, making us think, 'The hospitality here is great.'

Then we walked into our dressing room and there was nothing. Just a donkey. Literally, a big brown effing donkey!

So, we took the donkey out and dragged him into the Pogues' dressing room, where he ate everything on their rider. We nicked the booze. When they arrived they went berserk. What a laugh. I often wonder what happened to that donkey? I think it went solo.

I ended up rebuilding a new sound system in the style of a band PA with the help of Chris from Tractor. Chris had a lot of experience. He and I later co-owned Suite 16 recording studio in Rochdale – named, again, by Tony Wilson – which was formerly John Brierley's Cargo studios and where we'd recorded the first Factory single and later 'Atmosphere'. He now sells Joy Division mementoes. Any time there's something from Joy Division for sale, Chris Hewitt's the one selling it. He seems to have a nice sideline buying things that Joy Division used and selling them over and over again.

I was very proud of the new PA. It sounded miles better than the original, and it only cost £1000. I set it up and maintained it. I'd come in every Friday before opening to EQ it. For a special occasion, like a big group coming to play, we'd hire an extra PA as well, to augment it.

That set-up lasted until 1988, when we splashed out for a huge system from Wigwam Acoustics (although still not as much as we spent on the original PA) that made everyone's nose tingle because of the huge bottom end, and deafened audiences for a whole week. Eventually we had to turn it down from 140db to 130db because doctors were phoning up to complain – too many patients with Haçienda hearing problems. It also caused the baffling to fall down. We'd had this installed in the mid-eighties to improve the acoustics; it cost another thirty grand. The installation was designed by Peter Saville and Ben Kelly, in conjunction with Salford University, and was made up by a specialist company. Very stylish and looked fantastic. But it didn't make any bleedin' difference at all. Sometimes it would fall like a guillotine from the roof and always brought down half the ceiling plaster with it. There were some very lucky escapes. Ang Matthews was forever handing out free Life Memberships to dazed, white-haired people. In fact it became so dangerous we had to take most of it down. (Incidentally, most of the system is still going at a club in Oldham called the Tokyo Project, while the mixer and turntables are in Digital in Newcastle. The owner, Aaron Mellor, has also installed a huge chunk of the Haç dance floor at another of his clubs, Atomic in Ashton. That is what I call a true fan.)

Nude, on Friday nights, was launched in October 1984 by Pickering, who stepped up to man the decks. One of the club's most famous nights, and certainly the longest-running, it would go on make its name in 1987 and 1988, being one of the few places in the UK to play house music and providing a launch-pad for Pickering-as-DJ as well as for, later, Graeme Park.

Initially, however, Nude consisted of Pickering and Andrew 'Marc' Berry, from Swing, the hairdressers, playing jazz, salsa, Motown, pop, hip hop and electro. At last Pickering was providing the across-the-board blend of musical styles he'd witnessed in New York. It paid dividends, too. Within two or three weeks Nude was a capacity night plus it was attracting an even more mixed crowd than Greg Wilson had pulled in. Hairdressers and Goths were thin on the ground now. Punters wore trainers. It was the very beginning of the scally era.

Meanwhile, John Tracey's The End: A No-Funk Night, despite having started the year with a new intake of DJs (including Suzanne, who would later manage the kitchens), died a natural death. For some time it had been the club's most successful night. Yet now, perhaps because the regulars were having their ears tuned to different sounds – Nude on Fridays, Hewan Clarke's Hot night on Saturdays – it seemed oddly anachronistic. Arthur Baker's production of New Order's 'Confusion' had drawn lines between electro and hip hop and was establishing a link between rock music and dance . . .

WHAT'S ON AT THE HAÇIENDA IN 1984

JANUARY

Tuesday 3rd	THE END: A NO-FUNK NIGHT John Tracey; Suzanne
Wednesday 4th	CLUB NIGHT Hewan Clarke
Friday 6th	Easterhouse
Saturday 7th	John Tracey
Wednesday 11th	Red Guitars
Friday 13th	A Certain Ratio
Wednesday 18th	Specimen
Friday 20th	The Wake; Del Amitri
Wednesday 25th	Prefab Sprout; the Daintees
Friday 27th	*The Tube Live* (the Factory All Stars; Marcel King; the Jazz Defektors; Breaking Glass; Madonna *(in her UK TV debut)*

FEBRUARY

Wednesday 1st	The Chiefs of Relief *(ex Bow Wow Wow)*
Thursday 2nd	Reggae
Friday 3rd	Bourgie Bourgie
Friday 10th	Burning Spear; Spartacus
Wednesday 15th	The Cramps; Playn Jayn
Friday 17th	Pink Industry
Monday 20th	FILM NIGHT
Wednesday 22nd	Membranes; Tools You Can Trust
Thursday 23rd	Dead or Alive
Friday 24th	Thomas Dolby; Dekka Dance
Wednesday 29th	Fad Gadget

MARCH

Friday 2nd	My American Wife
Monday 5th	*Sanitorium (film)*

Wednesday 7th	Cook da Books
Friday 9th	Hewan Clarke
Saturday 10th	Whodini
Friday 16th	The Lotus Eaters
Thursday 22nd	Julian Cope
Friday 23rd	Johnny Thunders and the Original Heartbreakers
Wednesday 28th	Reflex
Thursday 29th	The Three Johns; Terry Duffy
Friday 30th	Orange Juice; the Go-Betweens

APRIL

| Tuesday 3rd | THE END: A NO-FUNK NIGHT |
| Friday 6th | The Chameleons |

Set-list: 'Don't Fall', 'Return of the Roughnecks', 'A Person Isn't Safe Anywhere These Days', 'Thursday's Child', 'Here Today', 'Pleasure and Pain', 'Perfume Garden', 'Monkeyland', 'Second Skin', 'One Flesh', 'Paper Tigers', 'In Shreds', 'Singing Rule Britannia (While the Walls Close In)', 'Splitting in Two', 'Up the Down Escalator', 'Don't Fall'

Wednesday 11th	Grandmaster Flash
Friday 13th	Xmal Deutschland
Thursday 19th	Nick Cave & the Cavemen
Thursday 26th	Spear of Destiny; the Shillelagh Sisters
Friday 27th	Swans Way

MAY

Thursday 3rd	Prefab Sprout; the Moodists
Friday 11th	Dead or Alive
Thursday 17th	FASHION SHOW
Friday 18th	Prince Charles and the City Beat Band
Monday 21st	SECOND BIRTHDAY PARTY
Wednesday 23rd	The Cramps
Wednesday 30th	Mary Wilson

JUNE

Friday 1st	Paul Haig; Lloyd Cole & the Commotions
Tuesday 5th	Cabaret Voltaire
Friday 8th	Sex Gang Children

THE HAÇIENDA

Saturday 9th	Sharon Redd
Thursday 14th	Play Dead
Wednesday 20th	The Bluebells; Friends Again
Thursday 21st	King
Friday 22nd	A Certain Ratio
Friday 29th	The Fall; Life

Set-list (the Fall): 'Smile', 'Lie Dream of a Casino Soul', 'Craigness', '2 × 4', 'God Box', 'Kicker Conspiracy', 'C.R.E.E.P.', 'Lay of the Land', 'Elves', 'Oh! Brother', 'Garden', 'Hey Marc Riley', 'I Feel Voxish', 'Pat Trip Dispenser'

JULY

Wednesday 4th	New York
Thursday 12th	The Go-Betweens; Microdisney
Thursday 19th	Pete Shelley
Friday 20th	Zeke Manyika; Colour Code
Wednesday 25th	Shriekback
Friday 27th	Jonathan Richman

AUGUST

Friday 10th	Section 25
Thursday 16th	The Armoury Show
Friday 17th	Salty Sea Dogs Birthday Thing
Tuesday 21st	THE HOMETOWN GIG
Thursday 23rd	Easterhouse; James
Wednesday 29th	Johnny Thunders and the Heartbreakers; Marc Riley

SEPTEMBER

Saturday 1st	HOT Hewan Clarke
Tuesday 4th	THE HOMETOWN GIG
Wednesday 5th	Section 25
Friday 7th	Arrow
Thursday 13th	The Cult
Wednesday 19th	Freddy McGregor; General Smiley
Thursday 20th	Lloyd Cole & the Commotions
Thursday 27th	Working Week

OCTOBER

Tuesday 2nd	THE HOMETOWN GIG
Wednesday 3rd	Tom Verlaine; the Room
Thursday 4th	Afrika Bambaataa *(rescheduled from 15 June)*
Wednesday 10th	Hanoi Rocks
Thursday 11th	Everything But the Girl
Friday 12th	NUDE Mike Pickering
Saturday 13th	HOT Hewan Clarke
Tuesday 16th	THE HOMETOWN GIG
Thursday 18th	The Fall *(rescheduled from 25 October)*
Friday 19th	NUDE Mike Pickering
Saturday 20th	HOT Hewan Clarke
Tuesday 23rd	THE HOMETOWN GIG
Wednesday 24th	General Public
Thursday 25th	Floy Joy
Friday 26th	The Gun Club
Saturday 27th	HOT Hewan Clarke
Wednesday 31st	Bronski Beat

NOVEMBER

Thursday 1st	New Model Army
Friday 2nd	NUDE Mike Pickering
Wednesday 7th	Orange Juice
Friday 9th	NUDE Mike Pickering
Thursday 15th	Alien Sex Fiend
Friday 16th	NUDE Mike Pickering
Saturday 17th	Circus Circus
Tuesday 20th	THE HOMETOWN GIG
Wednesday 21st	March Violets, Inca Babies
Thursday 22nd	NUDE Mike Pickering; Nasty's Mime Act
Friday 23rd	The English Menswear Collection
Wednesday 28th	The Kane Gang

DECEMBER

Tuesday 4th	Spear of Destiny
Wednesday 5th	Wah
Thursday 6th	STYLE IN OUR TIME *(hair/fashion event)* the Jazz Defektors; Frankie's Angels

THE HAÇIENDA

Friday 7th	NUDE Mike Pickering
Saturday 8th	DANCETERIA COMES TO THE HAÇIENDA Mark Kamins
Tuesday 11th	THE YEAR'S BEST OF THE HOMETOWN GIG
Wednesday 12th	The Durutti Column with the Riverside Orchestra

Set-list: 'Sketch for Dawn', 'Sketch for Summer', 'Mercy Theme', 'A Little Mercy', 'Without Mercy Suite', 'The Room', 'A Silence', 'The Beggar', 'Missing Boy', 'Ornithology', 'Prayer', 'Friends in Belgium'

Thursday 13th	Lee Perry
Friday 14th	NUDE Mike Pickering
Friday 21st	A NUDE NATIVITY Mike Pickering
Saturday 22nd	ELEGANT PARTY NIGHT
Monday 24th	HOLY SOAP the Jazz Defektors
Friday 28th	NUDE
Saturday 29th	GENDER BENDER PARTY NIGHT
Monday 31st	(UN)HOLY SOAP the Jazz Defektors

MISCELLANEOUS QUOTES
AND FACTS

At the Style in Our Time night in December, one of the models joining the Jazz Defektors and Frankie's Angels was Paul Cons, who later
became the club promoter and launched the seminal gay night Flesh.

In November, the Twentieth Legion performed at the Haçienda.
Among their number was Damian Lanigan, who was so inspired by the
experience that he decided to set up his own label. He thought better
of it, however, and instead wrote the sitcom *Massive*, which starred Ralf
Little (who played Peter Hook in *24 Hour Party People*) and was about
Manchester lads trying to make it big in the biz.

'I couldn't find a DJ. They all wanted to talk, they were all so pro-
grammed. So in the end, I just thought I could do better and started
doing the Friday night. It was a real *mélange* of music at first, everything
from salsa to electro to northern soul, and it really took off.'

Mike Pickering, djhistory.com

1985

'They shouldn't have allowed him in with a fucking drill anyway'

In February 1985 the German industrial-rock band Einstürzende Neubauten brought a pneumatic drill to their gig. They started it up during their set then attacked the central pillar with it. The crowd were mesmerized. We were, too. We may as well have been fiddling as Rome burned because none of us moved to stop the guy – even though that one beam held up the entire building. We just screamed, 'Yeah! Go on!'

I thought it was hilarious. Not so Terry Mason, who quite rightly panicked, ran over and started wrestling the guy with the drill to stop him from destroying the club. They shouldn't have allowed him in with a fucking drill anyway, the idiots. At last Terry – with the help of a bouncer – prised the drill off him. The band relented and the show continued regardless. Listening to the music, you wouldn't have known Einstürzende Neubauten were short a drill. They had another ten or so on tape.

One young lady, a very wacky Haçienda regular (she used to bring a train set with her, set it up in the cocktail bar and play with it for hours), decided to have a bit of fun with the band while they were playing. She enticed them off stage one by one to screw them in the stairwell. She got through three of them and the audience never even noticed, the noise was that horrendous. The gig ended when the singer's throat burst and he started screaming blood all over the mic. Our sound guy Ozzie got onstage and knocked him out. 'I'd warned him once,' he said.

I must admit, I'm not usually a fan of that type of their music or their sort of anarchy. But as loud as they were the noise actually sounded fantastic. Dead powerful. Mega. When they got that jackhammer going I thought, 'Wow, that's fucking great. I think New Order could use one of those . . .'

Though it ended in an outright ban for Einstürzende Neubauten, theirs was yet another legendary gig for the Haçienda.

Meanwhile, Hewan Clarke's Saturday nights were still a bone of contention. In January the name was changed to simply 'Party Night', then in April it changed yet again, this time to 'Body and Soul, Body and Mind'. Clarke's days at the club were numbered, though, and in May he was replaced by the DJ team the Happy Hooligans.

'Maybe the management felt they weren't getting their Loft or Paradise Garage, so I had to go,' he told writer Tim Lawrence.

However, the Hooligans' night, Will Saturday Ever Be, was not deemed a success and Clarke was invited back, only for there to be a final parting of the ways towards the end of the year. Clarke would be remembered with great affection by the Haçienda faithful, and it's to his credit that he introduced a dance floor expecting wall-to-wall Factory records to a broader selection of music; he had an inbuilt love of jazz-funk. But even so, he was old guard. He belonged to the era of Lulu and the Thunderbirds theme, and the winds of musical change were already beginning to blow at the club.

In June that year the Jesus and Mary Chain played, performing for just thirteen minutes under a hail of flying pint glasses as members of the audience attempted to storm the stage. 'There were ten glasses – real glasses – in the air at every point during the set,' gig-goer Andrew Perry told writer David Cavanagh. 'The Haçienda has a balcony so a lot of these glasses were coming from very high up.'

Even so, the Mary Chain returned in November of that year, shortly after the club reopened after being closed for acoustic baffling to be fitted. Some things at the Haçienda never changed: it was still cold, the roof still leaked and the sound still wasn't up to scratch.

I've got tapes of hundreds of shows I saw at the Haçienda. I recorded them all on the first-ever Sony stereo cassette recorder. Rob had bought us one each to record ideas and mine came in very handy; it was the same one I'd use to do all the New Order shows. Some of them sound fantastic. I'd stick the recorder on the stage or by the monitor board and capture them all.

When the Jesus and Mary Chain played on their infamous 17 Minutes of Feedback tour in 1985, I thought, 'That sounds quite interesting', so made sure I worked security that night.

They asked for a line of bouncers across the front of the stage, and I tell you they needed protection – they were shit. God it was awful,

Lou Reed had done it so much better. The show lasted exactly seventeen minutes, all of them excruciating. The entire set was just feedback, just as it said on the tin. It was done purely to provoke a reaction. To me, it came across as a real con. But if you're going to act that way, you've got to be ready to take the flak – and not expect somebody who's working security for a tenner a night to get battered on your behalf. I was so wound up after they'd finished, I pulled the bouncers off and let the punters at them.

The tour manager said to me, 'I'm getting the band out of here now. Take our gear off.'

I said, 'It's your fault, mate, take your own fucking gear off.'

Man, did they panic. God bless you, Manchester. I've never seen equipment loaded out as quickly in my life. They soon fucked off back to the hotel.

Funnily enough, Bobby Gillespie was on drums that night. He went on to form Primal Scream. Now, I fucking love Bobby and the Primals. One of the only true rock 'n' roll bands left. Us and them were separated at birth, I'm telling you.

In July the club hosted a Lesbian and Gay Miners' Benefit which featured the Redskins and Pete Shelley, among others. It was promoted by Paul Cons, the first night he ever hosted at the Haçienda, having appeared there as model the previous year. The event did well. So in June 'Gay Monday' was launched, again promoted by Cons. This featured music and entertainment in the Gay Traitor bar, and would go on to include performances from Divine, the Communards, Gina X and Bill Nelson. It marked the beginning of a long and successful relationship with the gay community.

Unlike those of us involved with the bands or Factory, who thought of the building's potential only as a concert venue, Paul Cons saw it as a theatre. He decorated the place fantastically so that when his customers came in it literally took their breath away. He certainly knew how to put on a production, that lad. They'd even send him to New York and other cities (lucky sod) to steal ideas or, as he put it, 'to gain inspiration', which he then incorporated at the Haç. Tony absolutely loved it.

For New Order 1985 was a watershed year. The Low Life *album had been released earlier that year and by mixing rock and dance was leading the way forward. They were also featured on the soundtrack of the John Hughes movie* Pretty in Pink, *before forging a huge link with the US . . .*

Suddenly things changed. We signed a licensing deal in America with Qwest, the label owned and ran by Quincy Jones – a great compliment to our production skills – and which was a part of Warner Brothers. So we went from being available only on import to being released on a major label, which meant massive promotion and distribution.

On the back of this huge increase in popularity, we set off on our first big tour of the States. It was a success, the first one where we made any money. We were ecstatic . . .

Until we were told we had to sign it all immediately over to the Haçienda to bail it out.

I remember the day well. We were called into Keith Taylor's office to pick up our money and it felt like Christmas. Better than Christmas. This was sixteen thousand dollars each. *Sixteen grand.* The first time we'd been paid by a company that wasn't Factory; the first time we'd had cheques made out to us, personally.

Then Rob asked us to countersign the cheques so the money could go to the Haçienda. *Shit.*

Well, we did it. I don't think we had any other choice, and perhaps the decision was easier because we'd always got by without money. Still, though, it bloody hurt. And never mind the missus' reaction . . .

But looking back there was one silver lining: after three years of ignoring what was going on, we started to take an interest. We became involved. At last my eyes were being slowly opened.

Because before that, mad as it sounds, I hadn't really been paying any attention. None of us had been. We earned our £100 a week (plus bonuses whenever Rob deemed fit) and got on with the business of being New Order and doing a lot of unpaid production work for Factory. I produced records for Stockholm Monsters, Royal Family & the Poor and loads more; Barney produced 52nd Street, Section 25 and even a young Happy Mondays; and Steve did Red Turns to . . . , Life and Thick Pigeon. And, while we might have been mad to do it for free, none of us minded. To a person, we loved music and wanted to use our status and state of the art equipment to help others – while gaining more experience ourselves, of course.

Which was all very well, but in the first two years of the club being open we'd put £667,000 pounds into it; money from record sales, which came in to Factory Records, then was passed on by Tony to Rob to invest in the club. Not the greatest investment in the world, surely?

So, for three years, we'd been blissfully unaware of the problems. But now that things had gone so horribly wrong – so badly wrong that we had to sign over all our tour money – New Order *finally* had to take an interest.

So the band began attending meetings. Well, I did. Steve and Gillian went to some while Bernard only attended the crisis meetings when he absolutely had to, and he stopped going altogether after 1987.

The first thing we discovered at the meetings was that there were no answers. None. For example, when it came to this management committee we found out that everyone was more or less setting their own wages. When they thought it was time for a raise, they'd give themselves one, never taking into account the fact that the Haçienda was losing money. When we found out about this, we went fucking mental. Although, in fairness, they weren't being told of the real scale of the losses.

There were so many stories like that. They had this huge safe downstairs; and for security reasons they changed the combination every week. This was too complicated for the staff; they kept forgetting the combinations and couldn't open it. So instead they'd stash the money in a filing cabinet – which, after a weekend, amounted to quite a lot for a filing cabinet. Guess where they put the files from the filing cabinet? In the safe! Meanwhile, someone blabbed about the cash in the filing cabinet and over the weekend it got robbed. Because the money wasn't in the safe, it wasn't insured. Brilliant.

That stress of it all didn't affect the quality of New Order's songs, but it did affect our thinking when it came to *why* we were writing them. Bernard, most vocal among us, would say, 'Why are we doing this if it's all going to the Haçienda?'

As soon as we finished that tour of America only to hand the money over, we started asking ourselves if we really wanted to work so hard for the club. (How hard? I'd been away for eight and a half years of the ten years my first relationship lasted, performing and recording all over the world.) New Order had always excelled at letting problems simmer rather than dealing with them. But now they boiled over and we all felt the same way.

The band never got into fist-fights, although I sometimes wonder if we should have chinned each other every now and then – perhaps there wouldn't have been such a build-up of resentment. Even Steve and Gillian, normally quite placid, spoke up when it came to what the club was costing us, because the fact was we still didn't have much cash to our names.

Why didn't we sack Rob and Tony, you might wonder. It never crossed our minds. Despite it all, we were an easy-going bunch. And loyal. We were all in this together, we felt, and as a band we disliked change.

In December, New Order took over the club to play two gigs – on the same day.

We performed two sell-out shows – a kids' matinee and an evening concert – in December that year. We did the former because of fond memories from when Joy Division used to play at Roger Eagle's club Eric's in Liverpool: Roger always scheduled a show for the under-eighteens. Really thoughtful, and the kids loved it. We felt we should do the same at the Haç.

In typical Haçienda fashion the staff allowed over-eighteens to attend the afternoon gig, so it turned into a complete debacle. All the kids got crushed. Then, because our bouncers in these early years were too nice, they wouldn't force the fans at the matinee to leave afterwards to make room for the evening crowd. A riot broke out on Whitworth Street as the evening audience struggled to get inside.

By now the management-committee situation had reached a head. The club began looking for an experienced, full-time manager, while the directors began casting around for ways to shore up the financial situation . . .

We were looking for ways to dig ourselves out this money-pit we were in. The directors' loans, our investment, made the Haçienda uninviting to outside investors because if we ever actually turned a profit the loans to us would need to be paid off. As soon as investors looked at the balance sheet, they left.

In the fullness of time, Rob and all of us in New Order simply agreed to forgive the club's debts to us, which by now totalled about £2 million.

We had no choice but to do that: we had no hope of ever getting the money back.

At that point, in 1985, Steve and Gillian relinquished their share-holdings and distributed them to the rest of us because they wanted to be free of the company.

They were so sick of it, they literally walked away. They still had their personal guarantees for the initial loans/mistakes, but at least they had the satisfaction of knowing that they didn't need to be involved in the business any more.

I don't blame them. We were all badly hurt by what had happened to us financially, and very angry about it. Bernard and I hung on; we stayed optimistic, hoping it could still succeed. Plus, the shares Stephen and Gillian passed to us were quite a juicy carrot: it meant that each of us possessed a greater percentage of the company. The shares were worthless, of course, but we felt like we'd gained something: we owned more of nothing. Then again, if a miracle occurred – like it reversed course and turned a profit – we might actually stand to gain more.

Meanwhile, Rob actively tried to eliminate all the personal guarantees. He knew it had been a mistake. We spent a fortune on lawyers and all of them told us the same thing: you can't get out of personal guarantees unless you pay them off.

I remember looking over the Haçienda's accounts. I did the sums and in the first five years it had been open we'd lost more than £20,000 a month on top of the set-up costs . . .

Also in December, the club hosted A Transatlantic Happening, featuring Pickering's Quando Quango and 52nd Street. The event was held to celebrate the birthday of Ruth Polsky, 'the Queen of New York City', and also included DJs Mark Kamins and Frank Callari. After this, Rob Gretton's health took a turn for the worse . . .

He was admitted to hospital suffering from a full-blown psychosis. It left him incapacitated for many months and with health problems for the rest of his life.

I presume Tony took over the running of the club. We briefly thought of getting our American manager, Tom Atencio, involved, trying to get him to manage both New Order and the Haçienda, but Tom didn't have a clue about running a club. He was quite honest about that:

he wasn't interested, plus he didn't want to move – living an ocean away in California suited him. Trouble was, this left both New Order and the Haçienda without leadership and with no money – we literally couldn't get money out of the bank without Rob. Taking pity on us, the promoter Phil McIntyre helped us out when he and Terry Mason arranged three gigs, starting in Warrington, and paid the band £10,000 in advance. That money literally allowed us to survive.

With all this on my mind, the daily operations of the club receded in importance for a while . . .

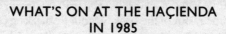

WHAT'S ON AT THE HAÇIENDA IN 1985

JANUARY

Friday 4th	NUDE Mike Pickering
Saturday 5th	Hewan Clarke
Friday 11th	NUDE Mike Pickering
Friday 18th	NUDE Mike Pickering
Friday 25th	NUDE Mike Pickering

FEBRUARY

Friday 1st	NUDE Mike Pickering
Friday 8th	NUDE Mike Pickering
Monday 11th	Milltown Brothers; Midwich Cuckoos
Wednesday 13th	James; A Certain General
Friday 15th	NUDE Mike Pickering
Friday 22nd	NUDE Mike Pickering
Thursday 28th	Einstürzende Neubauten

Set-list: 'Seele brennt', 'Zeichnungen des Patienten O.T.', 'Meningitis', 'Armenia', 'Yü-Gung (Fütter Mein Ego)', 'Sehnsucht', 'Sand', 'Negativ Nein', 'Letztes Biest (Am Himmel)', 'Hör mit Schmerzen', 'Tanz Debil', 'Die Genaue Zeit', 'Abfackeln!'

MARCH

Friday 1st	NUDE Mike Pickering
Saturday 2nd	Run DMC
Tuesday 5th	RAW POWER (The Tuesday Night. The Haçienda. The Real Music. The Cramps and Joy Division and Test Dept and Buzzcocks and T-Rex and the Fall and U2 and Bowie and the Inca Babies and Billy Bragg and Strongarm and Other Hard Stuff . . .)
Thursday 7th	The Pogues
Friday 8th	NUDE Mike Pickering
Thursday 14th	The Associates

Friday 15th	NUDE Mike Pickering
Thursday 21st	THE EASTER BALL Baby Go Boom
Friday 22nd	NUDE Mike Pickering
Wednesday 27th	The Redskins; Pete Shelley
Friday 29th	NUDE Mike Pickering

APRIL

Monday 8th	NUDE Mike Pickering *(rescheduled from 5 April)*
Friday 12th	NUDE Mike Pickering
Friday 19th	NUDE Mike Pickering
Thursday 25th	Nick Cave & the Bad Seeds; Sonic Youth

Set-list (Sonic Youth): 'Halloween', 'Death Valley 69', 'Brave Men Run', 'I Love Her All the Time', 'Ghost Bitch', 'I'm Insane', 'Brother James', 'Kill Yr Idols'

| Friday 26th | NUDE Mike Pickering |
| Saturday 27th | BODY AND SOUL, BODY AND MIND Hewan Clarke |

MAY

Thursday 2nd	Xmal Deutschland
Friday 3rd	NUDE Mike Pickering
Friday 10th	NUDE Mike Pickering
Thursday 16th	The Colourfield
Friday 17th	NUDE Mike Pickering
Saturday 18th	WILL SATURDAY EVER BE? the Happy Hooligans
Tuesday 21st	THIRD ANNIVERSARY CELEBRATION *(Three at last)*
Thursday 23rd	The Explorers
Friday 24th	NUDE Mike Pickering
Friday 31st	NUDE Mike Pickering

JUNE

Wednesday 5th	Gil Scott-Heron
Friday 7th	NUDE Mike Pickering
Monday 10th	GAY MONDAY
Tuesday 11th	THE SUMMER OF LOVE Martin Prendergast
Thursday 13th	The Pogues

THE HAÇIENDA

Friday 14th	NUDE Mike Pickering
Saturday 15th	WILL SATURDAY EVER BE? Chad Jackson
Thursday 20th	Afro-Caribbean Connection
Friday 21st	NUDE Mike Pickering
Monday 24th	Pete Shelley
Wednesday 26th	The Jesus and Mary Chain
Thursday 27th	War
Friday 28th	NUDE Mike Pickering

JULY

Tuesday 2nd	RAW POWER – RAW MEAT *(All the hard stuff)*
Thursday 4th	Johnny Thunders and the Heartbreakers *(American Independence night. Rally around the flag with Johnny Thunder and the Heartbreakers and many more Yank surprises.)*
Friday 5th	NUDE Mike Pickering
Friday 12th	NUDE Mike Pickering
Monday 15th	GAY MONDAY; the Communards
Tuesday 16th	New Order

Set-list: 'State of the Nation', 'Dreams Never End', 'Subculture', 'This Time of Night', 'Your Silent Face', 'Love Vigilantes', 'Weirdo', 'The Perfect Kiss', 'Face Up', 'Sunrise', 'Ceremony', 'Confusion', 'Temptation'

Friday 19th	NUDE Mike Pickering
Thursday 25th	Paul Blake
Friday 26th	NUDE Mike Pickering

AUGUST

Friday 2nd	NUDE Mike Pickering
Friday 9th	NUDE Mike Pickering
Thursday 15th	Playn Jayne; the Stone Roses

Set-list (the Stone Roses): 'Fall', 'Heart on the Staves', 'So Young', 'I Wanna Be Adored', 'Here It Comes', 'All I Want', 'Tradjic Roundabout', 'Getting Plenty', 'Tell Me'

Friday 16th	NUDE Mike Pickering
Monday 19th	GAY MONDAY
Wednesday 21st	George Clinton
Friday 23rd	NUDE Mike Pickering
Friday 30th	NUDE Mike Pickering

SEPTEMBER

Friday 6th	NUDE Mike Pickering
Monday 9th	GAY MONDAY *The Life and Times of Harvey Milk (film)*
Friday 13th	NUDE Mike Pickering
Wednesday 18th	The Pogues
Friday 20th	NUDE Mike Pickering
Wednesday 25th	Husker Du; Crime & the City Solution
Friday 27th	NUDE Mike Pickering; the Latino Beat *(Classic Dance-Floor Show Electro/Soul/Funk/Reggae)*
Saturday 28th	WILL SATURDAY EVER BE?
Monday 30th	MUSIC AND DANCE FOR LESBIANS AND GAY MEN Liz Wright; the Fallen Angels

OCTOBER

Tuesday 1st	THE SUMMER OF LOVE Little Martin; Martin Prendergast
Friday 4th	NUDE Mike Pickering
Monday 7th	MUSIC AND DANCE FOR LESBIANS AND GAY MEN
Tuesday 8th	FRESHERS' BALL
Wednesday 9th	The Fall
Friday 11th	NUDE Mike Pickering
Saturday 12th	WILL SATURDAY EVER BE?
Tuesday 15th	Everything But the Girl
Friday 18th	NUDE Mike Pickering
Saturday 19th	WILL SATURDAY EVER BE?
Wednesday 23rd	Primal Scream; Meat Whiplash; Weather Prophets
Friday 25th	NUDE Mike Pickering
Saturday 26th	WILL SATURDAY EVER BE?
Monday 28th	GAY MONDAY Miquel Brown; the Joan Collins Fan Club; Liz Wright; the Fallen Angels
Thursday 31st	Gil Scott-Heron

NOVEMBER

Friday 1st	NUDE Mike Pickering
Friday 8th	NUDE Mike Pickering
Thursday 14th	The Cool Notes

THE HAÇIENDA

Friday 15th	NUDE Mike Pickering
Friday 22nd	NUDE Mike Pickering
Tuesday 26th	The Jesus and Mary Chain
Friday 29th	NUDE Mike Pickering

DECEMBER

Tuesday 3rd — New Order *(two concerts, matinee and late show)*; the Happy Mondays

Matinee set-list (New Order): 'As It Is When It Was', 'Sunrise', 'Face Up', 'The Perfect Kiss', 'Your Silent Face', 'Sooner Than You Think', 'This Time of Night', 'Confusion', 'Temptation', 'Age of Consent'

Evening set-list (New Order): 'As It Is When It Was', 'Everything's Gone Green', 'Subculture', 'Blue Monday', 'Lonesome Tonight', 'Love Vigilantes', '586', 'Face Up', 'Ceremony', 'State of the Nation'

Wednesday 4th — MANCHESTER POLYTECHNIC CHRISTMAS PARTY *(produced by students and featuring their own DJs)*

Thursday 5th — A TRANSATLANTIC HAPPENING Quando Quango; 52nd Street; Mark Kamins; Frank Callari

Friday 6th	NUDE Mike Pickering
Monday 9th	GAY MONDAY
Friday 13th	NUDE Mike Pickering
Saturday 14th	STREET SCENE
Monday 16th	GAY MONDAY
Tuesday 17th	WINTER OF DISCONTENT PARTY
Thursday 19th	CITY LIFE PARTY
Friday 20th	NUDE Mike Pickering
Tuesday 24th	CHRISTMAS EVE PARTY
Friday 27th	NUDE Mike Pickering
Tuesday 31st	NEW YEAR'S EVE PARTY

104

EXCERPTS FROM COMPANY ACCOUNTS, 1985

FACT 51 Limited
Trading as: the Haçienda

REPORT OF THE DIRECTORS
The Directors submit their report and the audited accounts for the year ended 21 May 1985.

Principal activities
The principal activity of the Company is that of proprietors of a licensed club and recreation rooms.

Review of the business
The Directors consider that the Company's trading position will improve in the long term.

Fixed assets
The movement of fixed assets is set out in note 8 of the accounts.

Results and dividends
The trading loss for the year after taxation and extraordinary items was £52,528. The Directors do not recommend the payment of a dividend.

Directors
The Directors who served during the year and their interests in the Company at the end of the year were as follows:

A. H. Wilson (held in trust for Factory Records)
R. L. Gretton (Communications) Limited
H. M. Jones (Resigned 31.12.1983)
A. Erasmus

Mr A. H. Wilson retires by rotation and being eligible offers himself for re-election.

Political and charitable contributions
There were no political or charitable contributions in the year.

Taxation status
In the opinion of the Directors, the Company is a close Company within the meaning of the Income and Corporation Taxes Act 1970.

Auditors
A resolution to appoint Freedman Frankel & Taylor as auditors will be proposed at the Annual General Meeting.

BY ORDER OF THE BOARD

[Signed by Alan Erasmus]

Secretary

FAC 51 Limited
Trading as: the Haçienda

PROFIT AND LOSS ACCOUNT (for the year ended 21 May 1985)

	1985 (£)	1984 (£)
Turnover	476,893.00	499,566.00
Cost of sales	145,649.00	116,563.00
Gross profit	331,244.00	383,003.00
Administrative expenses	377,046.00	374,542.00
Operating profit	(45,802.00)	8461.00
Interest payable and similar charges	7736.00	11,119.00
Loss on ordinary activities before taxation	(53,528.00)	(2658.00)
Taxation	–	–
Loss on ordinary activities after taxation	(53,528.00)	(2658.00)
Retained loss for the year	(53,528.00)	(49,858.00)
Retained loss brought forward	(58,726.00)	(8868.00)
Retained loss carried forward	(112,254.00)	(58,726.00)

MISCELLANEOUS QUOTES AND FACTS

'About three years after opening the Haçienda we realized that every-body in Manchester was getting free drinks – except for the people who actually owned it.'

Tony Wilson

1986

**'We rarely had fights at all in
those days. The few times we did,
it was always our mates involved'**

In January 1986 Nico of the Velvet Underground, who had made
Manchester her home, played her last-ever gig. It was at the Haçienda. She
played with the Faction and was supported by Eric Random. Shortly afterwards – ever the trailblazer – she relocated to Ibiza.

Meanwhile, Paul Mason – the man who would later be credited with
turning the club around – arrived. He instigated immediate changes.

'[The problems were] big losses,' he told writer Jon Savage.

> There was no management structure at all. [It was] run by committees,
> chaos. Unfortunately, I arrived being known in advance as the hatchet
> man. I had no friends at all. I used to go back to Nottingham at the end
> of the week. That's the way it had to be for a few weeks. I started by
> explaining to the doormen that they couldn't have pints of beer on the
> door. That's how bad the situation was, There was no midweek club that
> was doing the business. The club was open Monday and Tuesday with
> about nine people in, it was costing a fortune. I saw the first Monday and
> Tuesday nights and we just didn't open the following Monday and Tuesday.

To his credit, Alan Erasmus realized very early on that we couldn't run
the Haçienda properly, and he insisted loads and loads of times we
needed new management –somebody who'd do things sensibly who
had experience. It just took everyone else a while to come round to
this idea. No one likes the truth.

But we all did come round, in the end, and we kicked out the committee and brought Paul Mason on board. He ran a club in Nottingham
called Rock City (New Order played and met him there in 1981), and
was a well-thought-of club manager, so Alan went along to Rock City,
sat down with him, and lined him up for the job.

When he agreed we were ecstatic: 'This is the one who's going to turn it around.' Our saviour.

He was very quiet. Studious. I remember coming in with him for his first day on the job in January and thinking, 'What a revelation!' He was all about doing things efficiently, asking the staff, 'Why is the boiler on, putting out heat during the day when there's nobody in the club? Turn that off until an hour before the doors open, to warm it up for when people come in.'

Pretty logical, but nobody had considered it before. He had an eye for detail the rest of us lacked. Little things like, 'Why don't you stop the staff stealing off you?'

He was a real, honest-to-God manager. A boss. For a while, he came across as a big authoritarian figure and everyone was scared him. For good reason: he hired and fired people like mad.

Because Paul came in as the golden boy, Rob and Tony basically offered him whatever he wanted. They gave him a lot of money, which he deserved. But he also wanted a company car. Now, Paul lived at Deansgate, which is 150 yards from the Haçienda, but they let him have any vehicle he chose. The one he picked was a £30,000 Lancia Delta Integrale 4X4, one of the fastest road cars ever made. To go from Deansgate to the Haçienda? They let him have it, though.

(We didn't agree with this decision. When the members of New Order got involved, one of the first things we asked was, 'Why has this guy got a £30,000 car when he lives across the fucking road?')

For his part, I think Paul was impressed by the reputations of Factory and New Order and had decided that an association with us would be a feather in his cap. Business-wise the club itself wasn't a success, so it can't have been that.

Staffing at the lower levels remained erratic. Without regular, experienced employees to rely on, all sorts of things would slip – even big things like the finances. As our accountants wrote it in one of Factory's annual reports: 'The subsidiary [i.e., the Haçienda] had a high turnover of staff in the accounts department during the year. The book-keeping was not up to the required standards and there was no system of internal control upon which we could rely or alternative accounting procedures which we could adopt to verify the accounting records.'

*

In other words, we trusted that Paul would turn our financial mess around, but we couldn't be sure by how much. We continued to move forward, blindly – but optimistically.

One story has it that Mason's introduction to the world of Factory and the Haçienda involved attending a management meeting during which Wilson threw chips at Gretton and the pair ended up grappling on the floor. Given Gretton's state of health at the time, however, this could be an apocryphal tale.

When Rob returned, unfortunately he was a shadow of his former self. Five stone lighter, he looked and acted a lot older. No longer as bombastic or as loud, he'd simply stopped being such a huge physical presence. He had to take things much easier, so a gentler, quieter side of him emerged, one that was much more thoughtful.

The axis of power shifted, and antagonism surfaced toward Rob, Factory and the Haçienda because the whole thing was such an absolute cock-up. To make matters worse, the taxman decided to fuck us all.

It all came out that while we were touring America, Tony didn't have time to give Rob New Order's royalties to invest in the Haçienda, so he put the money directly into the club without anyone paying tax on it.

That – technically – is fraud. It should have gone into New Order's company first, and been accounted, and only *then* could it be invested in the Haçienda.

To paraphrase *Scooby Doo*, we might have got away with it, too, if it hadn't been for a pesky member of staff.

The story goes that the PAYE/National Insurance contributions officer had asked to inspect the wages books – presumably to see if anyone was fiddling. We were informed of his impending visit, but unfortunately nobody advised the member of staff who was on the door when the contributions bloke came knocking.

Now in those days most business had two sets of books. The nice, clean set you gave to the taxman, which included all the PAYE, National Insurance details and so on, and another hush-hush set of books, the cash books for the cleaners, humpers, odd-job men, etc. Wouldn't happen these days, of course.

So anyway, there's our member of staff sitting scratching her arse when along comes the civil servant.

I wasn't there, but let's imagine he's wearing a bowler hat and carrying a briefcase, perhaps with a rolled-up copy of the *Financial Times* under his arm.

'Good morning to you,' he says to our staffer. 'I believe you're expecting me. I've come to collect the wage books to check the PAYE and National Insurance calculations.'

So she gave him the books.

Only, she gave him the wrong books – she gave him the cash books. An unbelievably stupid mistake, and they didn't even sack her. Someone must have been screwing her, I reckon.

This happening set in motion a very costly chain of events. The taxman investigated us under Section 105 of the 1970 Taxes Management Act, which regulates evidence in cases of tax fraud. He looked into the finances of Factory, New Order, Joy Division and all of the people involved. The only one he couldn't get hold was Will O'the Wisp himself, Alan Erasmus.

The inspector demanded to see all our financial paperwork and correspondence. On looking over the figures, investigators couldn't believe we'd put so much money into the Haçienda. We must have been taking it out for ourselves, they figured; we must have been living like lords. They simply wouldn't believe that we personally saw so little of what we were earning.

So one day three of the buggers turned up on my doorstep, demanding to do an inventory of the house. They even counted the tools in the garage and rooted through the knives and forks in the kitchen, thinking they'd find out where all the money had gone. They did the same to all of us.

One of the guys turned to me as he left, apparently satisfied – at last – that I wasn't salting millions away on cutlery and Black & Decker Workmates.

'Where's all the money gone?' he said, baffled.

'What do you mean?' I replied.

(A few months later, of course, I had the answer: the money he thought we were spending on ourselves? It had all been put into the club.)

At the end of the investigation a deal was done with the taxman where we agreed that the money New Order had put into the Haçienda was a promotional expense, not an investment. We and our lawyers had to fight really hard to get that, and it was a very expensive long-winded fight indeed.

That was how we escaped the fraud charge. Which was good – none of us fancied a trip to Strangeways, after all. What's the per-day money like inside? Do you get a rider? The downside was that we then had to write off our investment – it had become a promotional expense – so we no longer had any money in the club.

To add insult to injury the taxman fined New Order and Joy Division £800,000 for our own accounting irregularities – a record fine at the time.

It took us years to pay it off. Now we were working not only to keep funding the Haçienda – a club in which we no longer had a financial interest, remember – but also to pay off our own fine.

And we were pissed off about that because it meant we were no longer working for ourselves, or making music for the love of it. It felt like we were doing it for the taxman, or for the bloody Haçienda.

Even so, the music didn't suffer, and you could even argue that New Order hit its creative peak around this time – or was about to. Perhaps Tony was right when he told us, 'The taxman did you a favour, darling. You would have made shit music without that fine.'

Yeah, cheers, Tony. He definitely had a way with words.

Meanwhile, my growing-up period continued and I was starting to take an interest in some of the figures.

Or I was trying to. The accounts were very confusing. And when you could make head or tail of them, they simply didn't add up. For example, in the accounts were entries for 'records and CDs', which vary from year to year: £42,000 one year and £49,000 the next. A thousand pounds a week? That was physically impossible and the DJs brought their own stuff to play anyway. What a con.

It was unbelievable. I held long, drug-fuelled conversations about what was happening at the Haçienda with anybody who would listen, but there were no answers. Not from my high-as-kite mates anyway.

Despite the ongoing money issues, not everything at the club was doom and gloom. It was a very easy-going place back then, even the security were lovely. They were like chaperones. Fred was the head bouncer. Nice guy. Jasmine looked after the female punters. Ditto. She was really sweet. Back then, there was hardly any trouble and not many drugs, just a bit of whizz and dope, so their jobs were very easy. They even won an award in some magazine for being the best-presented bouncers in the UK. They all wore Crombies and were very smart. They left in 1986 when Roger Kennedy's firm took over. He had the door until 1991.

Frankly, we rarely had fights at all in those days. The few times we did, it was always our mates involved. Things would change in that department. The whole of Manchester and Salford would soon join in.

The other upheaval that year was that the golden period of Haçienda gigs finally drew to an end. Competing venues like the Free Trade Hall and the Apollo were offering bands better deals and the bands were defecting. There's loyalty for you.

It was decided that much more cost-effective were DJ-only nights. This decision would help to shape not just the club's future direction, but also the direction of UK club culture as a whole.

Nude night had shown the way. Nude meant 'nothing on' – there were no acts between DJs (or vice versa) – and it had proven successful. In May, Andrew 'Marc' Berry left. Now Pickering was joined in the booth by Martin Prendergast (who had been recruited by Ang on the back of the bus to work from Chorlton), the two playing as MP^2.

Together they were enthusiastic recipients of the new house sounds arriving in Manchester direct from Chicago: 'No Way Back' by Adonis, 'Love Can't Turn Around' by Farley Jackmaster Funk, J. M. Silk's 'Jump Back', 'Rhythm' by Marshall Jefferson. These were the very first house records and the Nude crowd loved them. Then, the style of dancing was 'jacking' and dancers the Foot Patrol would give virtuoso displays for the benefit of an appreciative crowd. Drugs had yet to enter the scene but, even so, clubbers sensed a change in the air at Nude, a shift from fashion to music, from 'being seen' to having a good time. The wardrobe was trainers and T-shirts; the night even saw the first appearances of what would later become the ubiquitous flares. This was the night that had attracted members of the Happy Mondays from the suburbs into the city, that would in retrospect be seen to have ushered in the era of the scally – who were at first known as Baldricks, according to a feature in iD magazine at the time. It was to provide the cornerstone of the club's policy from that moment on.

Not far behind Paul Mason came Paul Cons, whose official title at the club was PR. Together they would turn the club's fortunes around.

In May, Boardwalk DJ, Debris fanzine editor and Haçienda regular

Dave Haslam came on board to launch the Temperance Club on a Thursday night. Now the Haçienda had the two nights that would cement its reputation. Nude on Fridays, where house music was being tentatively explored, and the Temperance Club, where lies the roots of the Madchester phenomenon.

Temperance would play the funky end of hip hop and electro – Eric B and Rakim, Mantronix, the indie up-and-comers such as James and the Railway Children – alongside alternative favourites. On the one hand, Mark E. Smith once bought Haslam a pint for playing 'Little Doll' by the Stooges; on the other, Morrissey sat in his booth turning his nose up when he played Man Parrish.

For his part, Haslam, an ex-NME writer, was pleased to finally exercise a musical impulse he felt was stifled by the music press – a Londoncentric body that still tended to pit alternative music against dance music as two mutually excusive entities – yet was finding a voice in the club nights around the city. Thanks to Nude, and the groundwork of the DJs before him, he was able to reach an audience – a mainly student crowd — whose ears were already open to a mix of musical styles. Thursday nights did so well for the club that Haslam was asked to host a Saturday-night slot too, where he partnered Dean Johnson, who specialized in northern soul. The night was called Wide, and it began on Saturday 19 July during the Festival of the Tenth Summer.

If 1986 was a pivotal year for the Haçienda, and for the explosion of dance music and Madchester mayhem that was to follow and engulf the UK, then one event in that year can be said to mark its flashpoint: the Festival of the Tenth Summer. Aimed at marking ten years of punk – it being a decade since the Pistols played at the Lesser Free Trade Hall – the Festival of the Tenth Summer was a week of musical events helmed by Factory that ended with a gig at G-Mex. On the bill were the Fall, the Smiths and New Order, the latter of whom headlined, and it was followed by the launch of Wide at the Haçienda.

'At G-Mex I played "Stoned Out of My mind" by the Chi-Lites and then struggled round the corner to the Haçienda with my records in a cardboard box and my £40 wage in my pocket,' says Haslam. 'It was the dawn of a new era.'

At last things were falling into place for the club. Until August that year, the Haçienda had only ever been full for bands. This changed one Friday night when the club enjoyed a packed night. At the time, Wilson had been *in China brooding over the future of the club. While the Festival of the Tenth Summer would in retrospect be seen as a watershed moment, it hadn't had any financial effect on the club at the time. Exhausted from promoting the festival and downcast at not seeing the rewards through the door, Wilson was considering throwing in the towel. Then he put in a phone call to Paul Mason only to be told the good news. Times were changing.*

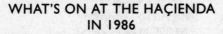

WHAT'S ON AT THE HAÇIENDA IN 1986

JANUARY
Friday 3rd	NUDE Mike Pickering
Friday 10th	NUDE Mike Pickering
Friday 17th	NUDE Mike Pickering
Thursday 23rd	Erasure
Friday 24th	NUDE Mike Pickering
Thursday 30th	Nico and the Faction; Eric Random
Friday 31st	NUDE Mike Pickering

FEBRUARY
Friday 7th	NUDE Mike Pickering
Friday 14th	NUDE Mike Pickering
Monday 17th	*Gone Hollywood (Jeremy Kerr art installation until 26 March)*
Tuesday 18th	The Swans; Gifted
Wednesday 19th	Cabaret Voltaire
Friday 21st	NUDE Mike Pickering
Thursday 27th	CHANGE
Friday 28th	NUDE Mike Pickering

MARCH
Thursday 5th	King Kurt
Friday 7th	NUDE Mike Pickering
Tuesday 11th	Kurtis Blow
Friday 14th	NUDE Mike Pickering
Friday 21st	NUDE Mike Pickering
Friday 28th	NUDE Mike Pickering

APRIL
Friday 4th	NUDE Mike Pickering
Saturday 5th	BIG NOISE: MUSIC FOR THE MODERN DANCE FLOOR

THE HAÇIENDA

Friday 11th	NUDE Mike Pickering
Saturday 12th	BIG NOISE: MUSIC FOR THE MODERN DANCE FLOOR
Tuesday 15th	Big Audio Dynamite
Friday 18th	NUDE Mike Pickering
Thursday 24th	The Blow Monkeys
Friday 25th	NUDE Mike Pickering; fashion show with Rosie Haywood/Armstrong Collins Sharp/Posh Frocks
Saturday 26th	DISCO NIGHT Chad Jackson
Wednesday 30th	LATIN QUARTER

MAY

Thursday 1st	TEMPERANCE CLUB Hedd-Dave Haslam
Friday 2nd	NUDE MP^2 – Mike Pickering and Martin Prendergast
Saturday 3rd	BIG NOISE: MUSIC FOR THE MODERN DANCE FLOOR Andy Miller
Friday 9th	NUDE Mike Pickering; fashion show by Su King
Wednesday 14th	Jesus and Mary Chain; Pink Industry
Friday 16th	NUDE Mike Pickering
Wednesday 21st	FOURTH BIRTHDAY PARTY
Friday 23rd	NUDE Mike Pickering
Wednesday 28th	Art of Noise
Friday 30th	NUDE Mike Pickering

JUNE

Wednesday 4th	Crime and the City Solution; Ghostdance
Friday 6th	NUDE Mike Pickering
Wednesday 11th	Gene Loves Jezebel
Friday 13th	NUDE Mike Pickering
Saturday 14th	i-D MAGAZINE PARTY
Friday 20th	NUDE Mike Pickering
Saturday 21st	BIG NOISE: MUSIC FOR THE MODERN DANCE FLOOR Rob Day
Monday 23rd	Sandie Shaw
Friday 27th	NUDE Mike Pickering

JULY

Tuesday 1st	Black Uhuru; the Wailers
Friday 4th	NUDE Mike Pickering
Tuesday 8th	The Alarm
Friday 11th	NUDE Mike Pickering
Sunday 13th	FASHION: CLOTHING THE NAKED FLESH WITH PLASTIC FLOWERS *(a Festival of the Tenth Summer fashion show)*
Friday 18th	NUDE Mike Pickering
Saturday 19th	WIDE Dean Johnson; Hedd-Dave Haslam
Friday 25th	NUDE Mike Pickering
Wednesday 30th	Zodiac Mindwarp; MC Evil Bastard

AUGUST

Friday 1st	NUDE Mike Pickering
Friday 8th	NUDE Mike Pickering
Friday 15th	NUDE Mike Pickering
Friday 22nd	NUDE Mike Pickering
Thursday 28th	TEMPERANCE CLUB
Friday 29th	NUDE Mike Pickering

SEPTEMBER

Friday 5th	NUDE Mike Pickering
Friday 12th	NUDE Mike Pickering
Friday 19th	NUDE Mike Pickering
Friday 26th	NUDE Mike Pickering

OCTOBER

Wednesday 1st	Trouble Funk
Friday 3rd	NUDE Mike Pickering
Friday 10th	NUDE Mike Pickering
Monday 13th	New Order

Set-list: 'Sooner Than You Think', 'Bizarre Love Triangle', 'Subculture', 'All Day Long', 'Every Little Counts', 'Paradise', 'State of the Nation', 'Everything's Gone Green', 'Weirdo', 'Sunrise', 'Temptation'

Tuesday 14th	Erasure
Friday 17th	NUDE Mike Pickering

THE HAÇIENDA

Wednesday 22nd	Full Force
Friday 24th	NUDE Mike Pickering
Tuesday 28th	The Fabulous Thunderbirds
Wednesday 29th	RESIDENTS *(thirteenth-anniversary show featuring Snakefinger)*
Friday 31st	NUDE Mike Pickering

NOVEMBER

Friday 7th	NUDE Mike Pickering
Thursday 13th	The Railway Children
Friday 14th	NUDE Mike Pickering
Friday 21st	NUDE Mike Pickering
Friday 28th	NUDE Mike Pickering

DECEMBER

Thursday 4th	David Mach *(art installation until 11 January)*
Friday 5th	NUDE Mike Pickering
Tuesday 9th	Spear of Destiny
Friday 12th	NUDE Mike Pickering
Thursday 18th	TEMPERANCE CLUB Felt
Friday 19th	NUDE Mike Pickering
Monday 22nd	CREATIVE CIRCLE PARTY
Tuesday 23rd	SOUTH MANCHESTER COLLEGE PARTY
Wednesday 24th	CHRISTMAS EVE PARTY
Friday 26th	NUDE Mike Pickering
Tuesday 31st	NEW YEAR'S EVE PARTY

EXCERPTS FROM COMPANY ACCOUNTS, 1986

FACT 51 Limited
Trading as: the Haçienda

AVERAGE MONTHLY OVERHEADS

	(£)	
Rent	2000.00	
Rates	1662.01	
Power: Gas	607.44	(estimated accounts being
Electricity	552.83	looked into)
Water	110.11	
Cleaning	1192.75	
(Lights, videos, etc.	1023.00)	
Electrician	1138.87	
Ads	400.00	(on two events per month)
Fly posting	140.00	
Printing	260.00	
Leaflets/artwork	180.00	
Bus – Temperance Club	300.00	
Full-time staff – gross earnings	2922.00	
PAYE and NI	2368.32	
Telephones	443.13	
Alarm system: Maintenance	123.05	
Rental	50.31	
Performing Rights Society	333.33	
Insurance	1000.00	
Total	21,407.15	

FAC 51 Limited
Trading as: the Haçienda

CURRENT WEEKLY INCOME FROM THREE NIGHTS

		(£)
Thursday	(average profit)	600.00
Friday	(average profit)	1600.00
Saturday	(average profit)	300.00
Total		2500.00

PROJECTED AUTUMN INCOME

		(£)	
Thursday	(average profit)	1000.00	(1000 admissions)
Friday	(average profit)	1800.00	(800 admissions)
Saturday	(average profit)	1200.00	(600 admissions)
Concert	(average profit)	750.00	
Total		4750.00	

Plus income from exhibitions and private parties.

MISCELLANEOUS QUOTES
AND FACTS

Ruth Polsky was killed by a runaway taxi on the steps of the Limelight club in New York on 7 September 1986. It was the first time she had ever queued to get in a club: this was one of the first AIDS benefits and the Queen of New York City was making an important statement.

From 1979 until her death she had been responsible for breaking innumerable British bands in the States thanks to tireless work in promotion and as talent buyer at Hurrah and Danceteria. She had booked the fateful Joy Division tour, then New Order's first tour as a three-piece. Others who owed her a debt of gratitude included the Smiths (who dedicated the 'Shoplifters of the World Unite' single to her memory), Sisters of Mercy, the Cocteau Twins, and Echo and the Bunnymen.

On 5 December 1986 New Order performed a benefit gig for her at the the Roxy in New York, during which they played 'Atmosphere' and 'Love Will Tear Us Apart' as encores – the first time the two songs had been played live since Joy Division was dissolved.

'Mason told me it was "full of art students" and although I couldn't work out whether he considered this a good or a bad thing he later called me up and asked me to start a Thursday at the Haçienda from 1 May 1986; the Temperance Club, the night was going to be called. I still hadn't met Mr Wilson or Mr Gretton. No one talked to me much, although I did have another conversation with Paul Mason, who said I could play what ever I liked and I would be paid £40 a week.'

Dave Haslam

1987

'I must be imagining this . . .'

The year began on an optimistic note. The latter half of 1986 had seen numbers steadily increase as the club's policy of staging DJ nights rather than live gigs (though prompted by necessity rather than choice) appeared to be paying off.

At the beginning of 1987 the Hacienda had three regular club nights: Thursday's Temperance Club, busy laying the groundwork for Madchester; the ever-popular Nude on Fridays, hosted by Pickering and Prendergast and preparing the city for the explosion of house music that was to come; and on Saturdays there was Dean Johnson with a night named after the music policy: Wide.

By 1987 New Order's constant touring of America had paid off and made us even more successful. We had graduated from playing clubs and theatres to headlining huge arenas and we were playing bigger crowds than Oasis or the Spice Girls ever did, plus we were still making great music (thanks to the taxman, remember), so it should have been a happy time.

It wasn't, though. As people, we'd grown apart. The music kept us together but we had no rapport and there was a general feeling of being in the doldrums. Partly this was because of the financial situation: we felt like we were a money-making machine, working just to get the Haçienda and out of a hole; plus Rob was sorely missed. He may not have been the most efficient boss in the world but, in the words of *Shameless*'s Frank Gallagher, 'he knew how to throw a party'. Everyone missed that when he was ill.

It took Rob a while to get back his health back and during that time Tony was number one, working closely with Paul Mason on all aspects of the club – a move I think a lot of the staff resented. Rob and Tony had very different ideas, and Rob was definitely the most popular with the staff. He was a man of the people.

I didn't get to many management meetings during this period because I was always off touring with New Order, but one thing I do remember was the strange phenomenon of 'financial projections', where they'd write lists and lists of projected attendances for the club. Well, you can write anything you want on a piece of paper. Who actually turns up is a completely different matter. It almost seemed like they made it up as they went along. Today, I know that you never open a club or put a night on until you can afford to lose the highest figure, but at the time we convinced ourselves that it was great to carry on as usual. We'd look at the projections (all of them based on wishful thinking) and go, 'Well, that's not too bad, is it?'

I compare it now to mass hypnosis. Furthermore, music goes in and out of fashion. Even if you had a great year in the past, there's no guarantee of even having a great week in the future. We learned that the hard way, too.

That year, New Order released the singles compilation Substance, *two singles, 'True Faith' and 'Touched by the Hand of God', and toured with Echo and the Bunnymen and Gene Loves Jezebel in the US.*

Being in a group, I went to a lot of different places. But this didn't educate me. Touring should have opened my mind, opened my thinking, but whenever I came home to Manchester and the Haçienda, I'd be so glad to be home. I knew exactly where I belonged, and it was here. I enjoyed the stability. I'd go off performing all around the world with New Order, come back and find my mates sitting exactly where I left them. Thank God. Rock stars have our cake and eat it. You go away, act like a complete idiot, then return and expect a nice, quiet life. They'd ask how the tour was and all of us would say the same thing, 'Quiet, you know?'

Of course, as soon as I became involved in the Haçienda, all of that changed. If you want a quiet life, take my advice: DON'T OPEN A FUCKING CLUB.

One cold Monday night in March 1987 the Chicago House Party Tour arrived at the club, featuring Marshall Jefferson, Adonis, Frankie Knuckles, Kevin Irving and Fingers Inc. Though the event signalled the impact house music was having on the club's owners and DJs, it was not tremendously

well supported. Still, the sound remained a staple at Nude and Wide.
Patiently, the Haçienda waited for the rest of the world to catch up.

The video screens never worked properly – this was blamed on the cigarette smoke, funnily enough – so when they completely broke, around 1987/1988, we did away with them for good.

They'd always had a bit of a chequered career anyway. After a while, Bessy had stopped doing his controversial installations and we'd hired Tony Martin to do the lights and video. Although not as confrontational an artist as Claude, Tony took his work very seriously. He was followed by two lighting guys named Jonathan Unsworth and Mark Smith, professionally known as Swivel, until they too left, to be replaced by Steve Page.

As for filming, we got an employee to film the shows at the Haçienda and project them on the screens. The bands were given the tapes for nothing at the beginning – in true Factory fashion – which is why that Birthday Party gig lives on.

It meant we had video footage, with sound, of performances by virtually every band that played in the club – which was just about every band playing in England at the time. Most groups demanded we erase the tapes. In the early days this was because they didn't like to see themselves playing to a half-empty club; later it was because we were asking for payment and they didn't want to cough up for them.

Luckily they never got erased, though, whatever the band demanded. Unluckily for all concerned the tapes disappeared when Factory went bust and later appeared when they were released by a number of third-party video companies, who even released New Order performances without our consent.

So, anyway, with the video screens broken we just stopped using the equipment and because of that we never properly filmed anything during the acid-house era that followed in 1988 and 1989. Again, we should have sent cameramen round to capture it all; it would have been gold. We never thought to do that. We were too off our heads, I suppose. Instead all we have are snatches, a few news items . . .

Zumbar launched in October 1987, promising 'an adventurous mix of live entertainment, fashion and disco, a night of exotic variety'. It boasted a Spanish theme, featured live acts and karaoke in the Gay Traitor bar and was hosted by Fred, who was better known as the club's maintenance manager. The opening included a 'wheel of fortune', which dictated the price of the booze, and legend has it that Tony Wilson fell out with manager Paul Mason when the needle stuck at 'free drinks' three times. (Maintenance manager Fred had weighted the wheel so this wouldn't happen and it never did during hours of rigorous testing. Mason was later reinstated.) Zumbar went on to become one of the club's most popular nights, and would host Julian Clary (as the Joan Collins Fan Club, with Fanny the Wonder Dog), Jerry Sadowitz and Frank Sidebottom. In November the night hosted a 'live happening' involving artist Phil Diggle doing 'action paintings', which saw the club hit with four insurance claims in its wake, including one from Barney, while the Christmas special featured a visit from Coronation Street's Vera Duckworth. A week or so later the club ushered in the new year with a 'mega firework display', and . . .

Our money went up in flames. We'd routinely hire guys to come to set up indoor fireworks; this was overseen by Paul Mason, who got them to set up the fireworks on top of the big main room bar.

We were taking so much money, it being New Year's Eve and all, they couldn't shift it so they started stashing it behind the bar, where there was a small room. When the fireworks went off at midnight the sparks rained through the gaps in the bar and set fire to the money, burning all of the notes inside.

I still have this drunken memory of Paul Mason on his hands and knees, patting all this cash, trying to put it out.

'Am I fucking tripping?' I thought. 'There is all our money, ablaze. No, no, no, I must be imagining this.'

That cost us, like, five grand or something. Happy New Year.

Little did I know, it would be. Maybe popular culture caught up to us. Maybe that pyrotechnic bungle served as a burned offering for good luck. Whatever the case, within the next few months, everything – and I mean everything – changed. For me, New Order, the Haçienda, Madchester and the entire world.

Acid house had arrived and the Summer of Love would soon be in full swing.

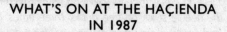

WHAT'S ON AT THE HAÇIENDA IN 1987

JANUARY

Friday 2nd	NUDE MP^2 – Mike Pickering and Martin Prendergast
Saturday 3rd	WIDE Dean; Hedd-Dave Haslam
Wednesday 7th	TEMPERANCE CLUB Hedd-Dave Haslam
Friday 9th	NUDE MP^2 – Mike Pickering and Martin Prendergast
Saturday 10th	WIDE Dean; Hedd-Dave Haslam
Wednesday 14th	TEMPERANCE CLUB Hedd-Dave Haslam
Friday 16th	NUDE MP^2 – Mike Pickering and Martin Prendergast
Saturday 17th	WIDE Dean; Hedd-Dave Haslam
Thursday 22nd	TEMPERANCE CLUB Hedd-Dave Haslam
Friday 23rd	NUDE MP^2 – Mike Pickering and Martin Prendergast
Saturday 24th	WIDE Dean; Hedd-Dave Haslam
Thursday 29th	TEMPERANCE CLUB Hedd-Dave Haslam
Friday 30th	NUDE MP^2 – Mike Pickering and Martin Prendergast

FEBRUARY

Friday 6th	NUDE Mike Pickering
Monday 9th	NUDE SPECIAL Mantronix; MP1 Dave Haslam
Friday 13th	NUDE Mike Pickering
Friday 20th	NUDE Mike Pickering
Tuesday 24th	*Neon (Peter Freeman art installation until 24 March)*
Wednesday 25th	Loma Gee; Hedd-Dave Haslam; Paolo Hewitt
Friday 27th	NUDE Mike Pickering; A Prophylactic Party *(Dave Dale in the Gay Traitor 'to launch the Haçienda condom Vendor')*

MARCH
Friday 6th	NUDE Mike Pickering
Sunday 8th	Frank Chickens; Hope Augustus; Sensible Footwear; Joolz
Monday 9th	NUDE Marshall Jefferson; Adonis; Frankie Knuckles; Kevin Irving; Fingers Inc.
Friday 13th	NUDE Mike Pickering
Saturday 14th	*Wide Art (performance-art installation by Adrian Moakes)*
Friday 20th	NUDE Mike Pickering
Friday 27th	NUDE Mike Pickering

APRIL
Friday 3rd	INTERNATIONAL AIDS DAY PARTY
Tuesday 7th	AIDSLINE BENEFIT the Woodentops; Everything But the Girl; Marc Almond
Friday 10th	NUDE Mike Pickering
Friday 17th	NUDE Mike Pickering
Friday 24th	NUDE Mike Pickering
Wednesday 29th	Mighty Lemon Drops

MAY
Friday 1st	NUDE Mike Pickering
Thursday 7th	TEMPERANCE CLUB the Bodines
Friday 8th	NUDE Mike Pickering
Friday 15th	NUDE Mike Pickering
Wednesday 20th	FIFTH BIRTHDAY PARTY *(Kung Fu Night)*
Thursday 28th	The Happy Mondays
Friday 29th	NUDE Mike Pickering

JUNE
Friday 5th	NUDE Mike Pickering
Wednesday 10th	New Order

Set-list: 'Touched by the Hand of God', 'Paradise', 'Way of Life', 'Shellshock', 'Ceremony', 'Thieves Like Us', 'Bizarre Love Triangle', 'Subculture', 'Age of Consent', 'Face Up', 'Temptation'

Friday 12th	NUDE Mike Pickering
Friday 19th	NUDE Mike Pickering

Tuesday 23rd	SLEEPING BAG FRESH REVIEW Joyce Sims; T-La Rock; Hanson & Davis; Just-Ice
Friday 26th	NUDE Mike Pickering

JULY

Friday 3rd	NUDE Mike Pickering
Friday 10th	NUDE Mike Pickering
Friday 17th	NUDE Mike Pickering
Friday 24th	NUDE Mike Pickering
Friday 31st	NUDE Mike Pickering

AUGUST

Friday 7th	NUDE Mike Pickering
Friday 14th	NUDE Mike Pickering
Sunday 16th	The Durutti Column
Friday 21st	NUDE Mike Pickering
Friday 28th	NUDE Mike Pickering

SEPTEMBER

Friday 4th	NUDE Mike Pickering
Tuesday 8th	FRESHERS' BALL Little Martin: the Legendary Stardust Cowboy
Friday 11th	NUDE Mike Pickering
Thursday 17th	TEMPERANCE CLUB *Westworld (art installation by Adrian Moakes and Andy Parkin)*
Friday 18th	NUDE Mike Pickering
Friday 25th	NUDE Mike Pickering

OCTOBER

Friday 2nd	NUDE Mike Pickering
Wednesday 7th	ZUMBAR MEGA OPENING PARTY Elvis *(impersonator)*; fashion PA by Vidal Sassoon; Jose & Pedro
Friday 9th	NUDE Mike Pickering
Wednesday 14th	ZUMBAR Joan Collins Fan Club with Fanny the Wonder Dog; fashion PA by Marc Benedict
Friday 16th	NUDE Mike Pickering
Wednesday 21st	ZUMBAR Hope Augustus; fashion PA by Aspecto

Friday 23rd   NUDE Mike Pickering
Wednesday 28th   ZUMBAR Jerry Sadowitz; fashion PA by Tristan Williams
Thursday 29th   TEMPERANCE CLUB Yargo
Friday 30th   NUDE Mike Pickering

NOVEMBER

Tuesday 3rd   All About Eve
Wednesday 4th   ZUMBAR fashion PA by Howl
Friday 6th   NUDE Mike Pickering
Wednesday 11th   ZUMBAR Bolo Bolo; fashion PA by Reiss
Friday 13th   NUDE Mike Pickering
Tuesday 17th   Micro Disney
Wednesday 18th   ZUMBAR Philip & Steve Diggle; fashion PA by Akimbo
Tuesday 24th   Edwyn Collins
Wednesday 25th   ZUMBAR The Amazing Orchante; fashion PA by Tailor of Two Cities
Friday 27th   NUDE Mike Pickering

DECEMBER

Tuesday 1st   Age of Chance
Wednesday 2nd   ZUMBAR Stevie Star; fashion PA by Woodhouse
Friday 4th   NUDE Mike Pickering
Wednesday 9th   ZUMBAR Staircase to Heaven; Frank Sidebottom; art installation by Hannah Collins
Friday 11th   NUDE Mike Pickering
Wednesday 16th   ZUMBAR Tot; fashion PA by Zipcode
Friday 18th   NUDE Mike Pickering
Wednesday 23rd   ZUMBAR YULETIDE SPECIAL Vera Duckworth/Liz Dawn; fashion shows by Geese/Tailor of Two Cities/Marc Benedict
Thursday 24th   CHRISTMAS EVE
Friday 25th   NUDE Mike Pickering
Sunday 27th   ZUMBAR Dead Marilyn *(Monroe impersonator)*
Thursday 31st   NEW YEAR'S EVE PARTY *(and mega fireworks display)*

EXCERPTS FROM COMPANY ACCOUNTS, 1987

FACT 51 Limited
Trading as: the Haçienda

THREE-MONTH ANALYSIS (1 January-31 March 1987)

Income		(£)	
Thursday average:	Door & cloak	905.00	
	Bars	862.00	
		= **1767.00**	
	Less expenses	575.00	
	Average profit	= **1192.00**	(× 13 weeks = 15,496.00)
Friday average:	Door & cloak	1632.00	
	Bars	688.00	
		= **2320.00**	
	Less expenses	605.00	
	Average profit	= **1715.00**	(× 13 weeks = 22,295.00)
Saturday average:	Door & cloak	1948.00	
	Bars	1172.00	
		= **3120.00**	
	Less expenses	637.00	
	Average profit	= **2483.00**	(× 13 weeks = 32,279.00)
Private parties		25.00	
Gigs		1720.00	
Machines (pinball & cigs)		691.71	
Merchandise:	Club	328.80	
	Mail order	757.00	
Telephones		124.80	
Total net income		= **73,717.31**	

FACT 51 Limited
Trading as: the Haçienda

Running costs	(£)
Bank charges and interest	1923.00
Rent	5500.00
Service charge	950.00
Gas	752.00
Water	2252.00
Electricity	2735.00
Rates	5957.00
Full-time manager and wages	14,640.00
Electrician	2665.00
Taxis	1491.00
Buses	653.00
Anagram	987.00
Insurance: Fire & theft	3125.00
Buildings	3000.00
Public liability	1000.00
PRS	1343.00
PPL	582.00
Keith Taylor	991.00
Sundries	5790.00
Acorn cleaners	3926.00
Cleaning materials	513.00
Cleansing department	478.00
Plumbers	114.00
Lifts	28.00
Larry Benji	492.00
Bessages (fire Xs)	53.00
Bolton BM (tills)	797.00
City Life	370.00
DJ Alarms	88.00
Euro Lighting	23.00
Sydney England	28.00
B. Gibbons	36.00

THE HAÇIENDA

H. Haworth (glassware)	1175.00
Johnstone Paints	63.00
Jonson Panas	1362.00
N. Klagg	510.00
MEN	485.00
Mainstage	89.00
Manders Paints	194.00
Rentokil	125.00
Petty cash: January	1350.00
February	1464.00
March	1337.00
Total running costs	**= 70,706.00**

INTERLUDE: ONE NIGHT IN IBIZA, JUNE 1988

Great excitement, we have Sham 69 visiting our Ibizan bolt-hole tonight. The Hersham boys are thinking of making their next album in the studio we've been using, Studio Meditterraneo – a grand name for a not-very-grand studio – so they're being given the full sales pitch and tour. One of the selling points, of course, is that New Order are currently using it, busy recording their next album, the one that will eventually become *Technique*, and if it's good enough for New Order . . . But actually we haven't been good enough for it!

We haven't exactly been busy, and we haven't done very much recording. Almost precisely none, in fact.

Instead, I've been partying. Every single night I've been out until the small hours only to rise some time the next afternoon, refreshed and ready to start again. Tonight, I suspect, will be no different.

Sham 69 arrive and are met by the two owners of the studio, a couple of right heavy-metal throwbacks: imagine Status Quo crossed with Judas Priest and you have an idea of the hair and wardrobe on these guys. They give Sham a tour of the studio then we all adjourn to the bar. There, I discover that Sham are doing a gig tonight at San Antonio harbour but have no soundman.

Step forward Peter Hook, a great fan, ably assisted by Andrew Robinson.

It's going to be wild, we're assured.

Oh, how right they are.

So we get to San Antonio where it turns out that Sham 69 will be playing the gig – an early Ibiza Rocks – on a big raft that'll be towed out into the middle of the harbour. Sounds good. Trouble is, they're not playing until much, much later – the early hours – and right now it's only nine p.m., giving us a suicidal amount of time to kill. You can see exactly where this is going, can't you?

We make for the backstage area, which is a barge with a public bar upstairs plus a downstairs dressing room with cabins and a private bar.

We get stuck in and by midnight everybody is off their face. I mean, completely out of their tree. Everyone's a right mess, not least of all Sham's lead singer, Jimmy Pursey, who's mithering me for coke: 'It's for me piles. They're killing me,' he moans.

Meanwhile, my mate has cornered the two studio owners. 'Have you tried this?' he says, holding out his hand. 'It's great. Everyone's on it.'

What he's offering them is the main reason I've done nothing during our four months in Ibiza. It's ecstasy, and I've taken to it like a duck to water . . .

We'd read about ecstasy before we arrived in Ibiza, of course, but none of us had seen or tried it; I'd never really used drugs up to that point. But every time we went out and about, buzzing around Ibiza, it looked like everyone was dropping E and having a fantastic time. They were, as we say, mad for it.

So, one day, after another half-hearted attempt at recording, we were sent to track some down.

There was a bloke named Paco who ran a bar near the studio and who once served the Rolling Stones up when they were on the island. Ronnie Wood was his favourite: '*Uno grande* guy: *uno* gram, *uno* line,' he'd say.

Paco introduced us to a dealer named Pedro, who we got to know well during our time in Ibiza. Pedro had only one arm. I kept asking him what happened to the other one but his English wasn't too good – or mine wasn't – so he never understood what I meant and I never found out. Pedro was shit hot on a moped. Work that one out.

Anyway, we got some off him. Spent a lot of money on them, too – £90, all told. We returned to the studio like the guy with the magic beans. What was he called? Oh yeah: Jack. Only, we didn't swap them for a cow. With hindsight I wish we had, but hindsight is good like that. Instead we went up our own beanstalk.

After we'd explained how much they cost everyone suddenly looked very uninterested, so we were stuck with these tablets. Very, very annoyed, we charged into San Ann. Once we'd pounded back a few drinks and calmed down I said: 'I know. Fuck it. Let's try a half.'

We swallowed. Waited ten seconds. Then, as soon as Andy said, 'Is yours working yet?' I experienced a need to shit like I'd never felt before and I ran around like a maniac trying to find a bloody toilet.

Once I'd accomplished that mission, the next sensation was like having a rocket up my arse. It felt like nothing I'd ever known before. My God, it was unbelievable. We lost control. We was off.

Tripping, we got split up in San Antonio. I came to my senses about ten hours later, five miles away in Ibiza harbour, sat on a bench and watching the sun rise. God knows how I got there but, as I stared blankly out to sea, I thought I saw a little black thing come out of the water. It looked like a periscope. It looked round; it *was* a periscope. A flaming submarine rose up and docked. All the sailors emerged from inside and lined up on the deck; someone whistled, they saluted, then all disembarked, walked past where I sat, then marched into town.

It was the most incredible thing I'd ever seen.

I still have no idea what navy they were. I just thought, 'Fuckin' hell. I'm going home.'

Once we'd recovered from that night, we couldn't wait to do it again. Like Alice in Wonderland we found we liked it down the rabbit hole and we spent all our time partying. We were on the guest-list for all the clubs: Pacha, Ku, Space, Eden ... My favourite was Amnesia – especially the roof terrace – but we haunted them all: the tranny bars of Ibiza Town, the after-hours clubs in San Antonio. And, God forgive us, we drove everywhere, too, all over the island – everyone did. Each morning there'd be a different set of rolled cars all over the place. We wrote off eleven hire cars ourselves.

It was fantastic. A permanent holiday and we'd tell anyone who'd listen at home how great it was – except the wives, of course.

Then somebody said, 'We're having such a good time, why don't we invite the Happy Mondays over?' Perfect.

The Mondays were friends of ours; they were like our naughty younger brothers. Though sometimes I absolutely hated their stinking guts, especially when they misbehaved. I remember them wrecking a room we'd hired at Birmingham NEC for a Dry staff party when we were playing there. They broke in, grabbed the booze and wrecked the room. I went berserk. Me and Terry were ready to throw them out but Rob said no. Shaun's only riposte was: 'What do you think cleaners are for, Hooky?' I was livid. Ah well.

That said, they embodied true rock and roll. Like Iggy Pop, Nick Cave and other people I admired, they didn't give a fuck what anybody thought. They made Pete Doherty look like Cliff Richard.

So I was delighted when they came to Ibiza. They arrived with our great friend Gordon the Chef ('Hundred and forty short orders, Hooky, one night'), and brought a couple of ounces of speed to sell to pay their way. They didn't manage to sell any of it because everyone preferred E – and after we'd introduced them to Pedro, our one-armed dealer, so did they. The rest is history. The last we saw of them they were driving off with a couple of our rentals. Into the night.

Needless to say, progress on the next New Order record now ground to a complete halt – in fact, if anything it went into reverse. There just wasn't enough time to party *and* make the record, and every night brought its tales.

Like the night Andy and I met Paul Oakenfold, and Brandon Block I think – or it could have been Danny Rampling – in a club. These were the guys who then took Ibiza and acid house back to London, so you can imagine: it was a massive night. Along the way we'd hooked up with two lads from Stretford and at the end of the night me and Andy offered to give them a lift home.

Which would have been a great idea if either of us had known where we were going. We didn't, but we weren't going to let a small thing like that bother us. Definitely not.

I was absolutely battered – no way could I drive. I could hardly even see straight. So it was Andy in the driving seat, me in the passenger seat, the two Stretford lads in the back. Tunes on. You've seen *Wayne's World*, right? The bit where they're all singing along to 'Bohemian Rhapsody'? That was us. Only we were doing the Ibiza version, the house remix, making boxes and gurning.

All the same, though, there was something wrong. Something not quite right.

'There's summat up here, Andy,' I was saying . . .

'No it's fine,' he said. Foot hard down.

'No there's something wrong? I can't figure out what it is . . .'

Then – *crash*.

We were on the wrong side of the road and we'd hit another car head-on. A right shunt. Andy and I both butted the windscreen – I swear the glass had a Peter Hook-shaped dent in it – and the two lads from Stretford came flying over the seats from behind us, scraping their shins on the seat backs and ending up in our laps, bleeding. Nasty.

'You ok lads?' I asked worriedly . . .

'HEAD ON COLLISION WITH NEW ORDER! YEH!' They cho-rused. Fuck me.

Still, no serious injuries sustained, we jumped out of the car to meet the driver of the other vehicle, also unharmed.

But very, very angry. He was a taxi driver, this guy, and he was ges-ticulating at his knackered car with one hand, using the other to wave a fist at us, screaming and shouting, 'Fooking English pigs. You on wrong side of road.'

Terrified, I went into full-on diplomacy mode.

'Sorry, mate, I'm really, really sorry. We'll pay for all the damage. We will, we're in a band.'

I was trying desperately to calm the guy down. He was having none of it. 'Eenglish pigs. I call police.'

The tunes were still on in our car and the lads from Stretford were dancing in the middle of the road. Andy, too. Still making boxes, throw-ing shapes and gurning – which for some reason seemed to annoy him even more.

'You ruin my livelihood, I no feed my children!' he was screaming.

Then, to make matters worse, I heard sirens in the distance. Uh-oh.

'You leg it,' I told Andy. 'I'll deal with it.'

God help us. I don't know what I was thinking.

So Andy and the two lads from Stretford did a runner to a grave-yard opposite hiding behind the gravestones, watching me as I stood waiting to deal with the police, who arrived like a Spanish Starsky and Hutch, two right big bastards. They didn't jump over the bonnet but both drew their nightsticks.

I gulped. One stood by the side of the car, glowering. The other one, the bigger of the two, fixed me with a stare. Then, very, very, slowly he walked round both of the crashed cars until he was standing in front of me again. He raised his nightstick and jabbed me in the chest.

'In Spain,' he said, 'we drive on zee right!' Then walked back to his car, me nodding inanely.

'Yes, sir. Thank you, sir!'

Meanwhile, Andy and the two lads from Stretford had decided to offer moral support from across the road in the graveyard.

'Hooky,' one of them called, head bobbing up from behind a gravestone.

The two coppers looked over at the graveyard, but there was no sign of Andy or the two lads. They looked back at me.

Behind them I saw the heads popping up from behind the grave-stones. Like that game with the moles. If only I'd had a mallet.

I grinned back at the coppers innocently. In the end, they'd had enough, got back in their car and drove off, leaving me a paranoid wreck in their wake. Now I legged it across the road and hid too, watching as the still-furious taxi driver managed to free his car of the wreckage and drive away, radiator steaming. With him gone, we emerged like Madchester zombies from the graveyard and pushed our car on to the side of the road. Another car wrecked.

'See you, lads.'

'Thanks for a top night, Hooky. See you in the Haç.'

That was the great thing about E. It made mates of you all. As a result, as soon as you'd had your first experience of it, you were always trying to convert other people to it.

Which brings us back to the barge, and my mate who is urging the two studio owners to get on one, offering them up in his upturned palm. 'Everyone's on one,' he insists.

Stuck in the album charts *circa* 1979 they may be, but these two don't pass up the opportunity to try out the new wonder drug.

They each take one.

Almost immediately owner number one goes completely off it, thinks Andy is a monkey and freaks out. We lock him in the car for a while to recover, but when we go back later to check he's OK he's disappeared. Ah well. Owner number two, meanwhile, goes hyper.

'I'm going to walk back,' he tells me, head nodding, hair shaking.

'The villa is about twelve miles away,' I say.

'I don't care. I'm going to walk back,' he insists. 'Which way is it?'

I'm just as trashed as everybody else, which is obviously why I point in the opposite direction to the villa and say, 'That way, mate', chuckling as he trots off. Oops.

Sham 69 haven't played a note and it's absolute pandemonium; nobody can even string a sentence together. But, hey, the show must go on. So the band find themselves on a raft being towed out into the middle of San Antonio harbour, where they begin to play.

However, by now it's three a.m. and the place is empty. God knows where everybody is, but they're not in San Antonio harbour. It's just Sham 69 on a raft, plus me, Andy, the PA guy, a few casualties and maybe a dog or two.

Of course we're going mad at the mixing desk. Andy is dubbing everything up and screaming, 'Woo, woo, woo . . .' The PA guy wants to kill him for it. We go so mad on the sound that even the casualties and the dogs are driven away, but it doesn't really matter. By the time the gig is over Sham 69 are completely incoherent with booze – they could have been playing Shea Stadium for all they know about it – so we ditch them, leave them dribbling on the barge and decide go to Eden instead.

Phew.

Out of the madness at last.

And then, into more madness.

Eden's one of my favourite clubs, and it's jumping. We make our way up to the balconies from where we can survey the devastation below, and there we spy some familiar faces. Paco's here. He's with a couple of our new friends, one a tranny, the other a lesbian, who always hang out together; plus we bump into a bunch of guys we've been meeting a lot – the air-traffic controllers from San Antonio airport. These guys are lunatics, I'm telling you. Total nutters. Tonight's a weird one even by their standards – tonight they're wearing make-up and half of them are in drag. It's the beginning of their holidays so they are celebrating; they leave Ibiza tomorrow.

So there we are in Eden, off our cake. The music's hitting the spot and we're all talking – well, shouting, really. Strange, intense conversations about how great the music is, how wonderful the club is, how beautiful Ibiza is, how life is great.

Next thing, this German guy comes over, bawls something in my ear and indicates a corner where it's quieter. I go with him and there he fixes me with a serious, probing stare and says, 'It is not a woman.'

He points at the tranny as he says it. He's really quite angry about the fact. Turns out he's been buying him/her drinks all night. 'It is not a woman,' he repeats.

'Yeah,' I think, 'and?' but trying to be polite, smiling and nodding. 'Thanks, mate. Cheers for the information.'

'It is not a woman,' he insists. 'It is a *man*.'

Yeah, right. Nod. Smile. Back away slowly.

Back to Andy. 'That dickhead over there has only just worked out that it's a guy,' I bawl, jerking a thumb back at the corner.

'This dickhead?' Andy points.

I turn. The German guy has followed me back to the table. He's now standing over us. Me, Andy, the tranny, the lesbian and the air-traffic controllers in drag. We all look at him. The tranny in particular looks scared. Now the German guy is screaming at the tranny.

'It is not a woman,' he repeats. He's getting a bit lairy. Andy – suddenly, surprisingly – is looking all protective.

Then it kicks off. The German guy starts throwing things at the tranny, moving around the table as if to get at her. She gets scared, jumps up and tries to run away. Thing is, she can't run too well in her stilettos. One of the heels breaks off and she crashes to the ground.

Andy, knight in shining armour that he is, rushes over and picks her up in his arms as though she's a princess or something.

'I'm in love, I'm in love,' he shouts, taking the piss. The German guy stops throwing things, looks at us as though we're the biggest bunch of degenerates he's ever had the misfortune to meet, and skulks off, muttering to himself.

'I'm in love,' shouts Andy once more for good measure.

Later, I find out that the tranny is a butcher. Funny old world, innit?

So anyway, we leave Eden. By this time we've picked up another member of the party, our one-armed drug dealer, Pedro. For some reason I never fully understand, it's Pedro's job to get the air-traffic controllers to the ferry in time, so we all pile in cars to make our way there.

'The ferry?' I say, settling into the driving seat. 'Why are we taking them to the ferry? Why aren't they flying out like everybody else?'

Pedro leans over to me. 'Nobody who works at Ibiza airport will fly from there,' he tells me conspiratorially, tapping his nose. 'It's far too dangerous. Too many near misses.' Looking at this lot I think I know why.

Great. Whether or not he was pulling my leg I never find out – I just hope he was.

By now it is very, very early in the morning and we're all hanging, coming down, a rag-tag convoy of casualties, rushing across the island to the ferry.

Then – *crunch.* Oh no, not again?

Shit. I've gone into the car in front of me. The one full of air-traffic controllers. We stop. Everybody gets out of the cars, everybody panicking. The air-traffic controllers, still in drag, are going mad, they're going to be late for the ferry. The tranny is panicking, the lesbian is panicking. Pedro the one-armed drug dealer is screaming and running around. Me and Andy are holding our heads and trying to get it together. The whole lot of us: a screaming, dragged-up, drugged-up, noisy, early-morning-coming-down mess.

Then, all of a sudden, we stop. Suddenly we're aware of being watched. We've crashed outside two massive tourist hotels and lining the pavements on either side of us are hundreds of holidaymakers sat there with suitcases, waiting for buses to take them to the airport. Mums, dads, children, grannies. Just normal tourists. All staring at us as we freak out in the middle of the road.

And, I swear to God, not one of them says a word.

There is a second or so of eerie silence. We stare at them. They stare back at us. All of us open-mouthed, like two different species meeting each other for the first time.

Then we just start freaking out again – even more.

We have to find an alternative mode of transport. *The taxi rank.* The air-traffic controllers continue on their way to the ferry; the tranny and the lesbian disappear. Andy and I get in the last one. The driver looks at me in the rear-view mirror, brow furrowed.

'A dónde vas, Gringo?'

'Studio Meditterraneo, mate, por favor.'

We drive.

'Hey señor,' he says, eyes narrowing, 'I know you?'

'No I don't think so!'

'Si Si, where I know you from?'

Then the penny drops. *Oh, shit.* My bruised and battered brain flashes back to month or so ago, a head-on collision, an irate taxi driver screaming. 'Eeenglish pigs.'

The same guy. Well, at least he was wrong – I hadn't ruined his livelihood. I shrink into the seat dumbstruck.

After all that, I get back to the villa. There, it's chaos, too. One of the Status Quo-meets-Judas Priest studio guys has been going round the island telling everyone he's New Order's manager. He's been posing as Rob Gretton and he's got himself in all kinds of trouble. He's pulled a girl, brought her back to the villa, then thrown her out of his room. She's running around the villa banging on all the doors, screaming, 'Let me in, you filthy bastard.'

'What's up, love?' I ask.

'New Order's manager, do you know him? He's locked me out,' she screams.

Can I be bothered to sort it out? No. And with that, grinning, I go to bed. Fuck me, what a life. Can't wait till tonight.

1988

'It's a miracle any of us survived'

Trouble was, we couldn't stay in Ibiza forever, even if we'd wanted to. We'd rented the studio for a set period of time, and eventually that time ran out.

Before we left, Tony came over to see us for a few days, bringing his son Oliver with him. I ended up babysitting while he checked Ibiza out. I drove them back to the airport a few days later, where I dutifully waited till he'd checked in then walked him to departures. They left, I waved, I walked away, I heard a shout.

'Hooky!'

It's Tony. He'd come back, beckoned me over.

'Yes, Tone?' I asked.

'This is the most expensive holiday you've ever had!' he spat, and disappeared again.

The next day Andy and I had been in Amnesia all night and we were shedded. We were walking through Ibiza town, looking for a cab to take us back to the studio, when we saw Nico with her son, Ari, sitting at a table, drinking coffee.

I said to Andy, 'Oh no, look, there's Nico. She'll do our heads in. Let's do one.' And shamefully we ran away.

Cycling home afterwards, she fell off her bike and hit her head; she died the next day. We must have been two of the last people to see her alive – of the last people who knew her, anyway. Now I really regret that.

Tony was dead right, though, at the airport. We'd wasted our time either out partying, or recovering, spent an absolute fortune and came home to England with just two songs ('Fine Time', inspired by a night in Amnesia, and 'Run', inspired by a night in San Antonio) and sixteen drum tracks (what can I say? Steve was always much better at concentrating than the rest of us) only to discover . . . In Manchester, acid house was in full swing.

Decadence. Complete madness. It's a miracle any of us survived.

Stories differ as to how 'acid house' was created. Some maintain that Chicago producer Marshall Jefferson and DJ Pierre were messing about with a Roland TB-Bass Line bass synthesizer when the machine began to make a strange, squelchy sound. A sound that would later become the defining characteristic of acid.

There's another story, also involving DJ Pierre: that he discovered the same acidic, squelching sound when the batteries on his TB-303 ran flat. Yet another has DJ Pierre and his mate Spanky messing around on a Roland TB-303, playing with the pre-programmed samples and discovering . . .

What's clear is that there was some combination of people messing around with a 303 and finding a sound that, combined with a flat 4/4 beat, led to the creation of acid house.

On the subject of which was the very first acid-house track, opinions once again vary: the credit belongs to either 'I've Lost Control' by Sleezy D or 'Acid Trax' by Phuture, both of which were produced by Marshall Jefferson. Of the two it was certainly Phuture's almost-twelve-minute epic 'Acid Trax' that had the greatest effect. It was a massive hit in the clubs of Chicago and New York, but it was in the UK that it had the most impact, arriving at the same time as the emerging Balearic scene from Ibiza and the drug ecstasy. Thus the acid of Chicago was but one element of the UK acid-house explosion in 1988. The scene had its roots as much in Balearic beat as it did in the Windy City and it stormed without focus, referencing 1960s hippy culture as well as house and techno and even early indie arrivals such as the Woodentops, Thrashing Doves and Finitribe.

Acid house spread like wildfire. Shoom had been opened by Danny and Jenni Rampling in November of the previous year and was followed by Paul Oakenfold's Future, held at Heaven on Charing Cross Road. In January 1988 Shoom adopted the smiley-face logo for its flyers and from there the symbol became the ubiquitous mascot of acid house.

In April that year it entered the charts, courtesy of 'Theme From S'Express', the first acid-house hit single. Oakenfold's Spectrum opened its doors that same month, ushering in the second Summer of Love. In June the Trip opened, held at the Astoria, the club that would become infamous for the spontaneous street parties that erupted after closing every night.

By August tabloids had begun to print stories about the movement. The Sun, which had initially been benign in its treatment of acid house – even going so far as to offer a smiley T-shirt – suddenly did an about-face when

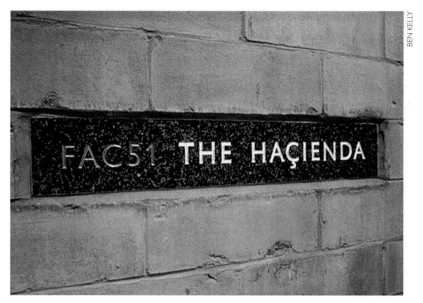

Our destiny set in stone!

The doorway to heaven and hell! Enter all ye who dare …

If we got that many in during the early 1980s, then it was a very good night indeed.

Here's Tony on the set of *So It Goes*, the TV show that introduced punk to Manchester and gave the Pistols their first ever TV appearance.

Tony Wilson's membership 'application'. Underneath 'What You Want from the Haçienda' he's scrawled: 'My money back'. You and me both, Tony.

The Haçienda, Whitworth Street, Manchester.

The beautiful interior, a Ben Kelly triumph.

The first birthday poster.

Me and Bernard when we played the Paradise Garage as New Order in 1983. Check out the ponytail. All the rage in those days!

Still in New York in 1983, and Rob's gone Flamenco. That's me with Gillian. On the right is Ruth Polsky.

The lads at the Swan in Salford. Home sweet home!

The Haç at dawn: me, Twinny and Bowser.

Ben Kelly and Peter Saville at the *Play at Home* video shoot.

(From left to right) Peter Saville, Paul Morley, Tony Wilson, me, Ben Kelly, Keith Allen, at the *Play at Home* video shoot.

New Order and Rob Gretton, 1985.

Me in Salford. What a great shot!

Me with Stephen Morris, probably 1985. (I'd spend the next ten years clinging on to the bloody thing!)

The front door.

TEMPERANCE CLUB

EVERY THURSDAY · THE HAÇIENDA
9PM-2AM · ADMISSION £1

25% OFF PRICE OF DRINKS
FREE BUS HOME TO CAMPUS / HALLS OF RESIDENCE

D.J. DR ROBERT   ·   ·FEATURING·   ·   EDDIE COCHRAN
TALKING HEADS   ·   THE WOODENTOPS   ·   FLOAT UP CP
ACR · GRACE JONES · FATS COMET · JAMES BROWN
B52S · LULU · JACKSON 5 · BUZZCOCKS · NEW ORDER
THE SMITHS · GO-BETWEENS · JUNE BRIDES · THE LOFT
THE FALL   ·   DADDY COLONEL   ·   GARY GLITTER

STARTS MAY 1 · BEER 60P A PINT

ADMIT ONE FREE

11/13 WHITWORTH STREET WEST MANCHESTER TEL: 061 236 5051

The Temperance Club flyer.

The sixth birthday flyer.

Andrew Robinson, my bike and me in Ibiza.

Sarah Sumner, Bernard Sumner, Peter Hook, Gillian, Danny, Steve Morris and Tom Atencio at Real World Studios.

Steve Morris, Chris Smith, Alan Erasmus and Tony Wilson at Real World Studios.

881-4152

Factory
Communications
Limited

Charles Street
Manchester
M1 7EB
England
Telephone:
44 (0)61 953 0251
Facsimile:
44 (0)61 953 2051

Fac 311

Directors:
Alan Erasmus
Anthony Wilson
Consultant:
Peter Saville

Sept 11th 1991

Factory™

Dear New Order

This is to confirm that Factory Communications Ltd will allot 1.5% of the Company Equity to the four musicians in New Order in return for £1.00. and the signing of the Polygram inducement letter.

Anthy H Wot

Brian Smith
0702 559723
Alison

Registered in England
No 1674772
Vat No. 3832 60632

Letter from Tony Wilson to New Order confirming our share in Factory.

Ben Kelly (left), Rob Gretton and Paul Mason, holding up the proposed interior for Dry.
Rob's skinning one up.

Me and Ben Kelly in Dry fiddling while Rome burns.

Bez, Tony Wilson and Paul Davies.

Laurent Garnier and Jon DaSilva.

This is how I'll always remember the Haç. Those were the good times.

The Haçienda after it was closed. Someone's painted on the door: 'The Haçienda must be built. Then lost by ~~cretins~~ Grettin.'

But its spirit lives on …

it published an alarming report about Spectrum that focused solely on drug use.

As we obviously hadn't finished the record in Ibiza, we booked into Peter Gabriel's brand-new state-of-the-art Real World Studios in the village of Box, near Bath, to start again. It was the UK's most expensive recording facility – now you're talking.

The recording of the album went in typical New Order fashion (i.e., the usual love/hate relationship. What's the easiest way to clear a studio? Answer: get your bass out!), but we loved the studio. It's like Disneyland for musicians at Real World – the technology, living quarters, staff, everything – so we ended up doing all our records there from then on. Peter Gabriel's had more of New Order's money than the taxman.

We called the album *Technique* and to celebrate finishing it we held a rave that Wiltshire will never forget.

By this time Rob was almost completely back to normal. Not his full pre-nervous-breakdown strength, but definitely back in the swing of things. The plan for the rave – in the usual manner – was to buy in drinks and about a thousand ecstasy tablets, sell the lot and make a profit that would pay for the party. We bussed down anyone who was anyone from Manchester. All the Haçienda and Dry regulars, the staff and management, etc. The idea was they'd party all night, spend their money and go home.

Two coachloads arrived carrying 150 maniacs. Everybody we knew had come down and the party turned into an absolute free-for-all: Es here, Es there, Es every-fuckin'-where.

We'd put two lovely girls, Michelle and Tracey who worked at Real World, in charge of running the bar. But everyone just grabbed what they wanted, waltzing off with bottles and bottles of champagne in their arms. The girls couldn't stop them.

It all went absolutely, madly fucking downhill from there. In the end the usual happened: 'Look, don't take money for it, it's too much trouble,' and we just gave the drugs and drink away. That bit of generosity alone cost something like ten grand.

Peter Gabriel hid himself well away. His only concern was that the party should be properly policed. To do that we'd brought in the security team from the Haçienda, who cordoned everything off and just about kept a lid on it. Just.

But as things got wilder the word spread and the good people of Bath got wind of the party and started arriving, trying to gatecrash. We just let most of them in, of course – the more the merrier – and those who came were introduced to ecstasy. No doubt they'd heard of it, but not seen it. We soon put that right. Here was a bunch of lunatics from Manchester handing it out like it was free. In fact, it was.

But it was insanity. Couples shagged in Peter's custom-built lakes, scaring his imported swans, and anywhere else they could too. I'm sure a lot of people woke up with sore arses and 50p, as we say in Manchester.

What was I up to, you ask? Well, I planned to drive home the next morning to see my kids, so I started early, DJed on my own to an empty room while still off my head, then went to bed. Later that night someone came and woke me, saying one of the partygoers had freaked out. 'You've got to sort this out, Hooky. He's your mate.' I was the only one in any condition to do anything about it, it seemed.

Apparently my mate Dylan had swallowed something like five Es (after all, they were free) and with one hand had grabbed some girl by the hair while holding a fire-axe to her throat with the other. She was screaming blue murder, and you could hardly blame her. But everyone was just walking past. I looked in his eyes, he had definitely lost his mind; there was no one in there. I took the axe off him and gave him a slap. 'What are you doing?' I said. No response, he just wasn't there at all.

The girl ran away, still screaming, and he wandered off too. He ended up shagging one of our female employees in a field full of cows and cow shit. Or so I heard.

After that bit of excitement I went back to bed and slept through the remaining madness of the party. I woke up the next day, got in my car and drove off with the party still in full swing. Then it was back to Madchester.

Which was perfectly poised to embrace the acid-house explosion of that year, not least because of the Haçienda's traditional insistence of bringing differing musical styles together. A year or so later the sound of the Happy Mondays – Madchester and Baggy – would be described as Sly Stone meets the Velvet Underground. It was in the Haçienda that Sly Stone had met the Velvet Underground.

This meant that acid house wasn't quite the Year Zero for the club in the way it was for nights like Shoom and Future down south, where rare groove had ruled for years. It was a near-seamless continuation of a music policy that had begun right from the moment it opened the club opened its doors. Thanks to its prescient choice of DJs; its alliance with electro, soul and hip hop, its ties with New York, its open-door attitude to music and its lack of snobbery, it was in the position not of responding to the rave revolution but rather of having created the very environment in which it would flourish.

And flourish it did. Within weeks of ecstasy sweeping the club it was packed for every club night. The place was finally reaping the rewards of its musical open-mindedness. Nude was packed out, as was the Temperance Club and Wide. The Hot night began. A Guy Called Gerald and Graham Massey of 808 State would arrive, banging on the DJ-booth door bearing just-made tapes of acid tracks that DJs would play in their entirety. Suddenly the club's acoustics sounded perfect. Phuture's 'Slam' – a favourite of DJ Jon DaSilva, boasting thunderstorm and rain effects among the squelchy acid and window-shaking bass – would fill and dominate the space as though made for it. Acid house and the Haçienda fitted perfectly together.

I felt great to be in Manchester then. I'd moved into a flat in Rusholme Gardens, Levenshulme. It felt like everyone I knew lived in that place, it felt like a little Haçienda. And the Haçienda felt like a little Ibiza.

On my return I found E culture in full swing. A massive change had occurred and it either swept you away or left you behind. Some of us involved took to it like the proverbial ducks to water, others weren't so keen, so we lost a lot of the old faces along the way.

I lost myself in it all, slipping into full-time party mode: I'd either be at the Haçienda or at one of the warehouse parties held by local crime families. E was readily available and I tried to introduce everybody to it, even the girl in the corner shop. I really did believe we'd found the world's salvation. Tony Wilson thought the same. He'd say, 'If the whole world took E, we'd all be all right.' We'd chorus along with him.

That said, I was always chasing that first high. It's generally the best one ever. Ecstasy is the same as crystal meth, coke, crack or smack in that respect. After that initial experience, you're never going to get back to that peak again. Nothing that follows is ever as good, and you always need more and more of a fix to even come close, and then it's too late – you're going to pay a very high price. Be warned!

Ecstasy changed my life. I shed my inhibitions. Tony Wilson said that it made white men dance. And he was right. I danced. Suddenly I felt like the world had changed and I loved the new perspective. There's another reason I took to it so passionately. The fact is that I was disenchanted with the group; I wanted to get away, to escape in my own head.

One of my favourite stories from this time involved a mate of mine. On his wedding day, he and his best man realized they didn't have anything for the evening. They went round to see the dealer, who said the cupboard was bare.

'But I've got these tablets from Amsterdam,' he told them, 'They're called ecstasy. I've not tried it yet. Do you want two of them?'

My friend had already had a few pints, so he said, 'Go on, then. We'll try 'em.'

He and his best man rode to the church and decided they'd each take one before walking inside for the ceremony. Next thing he knew, the bride's father was shaking him because he and his mate were lying in the cemetery on the gravestones, holding hands and watching the clouds drift by, telling each other how much they loved each other. Off their trolleys.

Ecstasy didn't have that effect on everybody. But it was a different experience from anything we had ever known before. Before, getting wasted meant beer and speed. Now it meant ecstasy.

The honeymoon period was short, though. The quality of E declined as the police clamped down. A lot of the time the shit that was sold to you did nothing but make you ill – dog-worming tablets, at best. One guy sold Nurofen and blotting paper in the alcoves at the Haçienda, passing them off as E and LSD. He got caught eventually and received the same sentence as he would have done for selling the real thing.

Spiking became a local sport in Salford. In the Swan you couldn't leave your drink unattended; you'd always take it to the toilet with you, otherwise someone would put a tab of acid in it as a joke. It happened all the time (still does: somebody spiked me at Mani's fortieth birthday party and it lasted three days, the bastards).

My mate Twinny was terrible for spiking people. We used to argue about it all the time. One night at the club he spiked Tom Atencio, our American manager. Everything was going off, a proper good night during the peak of acid house, and were sat in a corner with a bunch of Salford guys, when Twinny piped up, 'Hey, Tom you getting on one, mate? You having a pill?'

Tom, with his Californian drawl, said, 'No, no, man,' and went back to talking to someone else.

Once he'd relaxed, Twinny went, 'Hey, Tom,' and the moment Tom turned around, he threw it in his mouth.

Tom coughed loudly, then choked a bit but swallowed it.

I thought, 'Oh, you bastard,' while everyone around laughed hysterically.

Tom yelled, 'What the fuck, man,' and complained, but didn't make himself throw up like I said he should. He went for it, God bless him.

I just waited . . . It takes a while.

The anticipation built up. After about half an hour, I asked, 'Are you feeling alright?' Tom said, 'No, no, man, I'm fine,' but he got louder.

And louder.

And LOUDER.

Suddenly, he was on the table, whistling and yelling, 'Come on, Manchester. Woah.'

Now it was funny, cruel but funny. We'd got so used to ecstasy it no longer had that effect on us, but Tom was going mental. He ran around the club like a madman. Finally, he returned with this girl, and I'm not kidding, she was no oil painting, but he was all over her. She turned to me and said, 'Hey. Who's that fucking guy?'

'Him, you mean? Tom?'

'Yeah. 'E's just told me 'e's gonna take me to Hollywood and make me a fucking star.'

Apparently Tom was going round the Haçienda telling everyone he loved them and was going to make them famous. Funnily enough he told me the same. Finally, I dragged him back to his hotel room and left him dancing in the corner.

Twinny pulled that trick again later by throwing one into the mouth of another American visitor (talk about cementing Anglo–American relations), our accountant Bill. The little bastard had very good aim; he was an expert at it, should have played darts. Bill's experience went pretty much the same way as Tom's, only he ended up following girls around the Haçienda, stroking their hair. One of the doormen threw him out for being such a pest.

Artistically, all drugs – including ecstasy – affect me the same way: I can't make music. I am absolutely fucking useless when I'm high. I've always been that way. All it does to me is to send me to the pub, and they don't have mixing desks in pubs. They'd get in the way of the telly.

No, if you want to know what happens when you mix musicians with drugs, just look what happened to us. The drugs arrive and quality knocks off.

All this action had acid house as its soundtrack. To me, acid house was like a new punk – it had the same DIY aesthetic, the same freedom of expression. Technology had reached the point where people could write electronic music in their bedrooms, which was great, like a return to the punk-rock anyone-can-do-it ethos – which I liked.

The difference was that punk was aggressive. It was you against the world. It was all about anarchy, shock and upset. Acid house was inclusive. Its roots were in peace and love.

DJ Graeme Park had first played at the Haçienda in February 1988. A resident at Nottingham's Garage – the other northern house music stronghold – Park appeared as part of the club's Northern House Revue, and was there to witness the steadily growing popularity of house music in Manchester. After ecstasy arrived, however, things began to move more quickly; when he met Pickering for a magazine photo-shoot related to the burgeoning house phenomenon, Park was invited back to the club to cover for Pickering in July.

'The difference in there was quite amazing,' he remembers. 'There was something really exciting starting to happen.'

He watched the club reach its peak over the next two months. 'If it was wild in July, by August and September it was amazing, unbelievable.'

The legendary Haçienda queues were now beginning to form. '[The club] was full from the moment it opened until it shut every Friday,' Park recalled. 'Mike and I would arrive at eight thirty and there would be a huge queue. We would open at nine and people would run on to the dance floor. I'd never seen anything like it before. The Haçienda had a glass roof and there'd be a few nights in the summer where it'd be light for the first couple of hours, then when you left it'd be getting light again.'

'When ecstasy hit it was like a Mexican wave that swept through the club over a three-week period,' Pickering told the Observer. 'I could just stop a record and put my hands in the air, and the place would erupt. The whole club would explode.'

It wasn't like anything you'd ever experienced in a club before,' DJ and journalist John McCready told the Observer.

At the Haçienda it was almost as if a generation breathed a sigh of relief, having been relieved of the pressure of the chase. The baggy clothes desexualized the whole environment. The rising heat from 2000 people dancing, even at the bar, in the queue for the toilets, damped down everyone. We all looked crap. If you held on to on the handrail on the balcony above the dance floor, your palms would be dripping in accumulated human sweat. You could feel the down when the music stopped. The room quickly went cold as all the exit doors were thrown open and we were herded out. Back to forbidding reality. Until next Friday. The whole experience was always far more addictive than the drugs. You started wanting it all to go on for ever.

That summer the Haçienda's biggest nights were Nude, Zumbar and new arrival Hot, Paul Cons's Ibiza-themed night, which was launched in July and held on Wednesdays. It featured a swimming pool on the dance floor and free ice pops for clubbers. Legend has it that it was Hot that finally convinced Factory's Tony Wilson that dance music was the way forward.

Tony played an important part in promoting the acid-house scene. He saw that as his job and he was very good at it. Martin Hannett always called him 'that fucking talking head, Wilson'. The way he saw it, Tony didn't do anything, just enjoyed the limelight. If you ask me, Martin was wrong on the first count, right on the second. I remember Tony being voted the most-travelled record-company executive one year; somebody had worked out that he spent something like £300,000 flying around the world ten times, which – as Rob said – was very clever but achieved fuck all.

Throughout it all Tony maintained his career at Granada TV. He understood the power of the media. He saw it as a tool. He knew that the media likes a figurehead, so he set himself up in that role: to be the face of Factory, the Haçienda and Manchester, to get his message across. Mind you, he may have done a lot of talking but he didn't talk much to the bands. He freely admitted that he thought musicians were stupid; so, if a problem arose with the Haçienda, he wouldn't phone me up and ask my opinion. He'd never even get Rob to ask us. He couldn't see why he'd want to bring New Order into it, because in his mind we were just the investors.

We weren't close in the sense of being two friends who'd go out for a drink. I'd see him a lot, but you couldn't socialize with Tony because he wouldn't sit still for one fucking second. He'd dart in and out of everywhere. He'd never stay in the Haçienda for more than an hour at a time, and yet the public perception in Manchester was that we all lived together above the club, in bed together like Morecambe and Wise. They couldn't have been more wrong. He'd walk into the club, do what he had to do and walk straight back out. He used to say, 'When you want me, I won't be there. When you need me, I will be.' And God bless him he was. I still believe that now.

Tony hadn't been an early supporter of house music. He thought it wouldn't go anywhere. Mike Pickering brought Black Box to Factory hoping to get the band a deal for 'Ride on Time', but Tony rejected them because he thought they were manufactured. Acid-house acts weren't groups in the traditional sense of having a permanent, touring line-up, and he didn't like that. Of course 'Ride on Time' charted all over the planet. That was another of Tony's great missed opportunities: in the same way, he didn't sign the Stone Roses or the Smiths when he had the chance, and let James go from Factory to another label. Meanwhile, Rob's attitude was the opposite to Tony. His philosophy toward the Haçienda – as well as to the bands he managed – was that you don't talk about anything, you just do it, trusting the public to make the right decision and take an interest. He certainly wasn't interested in grabbing the headlines for himself, like, say, Peter Grant, the manager of Led Zeppelin, or even Tony. No, Rob liked to stay right in the background.

So, polar opposites, then, and I consider us lucky to have had both of them: Rob was more of a musicians' man; Tony, more the PR guy, banging the drum for Manchester.

As the Haçienda got bigger and bigger, Factory's cultural stock rose and the label was inundated by artists wanting a deal.

At Factory, they kept a huge tea-chest full of demo tapes that nobody except the A&R man Phil Saxe ever listened to. At the same time, the Haçienda had mix tapes by DJs looking for a chance to perform. None of the big names really started out that way, but some would be given a night or even a weekend if they sounded good. The other tapes were sent to Strangeways prison by Ang Matthews, so the prisoners there had something new to listen to. I heard some of them – the poor bastards. As if prison wasn't enough.

Mike was right about Black Box, of course. Him and Graeme loved pianos, vocals, and Italian house. None of it grabbed me – it sounded too samey – but there are loads of people who associate that period with the Italian-house sound, just as there are loads of people who remember it for the Mondays, or even for Lulu. Everybody remembers it differently. In America they know the Haçienda from *24 Hour Party People*. They associate it with the birth of indie music and Madchester acts like the Happy Mondays or the Stone Roses, but not with acid house and dance music. It all depended on what night you went; which DJs you liked.

Me, I went every night. I felt like I was truly, truly home.

I loved the vantage point from the DJ booth. It became one of my favourite places to observe the club in all its glory. I just walked to the bar, got a Special and hung out in the booth, watching the madness unfold. On the best evenings, I forgot all my problems. That was the wonderful part of it: no matter how bad things appeared on a Thursday afternoon during the directors' meetings, by the time I walked into the Haçienda the following night, everything felt magical, and would continue to feel that way until the drugs ran out – and I'd feel shite again.

On Monday morning, we'd deposit all the money we'd earned, guarded by our own armed men – boxes and boxes of it – into a Securicor van, only to see it disappear when it got to the bank: to cover our taxes, or our loans, or the costs of our daily operations. It was the night-time atmosphere we lived for, and every night was something different, new stories. I remember the indoor pool bursting during Hot, our summer theme night. Quite a laugh. Paul Cons also borrowed gimmicks from clubs in Ibiza, like the foam parties, which the punters loved. His knack for creating a dramatic setting took things to another level. Whereas we'd think about spending money on DJs, he'd focus his budget on decorating the building. These tastes didn't conflict; they complemented one another.

Hot ran for just that one summer, yet is remembered as being one of the early rave scene's defining nights. Dreamed up by Paul Cons after visits to Shoom and Future in London, it boasted all that we now associate with the acid-house era: freaky dancing, gyropscopes, fluorescent necklaces and ice pops. Thick dry ice was pumped into the club, while lighting played on the smoke to give dancers an unreal, glowing effect, the hands-in-the-air would seem to rise out of the fog. Plus, most importantly – and for the first time at the Haçienda – there were podiums to dance on. It was just as it names suggests, Hot, and the parties were intense, their reputation quickly spreading and boosting the profile of the other nights – Nude and the Temperance Club – taking the club to the next previously undreamed-of level of popularity. Queues stretched around the Whitworth Street building. A fanzine was even distributed free to keep clubbers entertained while they waited.

Not all of the gimmicks were without hazards. In an article in the Guardian *manager Paul Mason recalled the Hot pool being full of water from the previous night:*

> . . . and we had a bloody gig that night so had to empty it quickly some-how. Peter Hook turned up in the afternoon and said, 'I know what to do, my kids have got a paddling pool which is the same design, just smaller. You just take one of the panels out – it's much quicker that way.' But we lost control of it and tonnes of water burst out of the cargo doors of the club. This little old dear was walking past the club pulling her shopping trolley and it washed her about 300 yards down the road.

Everybody remembers the golden period of the Haçienda as being such a fantastic time. That may be because a lot of them settled down afterwards. There were a lot of rays of sunshine in the summer of 1988. Anyone who went to the club then will always feel like they're one up on anybody who didn't. In that sense, it's the same as the birth of punk in Manchester: everybody wanted to be at that first Sex Pistols gig at the Lesser Free Trade Hall. Factory cultivated that sort of 'us and them' mentality which made people feel like insiders or outsiders. If you lived through those times, it felt really exciting and special to be involved.

Really, though, the Haçienda experience doesn't need to be exclu-sive and cool. When you put aside the mythology of the place and the mythology of the era, both of which are now gone, the music still offers something special. There's a collective energy to it that's worth pursuing. The songs and the spirit live on.

If you were there, though, it consumed a big part of your life. How many kids would be devastated if they knew what their mums and dads got up to in there, dancing and going wild? I often like to imagine their parents reminiscing, 'Remember when we used to go to the Haçienda and get trolleyed, love?' How embarrassing . . . It's the same with my kids.

We regularly, constantly, enjoyed ecstasy-fuelled full houses raving like there was no tomorrow. It felt like admitting defeat if you went home. We all wanted more time to dance, more music, and/or more drugs – more, more, more.

Strange, because later studies showed that drug-takers in the Haçienda, or indeed any club, were very much in the minority. Even at the era's peak they reckoned that maybe 10 per cent of the audience – if that – took drugs. (Mostly the DJs, the doormen, our friends, and the key staff, I reckon.) That means that 90 per cent were just drunk or high on life – yet everyone presumed that they were all off it. Another myth shattered. Plus, back then, drugs were very difficult to get. You needed to know who to buy from to be really in on it. The image that normal people developed of the Haçienda was completely distorted.

In November New Order's 'Fine Time' was released, the band's first acid-house single and a massive worldwide hit. It was a declaration of the band's love of the new dance culture, and further established New Order as a band with its finger on the pulse. The links between the group and its club became even more pronounced in media reports and in popular thought. Also making their presence known were the Stone Roses, whose 'Elephant Stone' (produced by Peter) was released in October, swiftly becoming one of the era's defining records. Likewise the Happy Mondays, whose second album, Bummed, was proclaimed the rock equivalent of acid house, embodying as it did the spirit if not the sound of the scene, which could instead be found on the remixes. With the movement placed in a rock context, and thus easily understood and reviewed by the indie press, indie kids had yet another entry point into dance music: it was a landmark point in the development of the Madchester sound. And all of this was associated with the Haçienda, which was developing a reputation as the coolest club not just in this country but in the world.

The cash rolling through must have been immense. God, three nights a week × 2000 people × £10 each for admission + £15 per person spent on booze, plus cloakroom and food . . .

Except, they weren't spending that much on booze any more.

Ecstasy had stopped people drinking alcohol – they weren't inter-ested in it – so club owners were instead profiting from sales of overpriced bottled water. But Rob thought bottled water was the work of the Devil; he wouldn't stock it, insisting that we give everybody free water when they asked for it. A bit daft, really – you can't rave holding a glass of water, can you?

Suzanne in the kitchen cottoned on to this and started selling hun-dreds of bottles of water herself at £2 each.

She used to laugh at us, asking, 'Why don't you sell it?'

She earned a fortune, in direct competition with the bar. Rob knew this but didn't care. The public might have thought that the Haçienda sold bottled water, but he knew otherwise; to him, that kept his princi-ples intact.

Suzanne had previously DJed for a while (she was the first female DJ in Manchester). As kitchen manager she was the latest to try to make the kitchen profitable. Didn't work. She leased it from us in the end, but never paid any rent – for fifteen years, she proudly boasts.

Everyone thought she took the piss, but no one else would run the kitchen – for the simple reason that it made no money. We had to keep the kitchen open because we needed a supper licence to stay open late. In other words, a full menu, but all anyone wanted was chips. Suzanne sold more Rizlas, poppers, chewing gum and bottled water than she ever served food. Who wanted to eat anyway?

If Suzanne fell out with you, she wouldn't let you in the kitchen. She'd say, 'Fuck off. Fuck off. No, fuck off,' and refuse to have anything to do with you.

I'd stand there many times, dying for a piss, begging to be let in. She ran the kitchen like a club within a club with its own separate door policy.

We fought over daft things. One time I went in trying to get some drugs. She said, 'I've got a bit of speed here, but it's really strong. Be very careful with it.'

I went, 'Yeah, yeah. Fuck off, Suzanne.'

She gave me this wrap of stuff called Pink Champagne. And it was actually pink. I took a big fat line of it ('I'll show her') and was wide awake for four days. I got rather well acquainted with my ceiling during that time. She laughed her ass off, phoning me up every day, asking,

'How you feeling? Told you, didn't I, you fucking, greedy pig.' We really did enjoy a rather special relationship.

Another reason I needed the kitchen, remember: the Haçienda bogs were rubbish. The architects spent so much on the balcony, the plastic wall, the arches and all that crap, yet nobody had considered that for a club licensed to hold 1200 people we'd need more than four toilets for the men and eight for the girls. We let in 2000 people, so the bogs overflowed all the time and everyone in the basement walked around ankle-deep in piss and shit. Quite horrible, but it became a standing joke. 'Haçienda trousers', we called it. Everyone had to have them – or you weren't a fully paid-up member of the Experience.

We had lot of problems because of the queues for the toilets. They became legendary for fights because there were so many punters in the stalls getting twatted, which stopped anyone else getting inside for a shit (vicious circle: they needed a shit because they'd been taking drugs). They'd all be bursting. It was a nightmare right from the start. There simply weren't enough stalls. For years and years we tried to put that right but we could never afford to do it. Today, you wouldn't be allowed to open a club with so few toilets.

The mood could get heavy, though. I remember thinking one night that I'd rough it and use the toilets. I was waiting to go in one of the stalls when this kid pushed past: a thin, wiry, psycho-looking little fucker.

I muttered, 'Oh, fuckin' hell,' or something and waited for him to come out. When he did, I told him, 'Hey, there's a queue here, you know.'

He got right in my face – nose to nose – and went, 'Fuck off, you cunt.'

His eyes were absolutely empty, like a shark. *Shit.*

After that, I thought, 'Fuck that, I'll stick to the kitchen and my famous Hellmann's bucket.'

I'd stand there, peeing in my bucket, and Suzanne would be telling all the punters queuing up for chips and water, 'Do you fucking see him there? The dirty bastard. He's a director. He owns the fucking place and he's pissing in a bucket in the corner.'

To get back at her, I'd chase her around with it. Thinking about it now, I should have kept it – I could have sold it on eBay.

In addition to the problems with the toilets, the cloakroom wasn't big enough either (we had, after all, improvised with the location) and that turned into an issue as well. Everyone who worked there was so off it they'd sometimes just give the coats away. It was located right by the main doors and created a real bottleneck, so there was lots of jostling and lots of aggro.

One night I was stood talking to one of the bouncers and some pissed-up kid lurched forward. The bouncer told him, 'Back of the queue, mate,' but the kid tried to push his way past.

'Hey, mate,' repeated the doorman. 'There's a queue here.'

The kid muttered something then tried again, and again so the bouncer lamped him. Sparkled the guy.

'Well,' I thought. 'He did try to warn him . . .'

We were so busy – yet still strapped for cash – that maintenance on the building was impossible. The floor had originally been painted grey, which made the place look bright, but after a while it wore down to bare concrete. After all the money we had lost on the set-up, and the really bad business we'd suffered during the first few years (cue tumbleweed), every penny was needed just to keep it afloat.

Not that it stopped us partying. Nothing did. When we hosted the Disorder party in the basement, celebrating New Order's gig at the Manchester G-Mex in December that year, all of our friends were completely twatted. The party cost us £10,000, which was lucky because we'd just earned £10,010 for the gig. A profit of £10. But we just carried on. No one cared. We were that off it. I lasted ten minutes at the party before I got dragged home by the missus for being a naughty boy. I was gutted.

Present at that same party (which was assigned a Factory Records catalogue number, FAC 208) was Creation Records boss Alan McGee, whose label was struggling now that his biggest band, The House of Love, had left for a major label (although he remained their manager). All his hopes seemed to be pinned on an Anglo-Irish noise-rock band, My Bloody Valentine, who had been widely dismissed as third-rate by most critics in the years 1986 and 1987.

McGee had taken ecstasy that night – not for the first time, but it was possibly the most significant. As he stumbled on to the basement's dance floor, he had an epiphany.

'I heard acid-house music and suddenly I got it,' he told writer David Cavanagh. 'Something went click and I went into a new world. December 17 is when I got acid house. And that's when Creation changed.'

1988

McGee was then a regular visitor to the Haçienda. He, and Creation, spent 1989 partying, and by the following year he had introduced Primal Scream to acid house. Producer Andy Weatherall was found and the era's anthem, 'Loaded', was released.

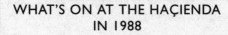

WHAT'S ON AT THE HAÇIENDA IN 1988

JANUARY

Friday 1st — NUDE YEAR'S DAY MP^2 – Mike Pickering and Martin Prendergast

Saturday 2nd — WIDE Dean; Hedd-Dave Haslam

Thursday 7th — TEMPERANCE CLUB Hedd-Dave Haslam

Friday 8th — NUDE Mike Pickering

Friday 15th — NUDE Mike Pickering

Wednesday 20th — ZUMBAR HOT FLESH Pedro; fashion PA by James

Friday 22nd — NUDE Spoonie G; Mike Pickering

Wednesday 27th — ZUMBAR Dead Marilyn *(Monroe impersonator)*

Friday 29th — NUDE Mike Pickering

FEBRUARY

Wednesday 3rd — ZUMBAR Dollar; fashion PA by Marc Benedict

Friday 5th — NUDE Mike Pickering

Wednesday 10th — ZUMBAR Eddie Burke

Friday 12th — NUDE Mike Pickering

Wednesday 17th — ZUMBAR Ruthless Rap Assassins; Kiss AMC; fashion show by Identity

Friday 19th — NUDE Mike Pickering

Wednesday 24th — ZUMBAR Oberton

Friday 26th — NUDE NORTHERN HOUSE REVUE T-Coy; T-Cut; Groove; Graeme Park; Mike Pickering

MARCH

Wednesday 2nd — ZUMBAR KARAOKE NIGHT fashion PA by Team for Hair

Friday 4th — NUDE Mike Pickering

Wednesday 9th — ZUMBAR Walking Hawk; White Dove

Friday 11th — NUDE Mike Pickering

Wednesday 16th	ZUMBAR Elvis (singer Jim White)
Friday 18th	NUDE Mike Pickering
Monday 21st	BHANGRA DISCO Naya Saaz; Tripple B
Wednesday 23rd	ZUMBAR Mr Boxman
Friday 25th	NUDE Mike Pickering
Wednesday 30th	ZUMBAR The Amazing Orchante; fashion by Aspecto

APRIL

Friday 1st	NUDE Mike Pickering
Wednesday 6th	ZUMBAR Big Ed & his Rockin' Rattlesnakes
Friday 8th	NUDE Mike Pickering
Wednesday 13th	ZUMBAR Frank Sidebottom; fashion by Geese
Friday 15th	NUDE Mike Pickering
Wednesday 20th	ZUMBAR DISCO DANCE CHAMPIONSHIPS hosted by Mike Baldwin; Miguel; Pedro
Friday 22nd	NUDE Mike Pickering
Wednesday 27th	ZUMBAR Boys Wonder
Friday 29th	NUDE Mike Pickering

MAY

Monday 2nd	NUDE BANK HOLIDAY SPECIAL Kid 'n' Play; Taurus Boyz; Julian Jonah; MP^2 – Mike Pickering and Martin Prendergast
Wednesday 4th	ZUMBAR Pope & Crocker
Friday 6th	NUDE Mike Pickering
Wednesday 11th	ZUMBAR KARRY-ON-KARAOKE Jimmy Corkhill; Miguel: Pedro
Thursday 12th	TEMPERANCE CLUB the Happy Mondays
Friday 13th	NUDE Mike Pickering
Wednesday 18th	ZUMBAR Les Bubb
Friday 20th	NUDE Mike Pickering
Saturday 21st	SIXTH BIRTHDAY HAUNTED HOUSE PARTY Dead Marilyn
Wednesday 25th	ZUMBAR Rob Gray
Friday 27th	NUDE Mike Pickering

THE HAÇIENDA

JUNE

Wednesday 1st	ZUMBAR Dead Marilyn; the Railway Children; Brilliant Corners
Friday 3rd	NUDE Mike Pickering
Monday 6th	BENEFIT GIG *(for the North West Campaign for Lesbian and Gay Equality)* Railway Children; Brilliant Corners
Wednesday 8th	ZUMBAR the King
Friday 10th	NUDE Mike Pickering
Wednesday 15th	ZUMBAR the Wee Papa Girl Rappers; fashion by Pebbles
Friday 17th	NUDE Mike Pickering
Wednesday 22nd	ZUMBAR Stevie Starr
Friday 24th	NUDE Mike Pickering
Saturday 25th	WIDE
Wednesday 29th	ZUMBAR Miss Zumbar 1988

JULY

Friday 1st	NUDE Mike Pickering
Wednesday 6th	*i-D* WORLD TOUR Mark Moore; MC Merlin; Sarah Stockbridge
Friday 8th	NUDE Mike Pickering
Wednesday 13th	HOT Jon DaSilva; Mike Pickering
Friday 15th	NUDE Mike Pickering
Wednesday 20th	HOT Brylcreem Contest
Friday 22nd	NUDE Graeme Park
Wednesday 27th	HOT BEACH WORKOUT Muscley Dream Boys
Friday 29th	NUDE Mike Pickering

AUGUST

Friday 5th	NUDE Mike Pickering
Saturday 6th	Jon DaSilva; Hedd-Dave Haslam
Friday 12th	NUDE Mike Pickering
Saturday 13th	Jon DaSilva; Hedd-Dave Haslam
Friday 19th	NUDE Mike Pickering
Saturday 20th	Jon DaSilva; Hedd-Dave Haslam
Friday 26th	NUDE Mike Pickering
Saturday 27th	Jon DaSilva; Hedd-Dave Haslam

SEPTEMBER

Friday 2nd	NUDE Mike Pickering
Saturday 3rd	Jon DaSilva; Hedd-Dave Haslam
Friday 9th	NUDE Mike Pickering
Saturday 10th	Jon DaSilva; Hedd-Dave Haslam
Friday 16th	NUDE Mike Pickering
Saturday 17th	Jon DaSilva; Hedd-Dave Haslam
Friday 23rd	NUDE Mike Pickering
Saturday 24th	Jon DaSilva; Hedd-Dave Haslam
Friday 30th	NUDE Mike Pickering

OCTOBER

Friday 7th	NUDE Mike Pickering
Monday 10th	TEMPERANCE CLUB the Train Set; Dave Haslam
Friday 14th	NUDE Mike Pickering
Friday 21st	NUDE Mike Pickering
Friday 28th	NUDE Mike Pickering

NOVEMBER

Friday 4th	NUDE Mike Pickering
Sunday 6th	*Wall of Surf (film screening in the Gay Traitor)*
Friday 11th	NUDE Mike Pickering
Monday 14th	TEMPERANCE CLUB the Waltones; Jerry Dammers
Friday 18th	NUDE Mike Pickering
Friday 25th	NUDE Mike Pickering

DECEMBER

Friday 2nd	NUDE Mike Pickering
Friday 9th	NUDE Mike Pickering
Friday 16th	NUDE, plus 'North', Mike Pickering
Saturday 17th	DISORDER New Order
Wednesday 21st	HOT: THE FINAL PARTY Jon DaSilva; Mike Pickering
Friday 23rd	WISE MOVES SEVENTH ANNUAL BALL *(and Creditors' Meeting)* live entertainments
Saturday 24th	CHRISTMAS EVE Jon DaSilva; Mike Pickering

THE HAÇIENDA

Wednesday 28th	HOUSE NATION guest DJs; the Steamer
Friday 30th	NUDE Mike Pickering
Saturday 31st	NEW YEAR'S EVE Mike Pickering; Graeme Park; Dave Haslam; Jon DaSilva

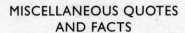

MISCELLANEOUS QUOTES
AND FACTS

'What made the Haçienda so special was the insane acoustics. I remember complaining about them on the opening night. But, five years later, when it all exploded, I realized that the nature of the building, and its high roof, made it feel like a Gothic cathedral, allowing hymns to be sent to the Gods.'

Tony Wilson

'The first couple of weeks of Hot were reasonably 'normal', but from the third week it was mayhem. It was almost scary. I came out of the DJ booth and there was this guy with dreadlocks who was almost hysterical, crying and laughing at the same time, just blown away by the atmosphere. You almost felt like you were missing out by DJing, you wanted to be on the floor.'

Jon DaSilva

'I was DJing at the Haçienda one evening and a girl came into the DJ box, lay down and took all her clothes off. She was naked, and started pulling at my trousers. I was wise enough to know it was E taking effect, rather than anything to do with me, but it was just one of those things; there was a lot of craziness in the air.'

Dave Haslam

1989

'We just weren't cut out to run a business'

The year began with the Haçienda enjoying unprecedented popularity. The Hot night had ended on a high at the end of 1988, to be replaced by House Nation, meaning that the Wednesday night never missed a beat. Dave Haslam's Temperance Club still ran on Thursdays; Nude, with Park and Pickering DJing, was on Fridays; then on Saturday nights there was Wide, featuring Jon DaSilva.

It was the year that Madchester took off, and indie-dance was born, kick-started by Paul Oakenfold's W.F.L. remix of the Happy Monday's 'Wrote for Luck' and further cemented by the Rave On *EP and remixes. In November the Mondays appeared with the Stone Roses and Inspiral Carpets on* Top of the Pops *and the Madchester phenomenon had its most defining moment. All eyes were on Manchester – and at the centre of it was the Haçienda, which was being credited with attracting tourists and students to the city and thus boosting the local economy.*

Before all of that, however, came The Hitman and Her, *the late-night clubbing show with Pete Waterman and Michaela Strachan. It paid a visit to the Haçienda in January 1989 and legend has it that Strachans' drink was spiked . . .*

They had a lot of trouble at that one: loads of young kids showed up trying to get in, and the usual tensions built up until a riot erupted. In desperation, the coppers had to shut off Whitworth Street yet again.

If you watch that episode of the show, there's a karaoke competition. The winner, at the ripe old age of seventeen, was Dave Potts 'Pottsy', who was soon to become my tape operator at my Rochdale studio, Suite 16, then my bandmate in Revenge and Monaco. Small world.

Personally, I missed most of the Madchester period because I was in America with New Order but, once our very successful *Technique* tour ended, Bernard and I stayed locally, working on projects of our own. He started Electronic with Johnny Marr of the Smiths, while I started Revenge, and the two of us became inveterate (although independent) partygoers, and pains in the arses for the staff.

What I found was that the city had changed a lot in our absence and the Haçienda had become a phenomenon. Reporters and tourists from all over the world descended on it. Journalists would wait for the staff to arrive in the morning and quiz them about the club, trying to get an exclusive insight.

Rave was now massive. Everything that used to be underground was suddenly overground and there was still an Ibizan vibe in the air. Even the weather was Ibizan, with the summers of 1988 and 1989 turning out to be really hot; and whereas it used to be empty all the time, now it was packed every Wednesday, Thursday, Friday and Saturday with upwards of 8000 sweaty, happy people, the bass pumping loud and deep. You couldn't move without bumping into Italian, Japanese or American tourists and the club became a holiday destination for music fans from all over the world, like the Salford Lads Club for fans of the Smiths, or the Cavern in Liverpool for the Beatles. Americans would immediately walk up to me and say, 'Oh, hi, Hooky, I'm here from Pittsburgh. How are you?' the way Americans do, whereas the European ones were a bit cooler but came for the vibe nonetheless. Even my normal friends, who wouldn't typically go to the club, started frequenting it. They came along for the vibe – and of course the free drinks and guest-list helped.

Speaking of which . . . During one of the weekly management meetings, somebody mentioned my drinks bill. It seemed that while New Order had been in America for our twelve-week tour, I'd continued drinking at the club. Impossible, given that I'd been thousands of miles away, right? Turned out that two of my best mates had set up a drinks tab while I was away, saying that Hooky would sort it when he got back. Once they'd done it, a couple of others joined in too. The staff just went along with it. I didn't mind, really – we're all fucking chancers, aren't we?

Even without my mates, about £4000 in free drinks was signed off per month. VIP stuff, I suppose. One month the figure dropped to £2000 and Rob gave the bar manager a bollocking, saying he wasn't hosting the club properly (which was odd, considering that Rob paid for every drink he ever had; no perks for him). Plus he kept giving me bollockings about my drinks bill, even suggesting that either I should pay it or the other members of the band should get the same.

In February, the Void club opened, taking over from House Nation. The night had a space theme: two giant spacemen floated over the stage, bar staff wore space-suits bearing the Void logo and there were distorting mirrors along the balcony. The music policy remained broadly the same as it had done during Hot and House Nation, though: house music courtesy of DJs Jon DaSilva and Mike Pickering. Void would go on to be remembered as yet another landmark club night.

In May the club celebrated its seventh birthday with the now-traditional party that saw staff and followers decamping to Amsterdam (at the club's expense) after Nude had finished on the Friday night.

And in July Factory opened the Dry bar . . .

Because acid house had saved our bacon, Tony and Rob seemed to think that everything we touched would turn to gold and so they decided to expand. Paul had had many discussions with Whitbread about putting money up for a bar, so with a bit on work on the dynamic duo . . .

We opened our bar, Dry, in July, as a place for people to visit prior to coming to the Haçienda. Rob and Tony felt we were missing out because a nightclub's hours were eleven p.m. until two a.m. They felt the bar filled the missing piece of the jigsaw. We now had somewhere to go during the day and early in the week, as per the original youth-club idea, and running a mere pub should be simple.

New Order were reluctant to get involved – which is the under-statement of this book – but Rob promised us it wouldn't cost us any money. All funds would be borrowed; we'd just be putting our name to it. It was a great opportunity to earn money all week, he said.

It was felt the Northern Quarter of Manchester was up and coming. At the time all there was for people to visit during the afternoon were working men's pubs. Dry would be the first new thing in the area.

However, Barney (who came up with the name Dry) disagreed: he complained that the Northern Quarter was run down, and insisted that the best spot was Oxford Road, where students from the university and polytechnic congregated. Rob and Tony said fuck off. They hated students. We all did. He was right, though.

The building, on Oldham Street, had belonged to the James Woodhouse furniture and carpet company (ironic because the first location for the Haçienda itself was a carpet showroom just up Oldham Street on the same side) and offered not just the ground floor but also three floors of offices above, a basement below and – as said the brief we received – 'a lift servicing all floors and rear loading off Spear Street'. All well and good. So well and good, I suppose, that everybody overlooked the implications of the final paragraph: 'I understand that the property is in a poor state of repair and decoration and consequently the freeholders are only seeking offers in the region of £80,000 for the benefit of their interest.'

Yup, so that's the one we chose. The other three floors were a hazard for the entire time we owned the place.

Once we went ahead with the plan to open Dry, Ben Kelly was the given the architect's job. It came in 50 per cent over-budget. We were told after we'd borrowed the down payment that if we didn't put our own money in too we'd lose everything again. Pretty soon we were almost £700,000 in the hole, including £69,647 loaned from Factory, £59,794 from Gainwest Limited (New Order's business partnership), £112,669 loaned from the Haçienda (done without the knowledge of any of the directors or investors), and a staggering £457,636 from Whitbread, the very same brewery whose loan to the Haçienda put us irrevocably in debt at the start (the associated loan charges that Whitbread hit us with cost Dry £23,106 in the first year alone, and they could never be paid off).

Once again, because of over-spending on the build, we'd over-extended ourselves, and once again our reliance on the brewery meant we'd never be able to buy the beer cheaply enough to make a profit. Unbelievable!

Ben Kelly's involvement again changed everything. We thought we'd have someplace warm and cosy – we wanted to model it on Nell's in New York, which was a great place even if it had just twenty people in it. What we got was a huge space, one that would accommodate 500 and again looked ridiculous with a small crowd. During the daytime, with only a few people in it, it looked deserted. We'd re-created the same problems. Dry was too light and too big to feel comfortable.

Everything was over-done: from the floor up it was way over the top. They intended to open all three floors and the basement to customers, and even build accommodation for the manager, Leroy Richardson, on the top floor. But when the estimates came in they were way too high because the building was in such a bad condition.

We had to scale it down to suit the budget (the first time we'd ever taken any notice of a budget).

The place became another burden on the Haçienda and Factory, causing more stress all around, the ripple effect being that we felt pressured into making rash decisions in search of any solutions to our financial woes.

Despite all of Rob's reasons for opening the place, Dry was built on wishful thinking, not on market analysis or whatever else people normally take into account when opening a bar. If we'd opened it on Oxford Road, as Bernard suggested, we'd have been close to the 15,000 students who attended classes there on a daily basis and we could have made a packet. Back then, the Northern Quarter was a wasteland. Now, of course, it's much more developed. Ahead of our time as usual, it was Dry that kick-started the area's regeneration. Hip little cafés and shops gathered around Dry, with many of them (most noticably Mantos on Canal Street) ripping off Ben's design to great effect. But, because we ran our bar so poorly, it turned a profit only on Fridays and Saturdays – when the money it made came from selling Haçienda tickets. The queues were so long at the club on Friday and Saturday nights that people invariably bought them at Dry in advance. Dry sold a thousand tickets a week, charging a £2 booking fee and making two thousand quid because of this surcharge to the regular ticket price. That was it. Otherwise it never turned a profit as a pub. We'd have been smarter to just open a daytime ticket window at the club. Looking back now, it does feel like we just weren't cut out to run a business, never mind two of them. Once again our managers wrote loads of budget /night projections, predicting income; once again, I felt they just made up numbers. All you can really do is look at the bottom line and ask yourself, 'How much can we afford to lose?' If the answer you come up with is too high, then don't do it.

Factory's accountant, Chris Smith, always thought the salvation of Dry would be the food. He insisted that it would earn money. He kept encouraging us to carry on until we could make the dining aspect of the place profitable. 'Get the food going and we'll clean up,' he'd say. 'Restaurants put a hundred per cent mark-up on food.'

Good idea, Chris. So what did we do? We got Vini Reilly's girlfriend, Pauline – a lovely girl – to open a vegetarian macrobiotic salad bar. On Tony's insistence.

A vegetarian macrobiotic salad bar. In Manchester. In 1989? We might as well have just chucked the stuff away.

Well, actually, that's exactly what we did.

At the end of each day, Pauline threw all the salad away because nobody ever wanted it. Heartbreaking for her. Nobody in Manchester had heard of macrobiotic food, let alone wanted to eat it. We were too far ahead of our time again.

I remember asking them, 'How do you lose £12,000 a year on salads?'

'No,' they said 'it's £1000 a week!'

Apparently I wasn't well versed in the vegetable world. I went fucking berserk.

Exit Pauline. After her we went through loads of people as kitchen managers: Suzanne, my friends Debbie Nightingale and Bowser (Little Red Courgette), and numerous others – all of them tried really hard. It should have worked but nobody could pull it off. They cooked well and had great ideas, just no customers. Laurent Garnier (later to become a huge DJ/producer) worked in the kitchen until he returned to France to do his national service.

In the end I said, 'Why don't we farm it out? Let's sublet it. Get somebody else to run it, then charge them rent.'

This actually happened when we opened Tommo's Tasty Tapas. Tommo – another great friend of ours, a great character, mad as a hatter – was supposed to sub-let the kitchen and pay us rent. He never earned enough to cover expenses, but we bankrolled him because we liked his food so much.

I had a butcher's assistant come up to me one night, completely off his head. 'You used to get your meat from us for Dry, didn't you?' he slurred.

I went, 'Did we?'

'Yeah, because we're doing that fiddle with you, weren't we?'

I said, 'What fiddle was that?'

'You know: we sent you a bill for three grand, but we only gave you £1500 worth of sausages and we'd split the money.'

Hmm . . .

Still we persisted with the food. What we didn't consider was the clientele: speed freaks and smackheads, coke addicts and pill heads who survived on little more than drugs and alcohol. They ate only out of necessity, to stop themselves from falling over and dying. Me included.

There's a saying in the pub trade that the time between lunch and evening is 'the graveyard shift' because there are no customers. Well, our friends were there then and none of our friends ate, and they looked so intimidating (the way only true zombies can) that normal people wouldn't walk the full length of the bar to get to the restaurant at the back. Everyone was scared of the lunatics who frequented it; the atmosphere kept them at bay.

At least we were consistent: we did everything wrong. We couldn't even get the drinking glasses right. Just as Tony had assigned the Haçienda a Factory catalogue number, FAC 51, he gave Dry its own, FAC 201. For years, we printed 'Dry 201' on the glasses, and people stole them all as souvenirs. That alone cost us a fucking fortune. You won't believe this, but we used to change the glasses depending on what night it was. The same at the Haçienda. So, if it was Zumbar night, they get out the Zumbar glasses. Hot would have Hot glasses and so on. I dread to think how much that little indulgence cost us.

Wish I'd have read Peter Stringfellow's book (*King of Clubs*) back then. Rob gave it me year's later to read saying, 'See? It wasn't just us?'

Then, because everything in the place was decorated in light colours, keeping it clean was again ridiculously expensive. Just like in the Haçienda, the second anybody put a hand on the brass handrail, the oil on their fingers made it look shit. It took an hour a day to polish it up.

The furniture was over-designed and over-priced. The customers wouldn't have been bothered whether they installed Yorkshire slate or Yorkshire Dales, and they routinely wrecked the place anyway. Tony loved the scallies at the cocktail bar carving their initials into the Morrison stools, and burning the Jasper Conran sofas with their fag-ends. He liked the idea of destroying art. A frightening thought. It wasn't just the customers, either. I spent the opening night cracking bottles of Budweiser open on the £40,000, one-piece thirty-feet marble bar top. Oops.

We had loads of staff, a lovely bunch. I missed them like mad when it closed. The interior was kept immaculately clean and bright, but even so . . . Very few people ever came.

It turned out the beer pumps and fittings had been installed incorrectly. Because the wrong taps were used, we lost something like one pint for every four we sold. We brought in loads of highly paid advisors to identify our problem areas, but they told us nothing we didn't already know: that we were overstaffed, that we were being ripped off and that we were idiots.

I could have told them that and saved us five grand a time!

Frankly, if Leroy couldn't make it profitable, no one could. Paul Mason tried, then Ang. Instead, the place was again more like a social club. That's how I used it, anyway, and I went through a phase when I was single when I socialized with the staff at Dry more than I did at the Haçienda; I even ate there occasionally before I fell over. I was the target audience. I loved it because I had somewhere to go during the day, before the Haçienda opened. I'd finish in the studio with Monaco at six p.m., go to Dry, eat there, stay there till it closed, go clubbing with Leroy, go back home, have a shower and go back to the studio. Sometimes I'd ride there on my Harley Davidson; then, when I was wasted, the bar staff would put me in a cab and wheel it into the bar until I collected it next day. It could be there for weeks sometimes.

Once again Rob complained about me getting my drinks for nothing and borrowing money from behind the bar.

One Saturday night, after eleven, when Dry had closed, Leroy cleared out the bar and bundled all the booze to one of the first raves in Manchester, where he planned to sell it at a profit. He'd asked our permission to do it and we'd given him our blessing. A nice little earner, we thought. Dry's holding stock of beer and spirits at the time would have been valued at around £5000.

Just our luck: the police shut down the rave. They took the sound system and lights (so the PA company were shafted) and the booze and all the money (so we were shafted). When we opened Dry the following day, the bar was bare and we hadn't been paid for anything we'd sold. It was all gone, dead and buried.

I also remember that rave because the cops arrested my mate Jim, saying, 'You must be the organizer.'

When he asked, 'Why the fuck would you think that?' the cops said, 'Because you're old.' Great detective work.

Barney had been there as well, but they let him and the rest of the crowd go because there were too many people for them to even attempt to interview or hold in custody.

The actual guy running the rave hid in a pre-prepared panic room, where he'd stored all the ecstasy he was going to sell plus all of his own coke, smack and the money he'd made. Right at the end, as the police cleared everyone out, they heard him cough but couldn't work out where the sound was coming came from. So they brought the dogs in and tracked him down. Sentences for drug dealing were strict in those days, so the guy (an arty, highbrow type who actually got married on stage at the Haç) turned Queen's evidence and fingered everybody he could think of. He literally sat there and gave the cops a long list of names, a who's-who of Manchester raving, many of whom had nothing whatever to do with the party. Weren't even there, most of them.

Including me.

The cops pulled Leroy, Rob and me in, saying it was our rave. I had to go in to the police station on Monday morning and tell them, 'I don't know what you're fucking talking about.'

Interestingly, the coppers were all my age -- and music fans -- so they were delighted at roping me in: 'Oh, let's get him out of New Order. That'll be a laugh.'

'Look,' I told them, 'You know by now that we've got nothing to do with this.'

Leroy got off by claiming he'd lent the beer for a private party and took the rap, getting a very stern warning. I think Tony had a word because only the main guy got charged. He'd been caught with so much ecstasy and so much cash (indicating that he'd sold either a lot of tablets or a lot of tickets) that I think he got about ten years in jail. The police became the enemies of acid house as they cracked down on all the unlicensed raves.

This wasn't the only rave to suffer. Tabloid hysteria over acid house had reached a crescendo by late 1989 and the authorities had started closing down 'rave' events such as Sunrise and Back to the Future, even though they were legal and well-organized. There was talk of an 'acid-house rapid-deployment task force' and MP Graham Stringer was pushing to introduce anti-rave laws. Manchester was one of the worst hit; the city's police force was run by James Anderton, who had a hard-line reputation gaining notoriety as 'God's cop' after claiming to be an instrument of divine judgment. As the second Summer of Love drew to a close, the clamp-downs marked the end of an era.

We bounced around the idea of franchising Dry, and had a hell of a lot of interest in it (the nearest we ever got was in Glasgow). But nothing came of it. We had so many problems with the Haçienda, we couldn't concentrate on anything else so any deal always fell through.

Now, every bar looks like Dry. Ben Kelly got it right again. Without a doubt, he revolutionized the industry's design.

Even so, the financial problems grew. Now Dry lost money hand over fist. New Order were again called in too late, and then started questioning things and looking at the accounts. Yet again, we discovered a list of cock-ups as long as your arm. The Internet, for example. In the mid-1990s Dry offered Internet access to its customers. One of the first. The concept was revolutionary. Unfortunately, when people booked a session at the computer to get online, we charged them much less per minute than we paid to the Internet service provider – Internet access was very expensive at first. Dry covered the difference. We lost money every second that people logged on, but Tony wouldn't let them raise the rates, saying that would price it out of the budgets of our customers. He used to say, 'The computer is the new hearth for the family.'

Eventually Leroy told people the computers were out of order, just to save us the expense. Good boy.

With Leroy moving over to run Dry, Ang Matthews (who'd been going to the Haçienda since John Cooper-Clarke's performance in June 1982) came aboard as assistant general manager, inheriting an operation that was now working on a huge scale and was beginning to attract the attendant problems. Manchester's gangs were beginning to make their presence felt, and there were problems with drugs in the club.

Ang bought herself a ring the week before she started work, which she got engraved with the anarchy sign to remind herself of her roots now that (she thought) she was getting a real job and settling down. Little did she know what she was in for. Her career with us would prove to be wilder than anything else she'd ever known.

At the start she and Paul Mason had a close working relationship. Ang followed Leroy around for a month, apprenticing with him, and soon became very good at her job. As she likes to say, she became a part of the club simply by virtue of being there so much (her boyfriend in the mid-1980s would come into the club to paint canvases of the archway and other features of the building to sell to people for their homes; that's how much it became a part of people's lives).

For the next eight years, she'd hire and fire staff – and she did both, loads of times. If she caught them stealing, they were sacked. Petty theft ended many careers at the Haçienda, whether that meant somebody swiping a bottle or giving free drinks to friends. Only one employee got kicked out for using drugs, however. If somebody could work while off their heads, she'd let them stay.

Still the financial problems persisted, despite our success. We'd weathered the tax investigations and I sided with Rob in trying to keep the Haçienda going – the old ego was out in full force – but we were still in the shit. At a director's meeting somebody joked that we should burn the place down, at which point our accounts guy – a proper businessman – said, 'If you're going to start talking like that, I'll have to leave the room.'

Either way, there was nothing in there that was flammable anyway. Just the dance floor and a couple of chairs.

We may have missed some opportunities to bring in extra profits, but we were denied the chance to pursue others. Today there are hundreds of mix CDs by Ministry of Sound, Creamfields and Renaissance – everyone, really – which have become a big part of our culture. When acid house took off, Rob immediately cottoned on to doing compilation LPs of the songs the DJ's played in the Haçienda, but in those days it was difficult to get the Black Boxes of the world to licence their songs; they figured they'd make more money on their own. Now, of course, the acts know there's a packet to be earned from compilations, so it's a lot easier to get their permission. Back then, they just said no.

We could have made a fortune – and made the bands a fortune – from selling albums that replicated the sound of a night spent at the Haçienda, but the big names all turned us down. In fact, the *Haçienda Classics* CD I did in 2005 has gone on to sell more than 175,000 copies and it's a triple CD; I was very flattered when Noel Gallagher voted it his favourite record of all time.

The closest we came to exporting the Haçienda experience was by hosting theme nights around Europe and America. Rob saw them as a way of promoting the brand further, which now is a very common thing to do but was difficult then. For a while, Ang co-ordinated them. She booked the talent, the idea being that that the promoters subsidized the tour. But the events all lost money, so what we hoped might be a source of revenue turned into a burden and had to be underwritten by us. You've got to be very, very clever to book a tour, because of the expenses. They proved to be demanding, and as soon as anything or anyone became demanding, Rob would always mutter, 'Oh, fucking pay them off.' He hated arguing about details. If a promoter argued about the hundred dollars it cost to take the DJs from an airport to a hotel, Rob would say, 'Oh, fuck it. Don't argue, we'll just pay it.' And that was it for the tours. However revolutionary the concept may have been, we never broke even.

At least people were still pouring through the doors. We still had that. And the club only got more and more popular as the year wore on. Madchester was in full swing and it felt like *everybody* was into it. The music had changed the way people dressed. Baggy trousers, T-shirts and Kickers, a floppy, summery fashion. Funnily enough, kids still wear it today. It's like dressing as a punk. At the time I first dressed as a punk, nobody had ever done it before – we made up our style as we went along. Now, each generation has its own punks, its Goths, its ravers, little sub-tribes that start in school.

The bands of that time sounded fantastic; it's one of my favourite eras of music. So many rock groups absorbed acid house and the result was a wonderful combination of styles, even though the two genres were completely different. If you listen to a lot of the Mondays' stuff, my God, they were fucking sloppy, whereas acts like James, the Stone Roses and the Farm were more mainstream. Primal Scream sounded very much like the Rolling Stones up until 1988, when their songs changed completely, becoming more like New Order's, a mixture of rock and dance music.

Our acid-house nights drew people from all over England – and soon even the world – because we offered a unique experience. The bands that performed at the Haçienda played around the country: fans wouldn't travel to Manchester to see them, because the groups would be coming their way – to Sheffield or Leeds – that same week.

But our club nights, such as Zumbar (where we had performers and acrobats, a real show), weren't happening in other cities, so we'd get coach-loads of people from everywhere, dying to see what our imaginations could come up with. That was unusual and a great compliment.

With the success of the Haçienda came the excess. And with it came dark times. We had a lot of drug overdoses, to the point where we'd have a ridiculous number of ambulances arriving at the club each night. Dealing with them took up a lot of time, as we'd bring people outside to wait for medical assistance. Eventually we employed somebody from LifeLine, a drug charity, to try to handle the problems.

I wasn't there on 14 July, the night that Claire Leighton died. Claire was a sixteen-year-old girl who took ecstasy in Stockport prior to travelling to the club. Once inside, she suffered an allergic reaction to the drug. She collapsed on the dance floor; the staff tried to help and called an ambulance. She was taken to hospital and died there after a prolonged fight for her life. Paul Mason found out when he received a call from a reporter the next day asking for a comment, then he phoned me to say that the media might contact me as well. I couldn't have done anything – I wish I could – but he believed I should be warned.

I felt sick when I heard. When I hung up, I went and checked on my kids. As a father it felt awful. I know how precious children are. I can only imagine what her poor parents and family went through. I couldn't understand how the scene had mutated from something so wonderful into something so hellish.

From then on, if something happened inside the Haçienda, we'd always get the nocturnal phone calls. I suppose Paul Mason felt we should know immediately.

And those panicked calls weren't unusual. Around this time I'd be home most weekends, single-parenting, and every time the phone rang after eleven p.m. I'd flinch, knowing something awful had happened. It really wore me down.

People collapsed in the Haçienda from heat, exhaustion, drugs and drinks all the time. They turned white non-stop – throwing a whitey, we used to call it. I hate to say it, but if the bouncers found somebody even looking wobbly or throwing up, sometimes they would just open the door and throw them out. People at raves are generally off their monkey. I remember seeing a kid at a Tribal Sessions rave in the Academy stagger up to a St John's Ambulance man and doorman who stood nearby, talking to each other. The kid wailed, 'Help. Help. I've had eight Es and I'm losing my mind.'

The bouncer and the St John's ambulance man looked at each other, then the bouncer kicked open the exit door, grabbed the kid, threw him out and shut the door behind him. Then the two of them carried on talking like nothing had happened. In the early days nobody thought they needed to worry. Ecstasy overdoses were infrequent. People came to view them as an occupational hazard.

A death, however, was unprecedented. Nothing like that had ever happened before in England, or even the world. We all lived life to the full, but the thing about ecstasy is that it's a bit like Russian Roulette. If you take it, you don't know what your reaction's going to be. If you're allergic to E it causes severe dehydration, which can kill you by itself. On the other hand, if you drink too much water to fight it, you can die of over-hydration; you flood your body with water, which puts pressure on the brain. Runners and athletes in general have to be careful when training for the same reasons.

The drugs started to sour everything around that time.

Later that year, in September, the Halluçienda night was launched for Monday nights. Music was indie-dance and the line-ups featured a mix of bands and guest DJs. That December, Sasha played at the Haçienda for the first time.

I spent the evening hanging out in the DJ booth with Sasha the first time he played, a sell-out. One of the best nights I've ever spent there; he caught the crest of the ecstasy-fuelled wave. He got paid £2000 for that night – which was back then the highest fee ever paid for a DJ. Once again we were ahead of our time.

The second time I saw him it was nowhere near as good – hardly anybody came.

I look at photos of the Haçienda in the 1980s and even though the crowds are small, and everyone is dressed strangely, the club looks fantastic. Very bright colours. Yet, funnily enough, I don't remember it being like that in the acid-house years. I remember it being dirty. Black. Dark. It's weird. I suppose a lot of the parties were in my head.

Or maybe it was because all the lights had been stolen.

WHAT'S ON AT THE HAÇIENDA IN 1989

JANUARY

Wednesday 4th	HOUSE NATION, RIP Evil Eddie Richards; Mr C
Thursday 5th	TEMPERANCE CLUB Dave Haslam
Friday 6th	NUDE Mike Pickering and Graeme Park; Hedd-Dave Haslam
Wednesday 11th	HOUSE NATION High on Hope; Norman Jay; Frankie
Thursday 12th	TEMPERANCE CLUB Dave Haslam
Friday 13th	NUDE Mike Pickering and Graeme Park; Hedd-Dave Haslam
Wednesday 18th	*THE HITMAN & HER* EXPERIENCES THE HAÇIENDA Mike Pickering; Jon DaSilva *(music-programme taping: 'Late-night TV will never be the same again')*
Thursday 19th	TEMPERANCE CLUB Dave Haslam
Friday 20th	NUDE Mike Pickering and Graeme Park; Hedd-Dave Haslam
Wednesday 25th	HOUSE NATION
Thursday 26th	TEMPERANCE CLUB Dave Haslam
Friday 27th	NUDE Mike Pickering and Graeme Park; Hedd-Dave Haslam
Monday 30th	The Stone Roses

FEBRUARY

Friday 3rd	NUDE Mike Pickering
Wednesday 8th	VOID Mike Pickering; Jon DaSilva
Friday 10th	NUDE Mike Pickering
Tuesday 14th	MID-CHESHIRE COLLEGE PARTY
Thursday 16th	THE HOUSE ON MARS Mike Pickering; Graeme Park
Friday 17th	NUDE Mike Pickering

Monday 20th	THE MONDAY CLUB the Train Set
Friday 24th	NUDE Mike Pickering
Monday 27th	THE MONDAY CLUB the Stone Roses; King of the Slums

Set-list (the Stone Roses): 'I Wanna Be Adored', 'Here It Comes', 'Made of Stone', 'Waterfall', 'Sugar Spun Sister', 'Mersey Paradise', 'Elephant Stone', 'Where Angels Play', 'Shoot You Down', 'She Bangs the Drum', 'Sally Cinnamon', 'I am the Resurrection'

MARCH

Friday 3rd	NUDE Mike Pickering
Monday 6th	THE MONDAY CLUB Spacemen 3
Friday 10th	NUDE Mike Pickering
Monday 13th	THE MONDAY CLUB McCarthy
Friday 17th	NUDE Mike Pickering
Monday 20th	THE MONDAY CLUB the Pastels
Friday 24th	NUDE Mike Pickering
Monday 27th	NUDE Bank-Holiday Special Kym Mazelle; Ten City; Mike Pickering; Graeme Park
Friday 31st	NUDE Mike Pickering

APRIL

Monday 3rd	Dub Sex; Slab
Friday 7th	NUDE Mike Pickering
Friday 14th	NUDE Mike Pickering
Monday 17th	Great Leap Forward; 1000 Violins
Wednesday 19th	VOID Mike Pickering; Jon DaSilva; Vanilla Sound Corp
Friday 21st	NUDE Mike Pickering
Friday 28th	NUDE Mike Pickering

MAY

Friday 5th	NUDE Mike Pickering
Monday 8th	The Happy Mondays
Tuesday 9th	The Happy Mondays
Wednesday 10th	VOID Free Dexters & Hypotonic
Friday 12th	NUDE Mike Pickering
Wednesday 17th	VOID
Friday 19th	NUDE Mike Pickering

Saturday 20th	WIDE
Saturday 20th	SEVENTH ANNIVERSARY PARTY
Wednesday 24th	VOID
Friday 26th	NUDE Mike Pickering
Wednesday 31st	VOID

JUNE

Friday 2nd	NUDE Mike Pickering
Wednesday 7th	Kraze
Friday 9th	NUDE Mike Pickering
Thursday 15th	Kazuko's Karaoke Klub; Janice Long; John Cooper-Clarke; Frank Sidebottom (chat-show taping)
Friday 16th	NUDE Mike Pickering
Saturday 17th	LAST SMILEY-FREE ZONE Jon DaSilva; Hedd-Dave Halsam
Friday 23rd	NUDE Mike Pickering
Saturday 24th	WIDE Nick Arrojo; Laurent Garnier
Friday 30th	NUDE Mike Pickering

JULY

Monday 3rd	Pere Ubu
Wednesday 5th	VOID
Friday 7th	NUDE Mike Pickering
Wednesday 12th	VOID
Friday 14th	NUDE Mike Pickering
Friday 21st	NUDE Mike Pickering
Sunday 23rd	DRY LAUNCH
Monday 24th	Primal Scream; Telescopes
Tuesday 25th	*Dry 201 opens in Manchester as a place to go to prior to clubbing at the Haçienda.*
Wednesday 26th	VOID
Friday 28th	NUDE Mike Pickering

AUGUST

Wednesday 2nd	VOID
Friday 4th	NUDE Mike Pickering
Saturday 5th	WIDE
Tuesday 8th	NUDE Colin Favor

Wednesday 9th	VOID
Friday 11th	NUDE Mike Pickering
Saturday 12th	WIDE
Wednesday 16th	VOID
Friday 18th	NUDE Mike Pickering
Saturday 19th	WIDE
Wednesday 23rd	VOID
Friday 25th	NUDE Mike Pickering

Set-list: Gino Latino – 'No Sorry', Kaos – 'Definition of Love', Inner City – 'Do You Love What You Feel' (Power 41 Remix), Royal House – 'Get Funky', Raven Maize – 'Forever Together', White Knight – 'Keep it Movin' ('Cause the Crowd Says So)' (Insane Mix), Sound Factory – 'Cuban Gigolo', Dionne – 'Come Get My Loving', 28th Street Crew – 'I Need a Rhythm', Adeva – 'Warning', the Bass Boyz – 'Lost in the Bass' (Mike 'Hitman' Wilson Mix), Julian Jumpin' Perez & Kool Rock Steady – 'Ain't We Funky Now', Monie Love – 'Grandpa's Party', Toni Scott – 'That's How I'm Living', Chubb Rock with Howie Tee – 'Yo Bad Chubbs' (Crib Mix), Akasa – 'One Night in My Life', Kid 'n' Play – '2 Hype' (Instrumental), Kenny Jammin' Jason & DJ Fast Eddie – 'Can U Dance', Jungle Crew – 'Elektric Dance', NWA – 'Express Yourself', Big Daddy Kane – 'Warm it Up', Queen Latifah – 'Dance for Me', MCs Logik – 'Get Involved' (In it to Win it Mix), Reese – 'Rock to the Beat' (Vocal Mix), Da Posse – 'Strings', R Tyme – 'R Theme', Doug Lazy – 'Let it Roll' (Dub), Frankie Bones – 'We Call it Techno', Seduction – 'You're My One & Only (True Love)' (C&C New York House Mix), Sandee – 'Notice Me' (Notice the House Mix), the Forgemasters – 'Track with no Name', Diskonexion – 'Love Rush' (Put On Mix), Black Box – 'Ride On Time', Sterling Void – 'Runaway Girl', Annette – 'Dream 17', Phase II – 'Reachinv', Orange Lemon – 'Dreams of Santa Anna', Shannon – 'Let the Music Play', Carly Simon – 'Why?', Imagination – 'Just an Illusion' (Pickering & Park Mix), Company 2 – 'Tell It as It Is', Roberta Flack – 'Uhh Uhh Ohh Ohh (Here It Comes)', 2 in a Room – 'Somebody in the House Say Yeah', Richie Rich – 'Salsa House', Redhead Kingpin & the FBI – 'Do the Right Thing', Digital Underground – 'Doowutchalike', Kariya – 'Let Me Love You for Tonight', Nocera – 'Summertime, Summertime', Lil Louie – 'French Kiss', Sylvester – 'You Make Me Feel (Mighty Real)' (Acapella), 808 State – 'Pacific State', Sueno Latino – 'Sueno Latino', Dynamic Duo – 'In the Pocket', Da Posse – 'It's My Life', Technotronic – 'Pump Up the Jam', Mix N' Tel – 'Feel the Beat' (Pierre's Mix), Gary Jackmaster Wallace – 'House Every Night' (Oh Yeah Mix)

| Saturday 26th | WIDE |
| Wednesday 30th | VOID |

THE HAÇIENDA

SEPTEMBER

Friday 1st	NUDE Mike Pickering
Monday 4th	Inspiral Carpets
Friday 8th	NUDE Mike Pickering
Monday 11th	HALLUÇIENDA
Friday 15th	NUDE Colin Favor

Set-list: Kariya – 'Let Me Love You for Tonight', Dionne – 'Come Get My Loving' (EZ Mix), Afro Erotica – 'French Kiss', Liasons D – 'Future FJP', Snowboy – 'Snowboy's House of Latin', Baby Ford – 'Beach Bump' (Wildflower Mix), Rhythim is Rhythim – 'Strings of Life', Blow – 'Think Love', Quartz – 'Meltdown', Kid 'n' Play – '2 Hype', Da Posse – 'It's My Life', Annette – 'Dream 17', Sterling Void – 'Runnaway Girl', Kenny Jammin' Jason & Fast Eddie – 'Can U Dance', 808 State – 'Pacific State', LA Mix – 'Love Together', Kechia Jenkins – 'I Need Somebody', Ce Ce Rogers – 'Someday'

Wednesday 20th	VOID Mike Pickering; Jon DaSilva; PA by K. C. Flight
Friday 22nd	NUDE Mike Pickering
Friday 29th	NUDE Mike Pickering

OCTOBER

Friday 6th	NUDE Mike Pickering
Friday 13th	NUDE Mike Pickering
Friday 20th	NUDE Mike Pickering
Friday 27th	NUDE Mike Pickering

NOVEMBER

Friday 3rd	NUDE Mike Pickering
Friday 10th	NUDE Mike Pickering
Monday 13th	The Shamen
Friday 17th	NUDE Mike Pickering; Graeme Park; Frankie Knuckles
Monday 20th	King of the Slums
Friday 24th	NUDE Mike Pickering
Tuesday 28th	Mega City Four
Thursday 30th	TEMPERANCE CLUB PARIS

DECEMBER

Friday 1st	NUDE Mike Pickering
Friday 8th	NUDE Mike Pickering

Wednesday 13th   Sasha

Set-list: Doug Lazy – 'Let the Rhythm Pump', MC Buzz B – 'How
Sleep the Brave', KC Flight – 'Planet E', Toni Scott – 'That's How
I'm Living', Armando – '100% of Dissin' You', Wood Allen –
'Airport 89', Renegade Soundwave – 'The Phantom', Bizz-Nizz –
'Don't Miss the Party Line', DJ Atomico Herbie – 'Amour Suave'
(Remix), Young MC – 'Know How', Phuture Pfantasy Club –
'Slam', Concrete Beat – 'That's Not the Way to Do It', KLF –
'What Time is Love', Rhythm Device – 'Acid Rock', FPI Project –
'Rich in Paradise', Jazz & the Brothers Grimm – 'Casanova', Musto
& Bones – 'Just as Long as I Got You I Got Love', the Stone
Roses – 'Fool's Gold', Guru Josh – 'Infinity', 49ers – 'Touch Me',
the Machenzie – 'Party People', Reese – 'Rock to the Beat', Kid
'n' Play – '2 Hype', Gino Latino – 'Welcome', Raul Orellana –
'The Real Wild House', Julian Jumpin' Perez – 'Stand by Me',
Sueno Latino – 'Sueno Latino' (Cutmaster G Mix)

Friday 15th   Jon DaSilva
Monday 18th   The Fall
Friday 22nd   NUDE CHRISTMAS Mike Pickering; Graeme Park
Saturday 23rd   WIDE CHRISTMAS EVE Nick Arrojo
Sunday 24th   SUNSET RADIO OPENING PARTY
Sunday 31st   NEW YEAR'S EVE Mike Pickering; Graeme Park

THE HAÇIENDA

EXCERPTS FROM COMPANY ACCOUNTS, 1989

FAC 51 Limited
Trading as: the Haçienda

TRADING AND PROFIT AND LOSS ACCOUNT (for the year ended 30 June 1989)

	1989		1988	
	(£)	(£)	(£)	(£)
Sales		1,095,693.00		841,318.00
Cost of sales		322,954.00		255,581.00
Gross profit		= 722,739.00		= 615,737.00
Overheads				
Operating expenses	439,426.00		326,002.00	
Establishment costs	171,973.00		157,468.00	
Administration costs	110,610.00		100,378.00	
Finance costs	6754.00		7844.00	
		728,763.00		591,692.00
Net trading profit		= 43,976.00		= 24,045.00
Other income				
Insurance claim	11,009.00		–	
Bank interest received	425.00		107.00	
		11,434.00		107.00
Net operating profit		55,410.00		24,152.00
VAT assessment		25,599.00		–
Profit for the year		29,811.00		24,152.00

FROM THE DRY
PROMOTIONAL POSTER

Fac 201 Dry
28-30 Oldham Street, Manchester, England

Function: bar
Proprietors: the people who brought you the Haçienda
Telephone: 061-236-5051
Public Opening: 25 July 1989
Capacity: 500
Area: 450 square metres
Bar length: 24 metres
Specifications: bead-blasted stainless steel, Delabole blue-grey slate,
    acid-etched coarse-stippled glass, Douglas fir, Japanese oak, utile,
    Junkers beech, black American walnut, telephone poles, mirror
    mosaic, blue-glazed bricks, Pantone 2685C Purple, International
    Orange, BS 10C33 Pollen, galvanized steel, Lapistone Marbo tiles,
    Turquoise MG35 glazed tiles, PVF2 Silver, polished stainless steel,
    linen-finish stainless steel
Lighting System: 18-channel Pulsar Rock desk, Lee low-voltage
    framing spots
Sound System: Reinforcement by Wigwam Acoustics, Denon
    multiplay compact disc
Approach: a bar on Oldham Street
Director: Paul Mason
Manager: Leroy Richardson
Design: Ben Kelly Design (Ben Kelly, Sandra Douglas, Elena Massucco,
    Peter Mance, Denis Byrne, Fred Scott)
Graphics: Peter Saville/Johnson Panas
Press Officer: Paul Cons

MISCELLANEOUS QUOTES
AND FACTS

'Whereas music in clubs is now pigeon-holed and segregated, in those first years of acid house, the dance floor was open minded. In retrospect DJs have tried to convince us of their purist underground credentials; that wasn't really the case. In the acid-house era you would have heard house, and techno, but also hip-hop records, like 'Know How' by Young MC, New Order and Euro-disco tracks by Italian production teams.'

Dave Haslam

'It was never just a club. It became just a club with ecstasy and acid house. It was an artspace. We had bands, we had art installations. We had William Burroughs reading *Naked Lunch*, we had David Mack doing huge installations with 12-inch record sleeves. It was supposed to be a space for everyone to use, a meeting place. We'd all been to New York, and hung out at places like Danceteria, and the great thing about them – yeah they were fantastic clubs – but they were meeting places for like-minded people, creative people. Ecstasy changed it all. Because obviously everything went to the beat and to the instance on drugs. You know, the first two summers of ecstasy, of love, was the most special time you'll ever have. But after that, it was just boring.'

Mike Pickering

From the minutes of a meeting held at Bromley House, Woodford Road, Bramhall on 8 February 1989:

20. RG [Rob Gretton] requested an up-to-date business plan to take account of all the revised costs [for the Dry bar].

(RG had a £100 bet with PM [Paul Mason] that costs would go up further and that the shareholders would be approached for more money).

1990

'The sheer volume of drugs we handed over made the cops very nosy'

As 1990 began, Manchester was at the centre of another cultural revolution. The city wasn't just raving: it had taken the sound, the ethos and spirit of rave and reshaped it into something brand new – Madchester.

Suddenly indie kids were dancing too. Everybody was, and they were doing it at the Haçienda. The club lay at the heart of a previously unimagined surge in the city's nightlife as the student population grew (at one point places for higher education in the city were ten times oversubscribed) and coach-loads of clubbers arrived in the city every weekend. Other clubs launched to capitalize on rave's popularity. There was Konspiracy at the old Pips/Nite and Day venue, which would go on to become one of the city's most infamous clubs – the subject of almost as many stories as the Haçienda itself. (The greatest of these being that Damien Noonan, who controlled the door there, was charging people to get out of the club – twice as much as it had cost them to get in.) On Osbourne Street, Newton Heath, was Thunderdome (the scene of one of Joy Division's first successful gigs); and at Legends, Princess Street, London club Shoom hosted a residency and the Happy Mondays filmed their video 'Wrote for Luck'. In the meantime a whole generation of music-makers were being inspired on the Haçienda's dancefloor. Those having their eyes opened included Laurent Garnier (who worked at the club as a pot-collector); the Chemical Brothers, then student ravers; the Charlatans; and even Noel and Liam Gallagher, jobbing as floor-sweepers before they hit the big time (Oasis in fact played their first-ever gig as support to Peter Hook's Revenge at the Hippodrome in Middleton in 1993); as well as the huge swathes of Madchester wannabes who sprang up in the wake of the Mondays and the Roses. London-based magazines began to pick up on the Madchester phenomenon and even America started to show an interest: that summer DJs Mike Pickering, Paul Oakenfold, Graeme Park and Dave Haslam went on a Haçienda DJ tour of America and were greeted like superstars; even Newsweek carried a Madchester cover story.

As the movement grew there were mutterings that it was already becoming too homogenized; that the baggy Joe Bloggs/Gio Goi look had become a uniform. The Fall's Mark E. Smith even wrote a song about it, 'Idiot Joy Showland'.

At the Haçienda the management continued to investigate ways in which to capitalize on the club's success. First Factory wished to buy the building, which would free them from the millstone of the twenty-five-year lease and make the club a much more attractive proposition. They'd made repeated offers to purchase since the club first opened and now, at last, the owner relented: Factory secured the property and immediately set about planning how best to utilize their newly acquired real estate.

I remember being asked about buying the building while New Order were backstage at the Free Trade Hall (although I can't remember why we were there). Rob gave us literally five minutes to make our minds up – as in yes or no. We again went with the flow; but, knowing how punitive the length of the lease had been, owning the building did seem like a good idea.

One of the biggest criticisms of the Haçienda was that there was no cosy, funky part of it for people to hide away in. So it was around this time, with the money being apparently available (we were on the crest of a wave, remember), that the idea of developing the basement first came up: to form a club-within-a-club and drum up business for off-peak weekday nights and the smaller club nights. We'd used it for the occasional private party but we figured we could put the space to more lucrative use. We thought that it would generate yet more revenue. In the end, the idea went on the back-burner until 1994.

The death of Claire Leighton in 1989 had begun a protracted and expensive battle between the Haçienda and Greater Manchester Police that would plague the club for the next eighteen months to two years. A blow for the club was legislation introduced in February of 1990 that gave the police greater discretionary powers over local magistrates granting nightclub licences. The police also launched Operation Clubwatch, aimed at targeting drug use within the city's clubs.

All of the Haçienda's troubles had the police asking whether or not we should be allowed to renew our licence. Shit. Without that licence, we were just another empty building.

We tried to get the local community involved, to see if that could help us solve the crime problem. There was precedent for this: in around 1986 Paul Mason had joined the pub- and club-watch safety committee. (He got into it by default: every time somebody applies for a licence, all the other pubs routinely object because they don't want the competition. We were a bit on the outside to say the least, so he joined the pub-and-club network to find out how the business worked. Paul became very passionate about it; he enjoyed being involved and even headed the organization for a while.)

To show our willingness to help solve the drug problems, we started a drug-confiscation scheme. When the door staff searched customers and found Es, dope, coke, whatever, the drugs were given to Ang, who put them in a safety-deposit box that was then locked in the safe. I'd harass her for it all the time, Pandora's box, I called it, saying 'gimme gimme', dying to see what I could find inside, rooting around like a ferret. The doormen would even tip me off: they'd say, 'I just handed over ten Es,' and I'd nag her for them, enjoying the wind-up.

She took her job seriously, though, and always refused (mainly telling me to 'fuck right off'). Happily, since I didn't know the safe combination, there was nothing I could do.

Each Monday she'd remove the drug box from the safe and take it down to the police station. Before long, the police decided that she was putting herself at risk not only of being robbed en route but also of being arrested for transporting controlled substances. At that point they decided to come by and pick them up from her; this lasted a week, after which time she had to mither them constantly to come and collect the drugs. She'd sometimes be forced to destroy them, the stockpile having built up for weeks.

The sheer volume of drugs we were handing over was making the cops very nosy. Ang soon realized that the more drugs she turned in, the worse it looked for the Haçienda, so she'd wash some down the sink or flush them down the toilet. That whole rigmarole became the bane of her life. Then the police said that if we found drugs on somebody we should turn their face towards the security camera, so there'd be documentation in case they wanted to press charges – not *when* they pressed charges. Please. We were just trying to run a club. Do your own bloody job.

Tony himself got very involved in taking the problems to the local government because we felt so powerless. His biggest beef was that nobody ever helped: the police, the CID, the licensing committee, the city council, none of them. We were so accustomed to going it alone, we certainly didn't come to count on any assistance. Tony even applied for grants from the city council to preserve the Haçienda and Factory as a vital part of Manchester's cultural and financial heritage, drawing up a detailed economic breakdown of how the club and the record-label earnings affected the entire UK. He didn't get very far with that one. He and Ang went so far as to petition local members of parliament on the club's behalf, with no results there either.

He'd leave the donkey-work (like meeting four thugs with Uzis at some scummy council house in Salford) for us to sort out, whereas he and Paul Mason took care of the airy-fairy work (like meeting with the chief constable for tea in police towers) –and good luck to them; I knew where I'd rather be.

We weren't pulling a good cop/bad cop act. More like posh cop/working-class cop. I don't think it would have worked any other way: the Haçienda, like Factory Records, crossed generations and social classes. It was gritty, down-to-earth and edgy and at the same time was arty and intellectual.

In fact, in an attempt to cater to everyone in Manchester, we offered free admission, food and drinks to the homeless once a month. (The night was called Itch! Ha ha.) And this as we tried to project the image of a ritzy nightclub.

'There were all kinds of undercover operations going on in the club,' Tony Wilson told writer Mick Middles. 'It was a bit bewildering, to say the least. We wanted very, very much to work with the police to help prevent the flow of drugs, but it seemed to be very much an us-against-them situation, which we didn't, and still don't, understand.'

In May 1990 the police told manager Paul Mason that they intended to oppose an upcoming licence renewal. In response the club beefed up security.

Nonetheless the authorities decided they wanted us all out of the way. Fearing any evidence of drug use that might play into their hands, we took the matter to our audience by issuing a flyer that laid out the facts:

FAC 51 The Haçienda A MESSAGE TO ALL OUR CUSTOMERS:

As you may already know, the Greater Manchester Police have told us that they will be applying to revoke the Haçienda's licence at the next magistrates meeting on the 17th of May.

We will of course be rigorously defending the action with all our energy.

Despite our major efforts in recent months, the police feel we must do even more about removing the use of illegal drugs inside the Haçienda – this is where you come in: do not, repeat, NOT, buy or take drugs in the club – and do not bring drugs on to the premises.

The prime role of your club is a place to dance to the most important music of the day; the only way it can continue in this way is by the complete elimination of controlled substances.

It's our club – and it's your club – we're going to fight to keep it alive and we expect you to be fighting with us.

PLEASE MAKE SURE EVERYONE UNDERSTANDS HOW IMPORTANT THIS MESSAGE IS. LET'S ROCK – LEGALLY.

Our licence actually came up for renewal in July 1990, and the hearing resulted in our case being adjourned until January 1991. We had the famous George Carman on our side.

George Carman QC was already a legendary barrister, having defended Ken Dodd and Jeremy Thorpe. Legend has it that, on meeting the Factory men, his first bit of advice was to 'Shut that loudmouth up' in reference to Tony Wilson, whose constant public proclamations Carman believed to be damaging the image of the club.

Carman was extraordinarily expensive but the money was proved to be well spent when he was able to get the licence hearing pushed back to 3 January 1991 – giving the club time to get its house in order. He did so by pledging the Haçienda's commitment to stamping out drug use and drug dealing within the club, as well as producing letters of support for the Haçienda – in particular from the city council's new leader, Labour's Graham Stringer, who had pointed out that the club greatly contributed to the economy and vibrancy of the city centre (obviously having revised his opinion of rave since 1989).

Carman beat the police in their attempts to close us down by refuting the evidence brought against us.

He was very theatrical. In court he brought up what had happened when police filed charges against the club Konspiracy. The cops said they'd seen 150 acts of drug-related offences, meaning people buying, selling or using inside there.

Konspiracy had fought the charges by pointing out that the club was so full of smoke and so dark that there'd be no way for someone to witness much of anything at all, illegal or otherwise. They took the judge, jury, police and everybody associated with the case inside Konspiracy, stood 50 people on the dance floor, started the smoke machine, put some music on and said, 'Tell me how you can spot 150 separate crimes in these conditions.' You couldn't.

By referring to the Konspiracy case Carman got the charges against the Haçienda thrown out. With so many people moving within the club, there was no way to see too much of what anyone was up to. Furthermore, anyone using drugs was careful about where they did them, making crime even harder to detect. The coppers had pulled a scam on us, but the legal battle cost us another £250,000 pounds. Carman charged £15,000 for his first day then £10,000 each day thereafter – for something like seventeen days in all.

The police were furious because they'd failed to shut the Haçienda. They were really pissed off and now we were all marked men.

Anyway, we put out an announcement to tell the clientele what had happened – and that they needed to behave:

GOOD NEWS:

The Haçienda licence hearing on 23rd July resulted in the case being adjourned until 3rd January 1991.

This means that the Haçienda will remain open as usual until this date. FAC 51 the Haçienda now intends to redouble its efforts to keep our club open. This must involve the complete elimination of controlled drugs on the premises.

In this we continue to rely upon your help and co-operation. Please do not, repeat, NOT, buy or take drugs in the club, and do not bring drugs on to the premises.

Please make sure everyone understands how important this message is.

Thank you for your support.

We followed this with another flyer (Tony, treating the whole thing as an art project, called this one 'Communiqué, Winter 90/91'):

Dear Friend,

Let's face it, 1990 has not been an easy year for the Haçienda.

Our problems began in May with the threat to our licence when we had no choice but to take drastic action in order to keep the club open.

A major problem which we have also had to deal with is the increase in violence in and around Manchester's clubs. This is an extremely worrying development to which there is no easy solution.

It must be apparent to you that both these factors have seriously affected the way in which the Haçienda is run.

We realize that things like searches on the door, video surveillance and high-profile security, while necessary, have had a damaging effect on the club's atmosphere and we would be the first to admit that we have found it difficult to get the balance right between law enforcement and partying.

We are particularly aware that the door policy at the Haçienda has provoked much criticism. One problem has been on the occasions regular customers have been turned away. We aim to remedy this situation in the New Year with a membership scheme for Saturday nights which will ensure that regulars are guaranteed admission, at a reduced price (details will be announced shortly).

However, we feel that it is worth remembering that the much-maligned Haçienda doorstaff are under a lot of pressure and while they may not always get it right they are having to work in a difficult situation and do deserve your support.

So, our court hearing approaches and from January the 3rd we will get an indication whether the Haçienda has a future. We are confident that it does. To the pessimists, piss off.

TO ALL OF YOU WHO HAVE CONTINUED TO SUPPORT US THROUGH THESE DIFFICULT TIMES, WE WOULD LIKE TO SAY A BIG THANK YOU.

This was the era of the DJ.

I didn't know many of the Haçienda's DJs very well, but took a dislike to some of them because of what I saw as their prima donna demands: £1000 and more per night (we still held the record for the highest payment to a DJ for a single night's work: Todd Terry took home £12,500), plus hotel rooms, transport, a backstage rider (i.e., booze and food) and 'sweeties'.

It seemed excessive to me, but Saturday nights stood out as our big earners.

On some nights we'd put three of them on. It's no wonder that we couldn't make a profit.

It's funny to think that the original DJ booth had been a hole in the wall. It evolved into a throne room, with locks on the door that were only unlatched to allow entry to the chosen few, friends desperate for a line, or to drug dealers dropping off their goods. Often I kicked that door for ages while those cheeky bastards just left me standing/fuming outside.

The worse case was the club's twelfth birthday, in 1994, when to celebrate we hired twelve DJs.

There wasn't a cat in hell's chance of making enough money to cover the expense. In fact, there wasn't a cat in hell's chance of finding time for them all to play. It seemed like a death wish. The costs were astronomical, ending up with half the DJs fighting in the booth about who was going on where and for how long. That wasn't even the first time we'd tried something like that. We'd had twelve hours' of DJs back in 1983; and, although I wasn't there, I'll bet nobody else was either. Even when DJing at the Haçienda became fashionable we didn't leverage its popularity to see if we could book people for less money. Rob continued to pay more for DJs, as he had done with bands. If a DJ asked for an extra £50, Rob would push his famous glasses up his nose and say, 'Give him another hundred and tell him to fuck off.'

Over time my own relationships with the DJs got better. Jon DaSilva hosted the midweek nights, which I'd occasionally attend, but I've since gone on to know him very well and I work with him a lot. A great DJ. He tells a great story about the *Technique* tour, when he and Graeme did a support tour with us, with me on one particular night offering the pair of them out for being a pair of big-headed bastards. Doesn't sound like me, does it?

Dave Haslam, in contrast, alienated himself from all of us. Dave hosted Temperance Club, the 1980s indie-rock nights, which became a popular evening for students. In some ways it offered the kind of music that people would expect from a club associated with us. He played a broad spectrum of styles, whereas I preferred a narrower focus on dance music.

He got into a fight with Tony, which culminated in October 1990 with him turning off the music to rant about Tony and Factory over the PA system. He slagged everyone off – hilarious – in front of the puzzled customers. Until the doormen kicked down the DJ-box door and threw him out. Tony rarely took exception to people or carried a grudge, but with Haslam he really did and literally took it to the grave.

Dave returned to the Haçienda later, much to Tony's indignation, and has since become an author of many books about Manchester.

According to Wilson in his book 24 Hour Party People, *even in 1990 – at the height of Madchester fever – the club still wasn't making money. 'There were huge crowds and a great atmosphere,' he wrote, 'but it was all fuelled by Ecstasy, not alcohol, and they didn't sell E at the bar.' (Presumably, in the post-hearing era, any drugs were taken before arriving at the club.) The money was going to the drug dealers, he said, and they weren't passing it on to the Haçienda.*

Wilson, the co-owners and other club promoters in the city were at the sharp end of an inevitable side-effect of rave culture. Where there were drugs there was money. And that meant gangsters. And guns.

The trouble had begun to snowball in September 1989, when the police had closed the Gallery, a favourite haunt for Cheetham Hill gangsters. The following weekend the gangsters needed somewhere to go and arrived at the Haçienda.

It all changed forever that night. Three guys came to the door and said to the bouncers, 'We're coming in.'

'Yeah! You and whose army?'

'Us and these,' and they opened up their coats and flashed their guns.

'Well, of course you're coming in.' And our doormen stepped aside. What would you do against three guns?

These guys went inside the club and just sat in a booth, quite normal, drinking and chatting; we were watching them on the closed-circuit TV.

The bouncers told Paul Mason what had happened. He phoned the police and the CID came down. They looked at these kids on the CCTV and told Paul, 'If they don't cause any trouble, leave them.' And then they left.

That was the moment. That's when we started having regular trouble with the gangs, because they knew that the police weren't going to do anything about it. We needed a ballsy, proactive police force and we didn't have one. We'd repeatedly ask for police on the door and they'd just laugh at us for thinking they'd even want to confront the gangs on our behalf. (I know: it's very easy to criticize them; and I don't blame them for wanting to avoid the danger. You wouldn't send someone to war without a gun, but in Manchester, England, we ask people without guns to face people with guns all the time. It's ridiculous.)

Tony knew how to get publicity and during this period that really helped. He highlighted our problems with the gangs in the press. The police really, really hated that he brought their shortcomings out for all to see. They were anti-Haçienda. They just wanted the club to disappear, which is ironic: I'd have thought that knowing where every lunatic and Salford gangster was located on a nightly basis would have been handy. Tony also complained about the cops' treatment of the club to Manchester city council every chance he got. He wouldn't let them get away with it.

Not that it helped on our door, of course – the attitude of the doormen had to change. They had to become much, much harder in order to protect themselves. Everything had to change. Eventually the whole axis of power in the club would shift, so that it was no longer the management running it – it was the doormen.

Throughout 1990 there were numerous instances of violence, with doormen and clubbers assaulted, guns pulled, knives used. Some gangsters saw the dealers as easy targets for muggings, or 'taxings' as they were called; others wanted a slice of the drug-money pie. At Christmas that year there was an incident at Discotheque Royale, where Cheetham Hill gang members beat up doormen, then 'taxed' dealers and clubbers at gunpoint. The most notorious taxing method was the 'scraping', which meant a dealer being kidnapped, driven to the M602 roundabout in Salford, then having his face held to the tarmac while the car drove round. There were incidents at Konspiracy and the Kitchen. The seeds of Gunchester were already sown.

WHAT'S ON AT THE HAÇIENDA IN 1990

JANUARY

Wednesday 3rd	VOID Jon DaSilva; Mike Pickering
Thursday 4th	TEMPERANCE CLUB Dave Haslam
Friday 5th	NUDE Mike Pickering
Wednesday 10th	VOID Jon DaSilva; Mike Pickering
Thursday 11th	TEMPERANCE CLUB Dave Haslam
Friday 12th	NUDE Mike Pickering
Wednesday 17th	VOID Jon DaSilva; Mike Pickering
Thursday 18th	TEMPERANCE CLUB Dave Haslam
Friday 19th	NUDE Mike Pickering
Wednesday 24th	VOID Jon DaSilva; Mike Pickering
Thursday 25th	TEMPERANCE CLUB Dave Haslam
Friday 26th	NUDE Mike Pickering
Saturday 27th	Tommy Musto; Frankie Bones
Wednesday 31st	VOID Jon DaSilva; Mike Pickering

FEBRUARY

Friday 2nd	NUDE Mike Pickering
Saturday 3rd	Paul Oakenfold
Monday 5th	Northside; Paris Angels; the Spinmasters
Friday 9th	NUDE Mike Pickering
Friday 16th	NUDE Mike Pickering
Wednesday 21st	COACH TRIP TO LOCOMOTIVE New Fast Automatic Daffodils; Paris Angels
Thursday 22nd	COACH TRIP TO LOCOMOTIVE James; Dave Haslam
Friday 23rd	NUDE Mike Pickering
Tuesday 27th	STAFF PARTY AT THE GREEN ROOM Revenge; Steve Williams

MARCH

Friday 2nd	NUDE Mike Pickering
Monday 5th	The Beloved
Tuesday 6th	The Fall

Set-list: 'The Littlest Rebel', 'Jerusalem', 'Sing! Harpy', 'I'm Frank', 'Telephone Thing', 'Hilary', 'Hit the North', 'Bill is Dead', 'Black Monk Theme', 'Popcorn Double Feature', 'Deadbeat Descendant', 'Bremen Nacht', 'And Therein', 'Victoria', 'Mr Pharmacist', 'U.S. 80's-90's', 'Fiery Jack'

Friday 9th	NUDE Mike Pickering
Monday 12th	Northside; Paris Angels
Friday 16th	NUDE Mike Pickering
Wednesday 21st	VOID Guru Josh
Friday 23rd	NUDE Mike Pickering
Friday 30th	NUDE Mike Pickering

APRIL

Monday 2nd	Dubsex
Friday 6th	NUDE Mike Pickering
Monday 9th	The Farm
Tuesday 10th	Jimmy Somerville
Friday 13th	NUDE Mike Pickering
Monday 16th	Adamski
Friday 20th	NUDE Mike Pickering
Monday 23rd	The Mock Turtles
Friday 27th	NUDE Mike Pickering

MAY

Friday 4th	NUDE Mike Pickering
Friday 11th	NUDE Mike Pickering
Monday 14th	New Fast Automatic Daffodils
Friday 18th	NUDE Mike Pickering
Monday 21st	EIGHTH BIRTHDAY PARTY
Friday 25th	NUDE Mike Pickering

JUNE

THE UNITED STATES OF THE HAÇIENDA: TRANCE AMERICAN TOUR Mike Pickering; Paul Oakenfold; Graeme Park; Dave Haslam

Friday 1st   NUDE Mike Pickering
Wednesday 6th   VOID Jon DaSilva; Mike Pickering
Thursday 7th   TEMPERANCE CLUB Dave Haslam
Friday 8th   NUDE Mike Pickering
Wednesday 13th   VOID Jon DaSilva; Mike Pickering
Wednesday 14th   TEMPERANCE CLUB Dave Haslam
Friday 15th   NUDE Mike Pickering
Monday 18th   Northside
Wednesday 20th   VOID Jon DaSilva; Mike Pickering
Thursday 21st   TEMPERANCE CLUB Dave Haslam
Friday 22nd   NUDE Mike Pickering
Wednesday 27th   VOID Jon DaSilva; Mike Pickering
Thursday 28th   TEMPERANCE CLUB Dave Haslam
Friday 29th   NUDE Mike Pickering

JULY
Friday 6th   NUDE Mike Pickering
Friday 13th   NUDE Mike Pickering
Saturday 14th   TRANCE AMERICAN TOUR HITS THE
                   SOUND FACTORY, NEW YORK
                   Paul Oakenfold; Mike Pickering; Graeme Park;
                   Dee-Lite
Friday 20th   NUDE Mike Pickering
Monday 23rd   *Licence-revocation hearing adjourned to*
                   January 1991
Friday 27th   Nude Mike Pickering
Saturday 28th   Nick Arrojo

AUGUST
Friday 3rd   NUDE Mike Pickering
Friday 10th   NUDE Mike Pickering
Friday 17th   NUDE Mike Pickering
Friday 24th   NUDE Mike Pickering
Friday 31st   NUDE Mike Pickering

SEPTEMBER
Friday 7th   NUDE Mike Pickering
Friday 14th   NUDE Mike Pickering

Friday 21st	NUDE Mike Pickering
Friday 28th	NUDE Mike Pickering

OCTOBER
Friday 5th	THE MIX Dave Booth
Saturday 6th	NUDE Mike Pickering, Graeme Park
Thursday 11th	TEMPERANCE CLUB Dave Haslam *(his last night)*
Tuesday 16th	CLASSICS IN MOTION Rolf Hind; Graham Fitkin; the Durutti Column; Steve Martland & Orchestra *(Factory classical in conjunction with the Haçienda present . . .)*
Wednesday 17th	SHIVA Jon DaSilva; Mike Pickering
Thursday 18th	TEMPERANCE CLUB Tim Chambers
Monday 22nd	Plenty; the Sandmen; Dave Booth
Monday 29th	The High; Dave Booth

NOVEMBER
Monday 5th	Synergy; the Shamen; Dave Booth
Friday 9th	THE MIX Bass-o-Matic; Dave Booth
Sunday 11th	Northside; plus guests
Monday 12th	Blur; Dave Booth
Monday 19th	Bridewell Taxis; plus guests
Monday 26th	Cud; the Popinjays

DECEMBER
Monday 3rd	The High; plus guests; Little Martin; Dave Booth
Friday 14th	DECONSTRUCTION RECORDS PARTY N-Joi
Monday 17th	New Fast Automatic Daffodils
Monday 24th	CHRISTMAS EVE PARTY Mike Pickering
Monday 31st	NEW YEAR'S EVE PARTY Mike Pickering; Graeme Park; Jon DaSilva

EXCERPTS FROM COMPANY ACCOUNTS, 1990

FAC 51 Limited
Trading as: the Haçienda

PROFIT AND LOSS ACCOUNT (for the year ended 30 June 1990)

	1990 (£)	1989 (£)
Turnover	1,369,245.00	1,070,094.00
Cost of sales	339,600.00	323,432.00
Gross profit	1,029,645.00	747,662.00
Administrative expenses	862,127.00	732,039.00
	= 167,518.00	= 14,623.00
Other operating income	–	11,009.00
Operating profit	167,518.00	25,632.00
Interest receivable	–	425.00
Interest payable	(4222.00)	(2551.00)
Profit on ordinary activities before taxation	= 163,296.00	= 23,506.00
Taxation	2633.00	–
Profit on ordinary activities after taxation	= 160,663.00	= 23,506.00
Retained deficit brought forward	(177,107.00)	(200,613.00)
Retained deficit carried forward	(16,444.00)	(177,107.00)

FAC 51 Limited
Trading as: the Haçienda

COSTS OF PURCHASE OF WHITWORTH STREET BUILDING

	(£)
Purchase of building	1,200,000.00
Stamp duty	12,000.00
Their solicitor's fees	4600.00
Land-registry fees	500.00
Transfer fees	15.00
Berger Oliver fees	13,800.00
Insurance Sun Alliance	5600.00
Commitment fee	4000.00
Total	**1,240,515.00**

A GUIDE TO MANCHESTER'S GANGS, 1990

Cheetham Hill
Although Cheetham Hill in the north of the city is a relatively small area of Manchester, it boasted one of Manchester's largest and best-organized gangs, a black and mixed-race outfit with a fearsome reputation.

Doddington
Operating out of the Moss Side area, this crew took its name from Doddington Close on the west side of the district and were notable for the youth of its members.

Gooch
Also based in Moss Side, Gooch was a mainly black gang formed in Gooch Close. Though it had many older, original members, it also boasted a youthful element with a fearsome reputation for violence.

Salford
Predominantly white, Salford was one of the older gangs if not the oldest in the city and was organized by family. As with other gangs, it was the younger members out to prove themselves who gained a name for extreme violence.

1991

'That was the first time I'd been in the girls' loo. It looked very nice, actually'

As the club entered 1991 it had a problem. On the one hand it was being asked to stamp out drug use; on the other, thanks to bands such as the Happy Mondays, it was helping to create a scene that glorified their use.

'We are not responsible for the backgrounds of our artists,' Tony Wilson told writer Mick Middles. Wilson was aware of the paradox, however: he was, after all, a casual user himself. So, to find his own moral cut-off point in the drug culture, he needed to look in the direction of organized crime.

'What I am not into and am, in fact, appalled by, is the violence that sometimes comes with drugs and has caused problems at the Haçienda. What people might take or smoke or drink is up to them until the point where they might harm other people. Then it becomes an issue and we would have no truck with that.'

At the postponed hearing on 3 January the magistrates announced their pleasure at a 'positive change in direction' and renewed the club's licence.

In order to try to build on the reprieve offered by the magistrates, the club revitalized its original membership scheme and imposed stricter conditions on the door. The fact that the Haçienda, cheerleader of the new rave revolution, was to impose such draconian measures didn't sit well with the clientele, however. Queues became even more lengthy; the distribution of the fanzine Freaky Dancing and the entertainment provided by the club did little to make this aspect of the experience seem appealing. Furthermore, the new system failed to keep the troublemakers out – and those troublemakers were armed.

Up until this point our bouncers had never seen any real trouble and we still had a reputation for having the most wonderful, peaceful security of any club in England.

That peace was about to end.

After the police shut the Gallery the gangsters moved on to the Haçienda, saw how it had flourished and thought, 'We'll have some of that.'

Don't forget that for a long time the club had had a reputation in Manchester for being empty and playing indie music. But now the dealers in the Haç could earn three to four grand on Fridays and four to five grand on Saturdays. Then they were mainly middle-class, university-educated boys from Stoke and a lot of them worked the club on a regular basis.

At first the gangsters were their customers, joining in with the hugging and general togetherness. But over a period of time they sussed out how much they could earn if they took over. They then began turning dealers upside down – literally, they used to shake them by the ankles – to take money and drugs off them and when that didn't work the beatings were savage. Dealers wouldn't press charges for obvious reasons.

As a result, crime increased nightly. And Dry suffered the same security problems as the Haçienda – the same gang members were regulars at both. There were some terrible incidents of violence that made us regret opening both places, but it was especially bad at the Haç. I don't know of any place in England that suffered with violence the way we did here. We were unique.

On Wednesday 9 January the club celebrated its licensing reprieve with Thanksgiving, a night that featured Haçienda institutions Mike Pickering, Graeme Park and Jon DaSilva as well as a live performance from Electronic. The first Nude of the year was held the following Saturday, for which a membership scheme was introduced in a bid to stop troublemakers gaining entry. The next Saturday was the second Nude of the year – and in fact it was the last ever Nude to be held at the club.

There was an incident. At the time it was reported that a doorman had been threatened with a gun but there were no shots fired. According to Tony Wilson in his book 24 Hour Party People, *however: 'A Cheetham Hill sub-head went walkabout in the Haç entrance. Waving a gun in the air. Shots were fired.'*

Apparently the punter had not taken kindly to being refused admission under the new membership scheme.

It was the last straw. The following Wednesday, after days of meetings, Wilson called a press conference, held on the Haçienda dance floor.

'The Haçienda is closing its doors as of today,' he told journalists (looking 'tired and haggard' according to reports).

> It is with the greatest reluctance that for the moment we are turning the lights out on what is, for us, a most important place.
>
> 'We are forced into taking this drastic action in order to protect our employees, our members and all our clients. We are quite simply sick and tired of dealing with instances of personal violence.
>
> We hope and we must believe we can reopen the Haçienda in a better climate. But until we are able to run the club in a safe manner, and in a way that the owners believe will guarantee the role of the Haçienda at the heart of the city's youth community, it is with great sadness that we will shut our club.

It had always been on the horizon. The police were focusing on the drug issue while the owners of the Haçienda understood that guns and gangsters were the bigger problems. Since 1987 shootings in the city had increased and gang-style executions were taking place, such as the killing of 'White' Tony Johnson, a well-known troublemaker. The gangsters were primarily interested in heroin and cocaine, and not in what they felt was the low-level dealing usually to be found in a nightclub; but, as writer Andy Spinoza noted, 'Gangsters like clubbing too' – and their preferred night out was the Haçienda, the world's most fashionable nightclub.

There they expected free and immediate entry and were not above flashing a gun in order to get it. In return the Haçienda had sent a message to the gangsters. Whether it was heard would remain to be seen.

At the press conference reporters were told that the club would be closed for about a month. It turned out to be five.

When the Haçienda shut its doors in January 1991 it was because of gang violence. It had become too dangerous. We had to press pause while we reassessed, which cost us a fortune: it actually cost more to run the club closed than open. In that five months alone we lost £175,000.

We fitted the building with an airport-style metal detector. Once everything fell into place, we issued a statement:

THE HAÇIENDA

The Haçienda Press Release, 11 April 1991

It is with some pleasure that the owners of the Haçienda announce the reopening of the club on 10 May 1991.

We believe that the climate in which we work has changed sufficiently to allow us to make a fresh start. At last their [sic] seems to be a new understanding in the city.

We reopen in good faith, our faith in other people's faith in Manchester.

For further information call Paul Cons on 061 953 0251.

In the meantime the Haçienda had a makeover: Ben Kelly came up with a new scheme, and the pillars were painted in brighter colours.

As far as security was concerned, an airport-style metal detector was installed (that never worked, according to Tony Wilson, because it was erected above a metal floor), thorough body searches were instigated, external cameras outside and inside infra-red cameras sweeping the areas police and the club recognized as being drug hotspots. The club was doing all it could to target the gangsters and eradicate drugs.

The revamp provided the opportunity for a DJ shake-up, too, and the club's reopening party the Healing heralded a new line-up. On Saturdays an unnamed night was headed by Graeme Park, who was by now one of – if not the – UK's biggest DJ names. On Thursdays Dave Haslam returned to his old Temperance Club spot, but with the night renamed Beautiful 2000. A new night was launched for Saturdays to replace Nude: Shine!, hosted by Mike Pickering with guest appearances by big-name DJs such as Sasha and David Morales.

It was at Shine! that a now infamous act of violence occurred.

When we reopened we hired Top Guard, an established crowd-management company that provided security at football games, venues and festivals to augment the few local doormen we'd chosen to keep. We even looked into getting them to escort Paul Mason to and from work, in case somebody with a grudge (or an eye on robbing us) followed him home.

Then we found out that, 'Paul never locked up anyway. Ang did.'

She'd be there each club night, the last to leave, having carried all the takings upstairs to the offices, an easy target for anyone. Every weekend we'd have a ton of cash on the premises until the banks opened on Monday morning – even more on a Bank Holiday weekend, when we were a particularly tempting target. When the insurance company finally realized that she was traipsing around an empty building, spending forty minutes locking and checking all the doors, then walking to her flat alone at three in the morning, they supplied her with a personal alarm to wear around her neck, an escort from work, and a deadbolt for her door at home. Big deal.

We focused on securing the Haçienda itself too. The three main doormen lived in a house on the outskirts of Manchester, while their crew travelled by coach from Birmingham. We reopened with something like twelve Dobermanns and fifty bouncers, who patrolled both outside and inside the club. Instead of dressing in white shirt, ties and Crombies (like our security used to), this lot looked like a paramilitary force – much more threatening. That opening night, strangely enough, was called the Healing, yet the Salford and Cheetham Hill lot kicked off immediately and nearly closed us back down. They were storming the doors trying to get in. I'd brought Arthur Baker along from New York to celebrate our reopening and we couldn't even get near the door, the fighting was that intense; we had to wait across the road for an hour while security tried to calm it down.

On that first night our new doormen, who were mainly from down south, didn't know what the hell they were taking on. Thinking that a show of force would take care of the problem, they clamped down on everybody, rather than negotiating with people and defusing situations. They didn't know who to show respect to; the mood got leery very quickly, and the gangs just stormed the door.

It was a taste of things to come.

On another night shortly after this a doorman let some of the Salford lot in and, as they passed, muttered under his breath: 'Salford dickheads'. A perceived slight.

In the club they calmly sat down used their mobiles to call the young firm. Then just sat in the corner waiting.

It was like a military operation. One lot came in normally, in ones and twos, slowly infiltrating us. Then a second lot arrived en masse. This lot again stormed the door – and then it really kicked off.

As our bouncers charged after them, the first bunch made their play, stabbing the bouncers in the arse as they ran past. A classic pincer movement. The bouncers were severely outnumbered and they 'retreated' (shat themselves and ran away), fleeing through the club, creating panic as they went. Then they were cornered, by the main bar on the right by the fire exits, and it was complete pandemonium. Blood everywhere, clubbers screaming. Fucking chaos.

It was a classic example of younger gangsters doing the bidding of the older ones. It was a perfectly planned manoeuvre. Someone called the police but the TAG took forty-five minutes to come – despite the fact that the police were filming the building from the railway bridge opposite, to observe and count the number of people going in and out (they were trying to nail us for overcrowding). They didn't want to help us. Can't blame them, really. The wounded doormen were laid in a row until help eventually arrived.

The attack took place on Saturday 22 June. Inside the club Mike Pickering was presiding over the Midsummer Night Shine!, which had a specially extended licence until four a.m. The street was cordoned off after around 200 Tactical Aid Group officers turned up and clubbers were led from the Haçienda to run the gauntlet of police, with helicopters buzzing overhead, searchlights on. As the clubbers filed out, each one had their photograph taken . . .

There were many more incidents, culminating in the head doorman being chased out of the club by an Asian kid holding an Uzi. The doorman ran out the back door, jumped into his car, sped home to London and never came back. Poor bastard. That ended everything. The other doormen packed up and left too. 'We're not fucking standing there, even if we've got a hundred Dobermanns. There are too many little kids running around with guns.'

Clearly we were fucked. We'd reopened but now we had no bouncers. With clubs, punters and even cops failing to stand up to them, the gangsters had just got more and more cocky. Obviously what we needed was someone a bit more sussed, someone who knew the score, exactly what was going on . . .

It was at this point that the Haçienda's owners turned to Paul Carroll (one of the advisers to Top Guard) and Damien Noonan. Both had underworld links and Damien was a member of the infamous Noonan family, a huge

*family in which all of the siblings' names began with the letter D. His
brother Desmond had been charged but then acquitted of the murder of
'White' Tony Johnson, and had a name as a gangland fixer, while his younger
brother Dominic had more than forty convictions for armed robbery, assault-
ing police, deception, firearms and fraud. Together, Carroll and Damien
Noonan would now run the club's door.*

Yes, they were the bad boys but they were all we had left to turn to.
We hoped that with the protection of the Noonan family we could
control the violence. That was the idea, anyway.

Talk about out of the frying pan and into the fire. My mate is a
policeman in Salford. He told me about an unwritten rule whereby if
Damien Noonan got pulled over they had to let him go, no matter
what he'd been doing.

One time a new recruit on the force was patrolling Langworthy
Road.

He stopped some guy for drunk driving, got on the radio and said,
'Can I have some assistance? I've pulled over a guy called . . .' and then
nobody could make out what he'd said, but it sounded like 'Oonan'.

Everyone at the station froze. 'Noonan? Did he just say Noonan?'

Everybody started shouting, 'Let him go!'

'What?' he said back at them. 'You're breaking up.'

They all shat themselves because they had to go give him assistance
and they knew Damien would leather them all. That kid got a right bol-
locking when he eventually returned to the station.

You felt like other gangsters did things just for sport, but the
Noonans acted like proper businessmen. When I'd drive past Damien's
house – before I knew him – I always wondered, 'Who lives there?'
He'd create the most outrageous Christmas-light display you've ever
seen in your life. It used to cheer up the neighbourhood a treat.
Nobody else would have dared do it – it would have got stolen or
wrecked – but Damien dressed his home up like a fairy castle.

The Noonans ranked very high up in the gangs' pecking order, which
was just what we needed.

Many of the Salford gangs were family-based. The older ones –
including a lot of my mates from school – were pretty civilized and
enjoyed partying (too much). They weren't as violent as the younger
Salford lot, who loved fighting. The young guys were heavy, bad boys:

violent and unpredictable, very territorial, sensitive to any perceived slight, yet very loyal to their area and the elder statesmen. You needed to be careful not to cross them, and the older ones would get the younger ones to do their dirty work for them.

There were also a lot of these great characters around. One of my great mates could be a really nice guy, but he turned super-bad when he was off of it. He'd bait the police by driving around drunk in stolen cars, wait until he'd been spotted by a copper, then get in a car chase. To him, this was a great laugh, and he was gutted if he ever accidentally stole something a bit too fast because that meant he could outrun the police. He'd start a chase with the coppers then, if he lost them, go back looking for them. One time, he engineered the chase so that a police car got stuck in an entry and the officer inside couldn't open the doors. He was waiting and beat the shit out of the cop car before it could escape. I had a first-hand witness account of that one because Suzanne from the kitchen was in the car with him. She ended up screaming trying to get out but he'd locked her in. Took ten years off her life she said.

He wasn't the only one, either. The bad boys knew where the police patrol cars went for repair, so they'd go round to the garage, smash them up, burn them, film the whole thing and send a VHS of it to the Crescent, the divisional police headquarters. It was a game to them. A wind-up.

Under our new arrangement, these were the kind of guys we now had running our door.

Looking back now, the whole thing could have been a bit of a set-up. Talking hypothetically, the gangsters could have engineered the assaults on the door. Word had spread about how much we were paying, with people joking that even the Dobermanns were on great wages. So maybe the gangsters, thinking we had money to burn, decided to move in.

They charged us £400 a night each for two controllers' services, plus about £150 per night for each member of their team, who they then commissioned I heard (in other words, the Haçienda paid £150 but the bouncers only pocketed £80).

We had no choice but to pay. We even defended Damien before a special tribunal with a barrister and lawyer to get him his Doorsafe badge. He had a criminal record for aggravated violence and armed robbery. We needed him to run the door, so Tony told the judge that he'd reformed – 'he's learned his lesson now m'lud' – a very dodgy wicket, really. How we got through it all is a miracle, but the Doorsafe badge made his position a bit more solid. He was very proud of that badge, too; he loved the respectability he got from doing the door.

Paul and Damien were neutral when it came to the gangs, so their job was to act as a peace-keeping force, or like teachers trying to keep the hard lads from killing each other in the playground. Gangs were still allowed in, but rival gangs had to stick to their corners, and violence against staff was strictly off-limits. Every so often in the past, when the gangs had felt particularly cocky, they'd raided the bar just to prove they were invincible. Two or three would hop over and grab a few bottles. If a bartender tried to stop them, he got a slap.

That stopped. Damien wouldn't tolerate attacks on the staff – he was very protective of them – and he'd retaliate if anyone stepped over the mark. Eventually the raids stopped, too, when he cut a deal with the gangsters, giving them cut-price drinks.

This compromise we reached allowed all the big knobs in the Salford lot to buy their champagne at cost. As long as we gave it to them cheap, they wouldn't steal outright or harass the staff. If someone else tried stealing from us, however, they'd get battered. The Gooch and Moss Side gangsters kept pretty quiet at the Haçienda because Salford controlled the door. To my knowledge, Salford and Cheetham Hill had an uneasy alliance.

Again, as had been the case with my mates freeloading, we gave booze away. There are two kinds of bad treatment. Your friends do it with a kid glove. The gangs do it with a gauntlet.

Initially the gangs had just enjoyed the buzz of the acid-house scene; they were content to sit back and watch all the characters who turned everybody on, like Gordon the Chef standing on the podium shouting, 'Come on, Manchester. Come on, Salford.' He was the ringleader and cheerleader of the Haçienda before the hardened criminals moved in.

Gordon was a great character: a small, cheery guy of about my age on the fringes of the Salford gangs. He made a name for himself when he and his brother ran raves in Manchester. They threw a really big one in Rochdale called Joy, which was fantastic, then ran off with the money. Everyone thought that was hilarious – apart from the poor sods who had invested in it.

I'll remember Gordon that one night when we were both off our tits. I was moaning, 'I'm really bored with the Haçienda.'

'Well, let's go somewhere else. Number One?' he suggested.

We ended up at the Number One club in Manchester, One Central Street as it is now, run by Leroy. Then we moved on to DeVille's, by which point we were proper off it, both of us high as kites – especially him, because he had the bag. I spotted this beautiful older woman dressed all in silver, with silver thigh-length boots and really dark, coppery-red hair. She sat at a table with a friend, and I was entranced.

'Oh my God,' I thought. 'She's gorgeous.'

Emboldened, I walked over and said, 'Hello, hello. I love your outfit.'

She replied, 'Oh gee, thanks.'

Ah, an accent.

'You're American?'

'Yeah, I'm from Georgia.'

'What you doing here?' I asked.

She said, 'I'm a singer.'

'Oh, you're a singer. I play in a band as well. What band are you with?'

'I'm the singer of the B-52s,' she said.

At that moment Gordon the Chef walked up, poking me and pulling my arm. I was so off my head I thought I might make it with this bird from the B-52s, so I whispered, 'Gordon, fuck off, don't bother me.'

'Hooky. Hooky,' he exclaimed. 'We've got to go. We've got to go.'

'Fuck off, will ya,' I repeated.

At which point the girl asked me, 'What band do you play in?'

Just as I said to her face, 'I'm the bassist of New Order,' Gordon the Chef threw up all over her boots.

She screamed. I grabbed Gordon and rushed him out the door. Dear God in heaven. We went back to the Haç then. I still wonder to this day if she remembers that. I hope not.

At the Haçienda queues continued to stretch around the block. Madchester raved on. In a poll that year 40 per cent of with-it New Yorkers said that Manchester was the UK city they most wanted to visit. Meanwhile the music was evolving. It had moved from house to acid, then to garage. The Haçienda crowd hadn't really taken to the harder end of techno, which was becoming a 'British' sound, and Manchester has always preferred soul and funk from overseas; so, very gradually, the Haçienda began to carve a

*niche for itself as the club for house connoisseurs. On one hand this was for-
tuitous, in that it would help distance the club from the nuttier end of the
rave scene's ongoing love affair with ecstasy. On the other, it left the club a
little out on a limb when it came to adapting to the fast-shifting trends in
dance-music culture.*

You've heard about the drugs and the rock 'n' roll. What about the sex?

The fact is that very little of it actually occurred – well, to me anyway.
Everyone was so off their heads, I'm sure they only thought about it
when they were at home coming down, when even the keyhole looks
appealing.

I still enjoyed the Haçienda, standing on tables, dancing with a load of
fucking idiots whom I thought I knew but whom I wouldn't have recognized in the morning at all. And, while I was single (my two years of
freedom, before I met my first wife), I hung out with the staff from Dry,
Ken and Pottsy, the bouncers too, the Swan lot, as well as Paul Mason
and his wife, Karen – a really nice, friendly bunch.

I literally spent seven days a week at Dry before going on to the
Haçienda. Others fell into the same pattern. The staff became very
incestuous; inter-staff relations and affairs happened, and some lasted
but some didn't. Despite all the bad stuff associated with the club, I
could run about flirting with the female punters; but it was more of a
hangout for meeting friends and getting off your head than a copping
joint.

For the most part.

One night my mate Rex and I were bored so we stopped in to the
Jolly Roger night. There were about twelve people in, including these
two pretty student girls, both pissed as farts. Because I had the devil in
me, I went to Rex and said, 'Go talk to them.'

He started chatting them up and – gesturing toward me –
announced, 'This guy owns the club.'

The girl said, 'Oh, fuck off, I bet you always say that.'

Now, I'd always told the staff: 'If anyone asks you if I own the club, just
deny it.'

As a rule, I avoided explaining myself to strangers, because it'd take
up too much time. Well, this girl expressed an interest, and I figured that
it would help the evening along if she believed me. Now I needed
somebody to verify my credentials.

This nice little fat lad worked behind the bar. He wore a hat and I always sent him running around looking for drugs for me. He would vouch for me, I thought. I told the girl: 'I know. I'll prove to you that I own the Haçienda.'

I took her behind the bar, called this kid over and said, 'Go on, tell her that I own the club.'

'You don't.'

'No. It's OK. Tell her that I do.'

'No, you don't.'

'Oh, you bastard.'

It all went proper tits-up from there.

One time our bouncers actually caught me in the ladies' loo – with a lady, of course. It looked very nice, actually. The girls' bathroom was much nicer than the boys' and about three times the size. I never realized.

Everybody said that if you wanted to cop in Manchester you'd just have to go to the Ritz. On occasion you'd hear about people fucking in the DJ booth, or getting blowjobs in the lighting booth, and now and then you'd see a couple getting carried away in a corner. I remember one couple going at it on the shelf by the staircase and everyone was walking past cheering on their way to the cocktail bar.

One of the Haçienda's biggest nights around this time was Flesh, promoted by Paul Cons and Lucy Scher. Staged on Wednesdays, it boasted a controversial 'no straights' door policy and soon gained a name as the UK's most outrageous gay night out, attracting a nationwide clientele. It went on to win the Best Gay Club Night of the Year in the Pink Paper and, along with Nude and Hot, is recognized as being another of the landmark nights of the era.

The 'no straights' policy did ruffle a few feathers, though, with Paul Cons labelled 'Third Reich' by one punter who screamed, 'Fucking came marching with you for Clause 28 and now you don't want me at your club for being straight. Fucking fascist.'

Flesh kick-started a series of Wednesday-night events: DJ Sasha was given his own night; he had by now become legendary on the rave circuit but had first been inspired on the club's dance floor. It was a sign of the times, a gratifying acknowledgement of the huge part the Haçienda had to play in the birth of dance culture. The first of Sasha's nights played host to

K-Klass – another well-travelled rave-era act who had met and found inspiration at the Haç.

Flesh nights were wild. They'd put shower cubicles by the toilets and hang cages from the ceiling with male dancers writhing inside. Later they added massage tables. Drag queens from all over England made the pilgrimage. Even by our standards Flesh could be really debauched. It was completely over the top.

The bouncers resisted it at first, as they resisted every new club night they didn't understand – be it Asian, black, or whatever. But the bouncers were very popular at Flesh because the Muscle Marys fell in love immediately with them and their uniforms; it was a gay fantasy come to life. Initially the gangsters were scared off by it, too, but soon changed their tune when Flesh became a runaway success. They'd come in to sell drugs, or just to enjoy the wild atmosphere. No-one dared say no to them.

Mick Hucknall told me that a couple of them (who shall remain nameless) decided that they'd try a blowjob off the greeter, just to see what it was like. So Flesh introduced them to a whole new culture; and, if any of them already leaned that way or were curious, this was their opportunity to experiment.

The weirdest Flesh night involved an employee running up to Ang in tears because two guys at the back of the stage were dancing around with bottles shoved up their arses. He was worried about collecting the empties, I suppose.

I can't tell you how many times Paul Cons suggested that we make the Haçienda a gay club. One of our friends, Kevin Millens, ran Heaven, which was for years the biggest gay club in England, and they never had any trouble there. Paul would make his pitch to us at the directors' meetings.

'Why do you bother with these straight fuckers?' he'd say. 'The gays spend more money. They're less trouble. They smell better . . .' etc., etc.

In fact Flesh nights proved to be so profitable that when Paul eventually left us he'd rent the Haçienda and host his own nights. Paul was ambitious – I liked that about him – and at one point we were so sick of the fighting that we really thought, 'Oh fuck it, let's knock it on the head and go gay.' Never did, though. It would have been too radical a departure. Rob wanted the club to be for everybody. Plus he wouldn't have been able to ogle the girls then, would he?

Flesh ushered in the era during which we could stay open until seven a.m. and serve drinks until three a.m. We could never get a late licence until Paul applied for one. Rob went off: 'Why was he able to get one and we weren't?'

Then we heard that the licensing committee were very 'gay friendly'. They did Paul and the Haçienda a very big and important favour. They also set a precedent: once they'd accommodated Paul, they couldn't refuse our other late-licence requests – nor those made by anyone else, unfortunately. So getting what we wanted did backfire slightly because we ended up in competition with a lot of other bars and clubs that also got late licences.

Meanwhile, the cost of maintenance had become astronomical. On popular nights, when it got hot and wet inside the club, and the bass made everything throb, huge lumps of plaster would fall from the roof and hit people. Ang used to compensate them with free memberships, free drinks and/or sexual favours (only joking, Ang!) so that they wouldn't file claims against us.

Towards the end the building decayed even more and skylight glasses started slipping off too; by this time incidents were occurring on an almost nightly basis.

The licensee was required to be on the premises at all times, but Paul Mason was also in control of the Dry bar so it became difficult for him to remain Haçienda licensee. Thus he moved across to Factory Leisure, which ran the Dry bar. The day-to-day running of the club was then put in the hands of Ang Matthews, who became the Haçienda licensee.

As the years passed, stress wore Paul Mason down. He was a good bloke with a good heart and he tried to deal with issues in a businesslike manner. He also worked hard to change the relationship between the police and the Haçienda, and to improve the licensing magistrate's standpoint, too. He wanted to earn us money and he tried to stay optimistic – he'd phone me sometimes, really happy: 'Hooky, two thousand two hundred in tonight; you can't move.'

Once they were in, though, they were difficult to control. And that was the bit he found more difficult. Overall I'd say he worked best in pub culture, which was calmer. That's why he came to prefer working at Dry.

Tony could convince Paul to do things just to annoy Rob. Arguing with Tony gave Rob something to do and they'd get into some almighty rows, which Rob always won because whenever he ran out of retorts he'd get right up in Tony's face. Tony didn't like that and he'd just say, 'Fuck off,' and storm off. To his credit I never saw Tony angry, whereas I saw Rob angry millions of times.

Paul also put himself in danger. In the early days, if the alarm went off at five a.m., or something, he'd have to investigate. God bless him. The place was so big and so lonely, if anyone had asked me to do it I'd have told them to fuck right off. You'd need to be mad to walk through that place by yourself. For a time the police responded to our alarm, but eventually stopped doing so because there were so many false alerts – mainly birds flying through the broken glass panels on the roof and triggering the alarm.

I liked Paul. He and his wife Karen were always wonderfully sweet to me, especially when I needed help, and I couldn't be more grateful. But I didn't work at the Haçienda any more, so my opinion of him didn't matter. What did matter was what the staff thought. And they didn't like him. It got so bad in the end that no one would work with him or take any notice of him as manager. At that point he'd had enough and wanted to leave – you couldn't blame him.

He'd had a tough time, poor bastard: death threats and everything. I felt really sorry for him. Funny that when he left I bought his Lancia off the club (I paid £7,100), then couldn't sell it. It was very fast but was left-hand drive, totally useless. I lost money on it twice.

When Paul handed over the club's management and licence to Ang, he became operations manager of both the Haçienda and Dry. This ensured that he wouldn't work in the club. Obviously Ang in her new role assumed more responsibility, but Paul Cons also took over some of Paul Mason's duties; it became his job to decide our stylistic direction.

Rob always looked for ways to earn money and to make the building profitable, but it was always on his terms. In 1991 he started his own music label, Robs Records, which he operated with great success out of an upstairs office that he shared with his assistant, Rebecca Boulton (who took over the running of New Order when Rob died). He specialized in finding home-grown talent: most of the acts on Robs Records came from Manchester. He didn't extensively scout for talent, either – he relied on John Drape (Ear to the Ground), Dave Rofe (Doves'

Manager) and people like that to bring him *the* Manchester acts. Despite all the power at his disposal, he ignored anyone outside of our area. He hated everyone south of Chorlton. He wasn't looking for the next Black Box. He preferred to back a group from Wythenshawe, like the Doves or A Certain Ratio. It was a very purist attitude, but then he was a proper Wythenshawe boy.

WHAT'S ON AT THE HAÇIENDA IN 1991

JANUARY

Thursday 3rd	TEMPERANCE CLUB Tim Chambers
Friday 4th	THE MIX Dave Booth
Saturday 5th	NUDE Graeme Park; Mike Pickering
Wednesday 9th	THANKSGIVING: CELEBRATING SIXTH-MONTH REPRIEVE Graeme Park; Mike Pickering; Jon DaSilva; Electronic

Set-list (Jon DaSilva): Off-Shore – 'I Can't Take the Power', MCJ feat. Sima – 'To Yourself be Free', MDA & Lilian Vieira – 'Batucada Tropical', Nexus 21 – 'Self Hypnosis', N-Joi – 'Anthem', Double Dee Feat. Danny – 'Found Love' (Caipirina Remix), the Beloved – 'It's Alright Now', Nomad – '(I Wanna Give You) Devotion', C & C Music Factory – 'Gonna Make You Sweat', Alison Limerick – 'Where Love Lives' (Red Zone Mix), Cappella – 'Be Master in One's Own House', Systematic – 'Dancin' the Whole Night', African Jungle – 'Jungle Beat', Disco City – 'Future' (Techno Mix), 2 Men From Jersey – 'So Special', Katherine E – 'I'm Alright', Pako – 'Pakito Lindo', Baffa – 'Piano On', Tingo Tango – 'It is Jazz', Circuit – 'Shelter Me', Blanca e Negro – 'Get Down (It's Party Time)', 2 in a Room – 'Take Me Away', Pierre's Pfantasy Club – 'Dream Girl' (Ralph Rosario Mix), Loleatta Holloway – 'Love Sensation', Plus One – 'It's Happenin'', Inner City – 'Big Fun' (Juan's Magic Remix), Rickster – 'Night Moves', Annette – 'Dream 17', Seduction – '(You're My One And Only) True Love' (New York House Mix 2), Kariya – 'Let Me Love You for Tonight' (The Pumped Up Mix), Kechia Jenkins – 'I Need Somebody'

Thursday 10th	TEMPERANCE CLUB Tim Chambers
Friday 11th	THE MIX Dave Booth
Saturday 12th	NUDE Graeme Park; Mike Pickering
Monday 14th	DMC Mixing Championship Heat
Thursday 17th	TEMPERANCE CLUB Tim Chambers
Friday 18th	THE MIX Dave Booth
Saturday 19th	NUDE Mike Pickering; Graeme Park
Thursday 24th	TEMPERANCE CLUB Tim Chambers

Friday 25th	THE MIX Dave Booth
Saturday 26th	NUDE
Wednesday 30th	*Violence forces the Haçienda to close its doors*

APRIL

Wednesday 17th	*New Order/Joy Division producer Martin Hannett dies*

MAY

Friday 10th	THE HEALING: A REOPENING CELEBRATION
Saturday 11th	Graeme Park
Tuesday 14th	New Fast Automatic Daffodils; What?; Noise
Thursday 16th	BEAUTIFUL 2000 Dave Haslam
Friday 17th	SHINE! Mike Pickering; Sasha
Wednesday 21st	NINTH BIRTHDAY PARTY

JUNE

Friday 7th	SHINE!
Wednesday 12th	Cabaret Voltaire; Sub Sub; Amok; Winston & Parrot; Dave Haslam *(cancelled)*
Friday 21st	MIDSUMMER NIGHT SHINE! Mike Pickering

JULY

Friday 12th	SHINE! Mike Pickering; PA by K-Klass
Tuesday 16th	DEFINITION OF SOUND Mike Pickering
Tuesday 23rd	Primal Scream
Wednesday 31st	The Adventure Babies

AUGUST

Friday 8th	Graeme Park
Thursday 22nd	BEAUTIFUL 2000 World of Twist; Dave Haslam
Thursday 29th	BEAUTIFUL 2000 Intastella; Dave Haslam

SEPTEMBER

Wednesday 4th	Inspiral Carpets; the Bridewell Taxis
Thursday 5th	BEAUTIFUL 2000
Wednesday 25th	HARMONY Sasha; Nipper; Justin Robertson; PA by PKA/ Together/ Evolution

OCTOBER
Wednesday 30th   FLESH Cicero; Tim Lennox: Michelle

NOVEMBER
Wednesday 6th   Sasha; K-Klass
Wednesday 13th   WEDNESDAY-NIGHT FEVER Sister Sledge;
                    Jon McCready
Wednesday 20th   Dr Phibes; Puressenc
Wednesday 27th   FLESH Tim Lennox; Princess Julia; Luke Howerd;
                    PA by Army of Lovers

DECEMBER
Tuesday 3rd   Venus Returning
Wednesday 4th   Sasha; PA by Altern-8
Saturday 14th   Graeme Park
Tuesday 17th   Northside
Monday 23rd   FLESH: 'QUEER CHRISTMAS' the Amazing Pippa
Tuesday 24th   CHRISTMAS EVE PARTY Odyssey;
                    John McCready
Tuesday 31st   NEW YEAR'S EVE PARTY PA by K-Klass

EXCERPTS FROM COMPANY ACCOUNTS, 1991

FAC 51 Limited
Trading as: the Haçienda

PROFIT AND LOSS ACCOUNT (for the year ended 30 June 1991)

	(£)	(£)
Takings		
Mondays	33,374.00	
Tuesdays	9359.00	
Wednesdays	46,286.00	
Thursdays	101,368.00	
Fridays	83,426.00	
Saturdays	139,547.00	413,360.00
Loss cost of sales	18,416.00	
Opening stock	229,226.00	
Purchases	26,259.00	221,423.00
Closing stock		191,937.00
Wages: bar staff	42,082.00	
Bar management	22,578.00	
Bar consumables	300.00	64,960.00
Bar trading profit		**126,977.00**
Takings		
Mondays	15,558.00	
Tuesdays	12,047.00	
Wednesdays	30,551.00	
Thursdays	69,988.00	

Fridays	66,530.00	
Saturdays	168,998.00	363,672.00
Wages: doormen	59,503.00	
Topguard fees	25,180.00	74,682.00

Door net income   **288,990.00**

Other income

Cloakroom	8298.00	
Hire fees	4617.00	
Merchandising	32,569.00	
Miscellaneous	39,543.00	85,027.00

Trading profit   **500,994.00**

THE HAÇIENDA

FAC 51 Limited
Trading as: the Haçienda

EXPENSES AND COSTS (for the year ended 30 June 1991)

	(£)	(£)
GROSS REVENUE FROM TRADING ACCOUNT		500,994.00
Management Charges	34,084.00	
Wages: admin & management	64,647.00	
maintenance	32,829.00	
reception & cloakroom	3339.00	
merchandising	6794.00	
DJs	61,291.00	
Health insurance/pension	6475.00	
Bands & entertainers	45,092.00	
Concert labour	1310.00	
General staff costs	1994.00	
Catering goods	3985.00	
Light & heat	13,788.00	
Water	2392.00	
Rates	29,294.00	
Rent/service charges	87,157.00	
Insurance	40,036.00	
Telephone	10,237.00	
Stationery/printing/posters	31,542.00	
Design & artwork	36,007.00	
Advertising	5233.00	
Cleaning	24,402.00	
Waste disposal	521.00	
Glassware	6418.00	
Security	16,234.00	
Stocktake	1000.00	
Flowers	656.00	
Sundry expenses	9377.00	

Subscriptions & donations	850.00	
Professional fees	55,782.00	
Audit & accountancy	5368.00	
Repairs & maintenance	25,374.00	
Lights & video	26,024.00	
Records & CDs	1296.00	
Equipment consumables	7440.00	
General consumables	20,466.00	
Taxis	6969.00	
Motor expenses	6982.00	
Travel & accommodation	13,697.00	
Entertaining	1844.00	
Carriage/couriers	6404.00	
Licences	13,204.00	
Promotional retainers	4387.00	
Bank charges	3719.00	
Bank interest	10,442.00	
Whitbread loan charges	338.00	
Leasing interest	1640.00	
Depreciation	32,789.00	831,129.00

Profit/loss for period   **-330,135.00**

RIP

Martin Hannett died of heart failure in April 1991, aged forty-two. During the last few years of his life his career had gone into freefall because of his heavy drinking and heroin abuse; his weight had doubled, to almost twenty-six stone. Ironically, however, he had cleaned up his act four years before his death, only to die moving house. He was one of Factory's, if not the world's, true musical geniuses.

1992

'We had a problem. We were still off our heads'

By 1992 the whole rave scene had changed and a new generation had come on board – kids who knew acid house only from reading about it in the media – and many of the people I knew stopped going clubbing (strangely, the old-timers would return religiously for our New Year's Eve celebrations every year). Most of the time I'd look around the club and barely recognize anybody.

By now the Haçienda's wildest period, from 1988 to 1990, was well behind us; looking at the accounts for the years that followed, the profits came down very gradually by about 10 to 15 per cent per year. As Manchester had got hipper, more clubs had opened and investment came into the city. In some ways the Haçienda became a victim of its own success: people we'd drawn to the area opened their own places, which took our customers and made us look old-fashioned. And, because of our ongoing financial dire straits, we couldn't afford to fully renovate the club to keep up with the times.

Furthermore, like punk before it, acid house lost something as it got older: the innocence of nobody knowing the rules, or even if there were any. That initial explosion of ecstasy – coupled with the music – had revolutionized the world. Everything that followed could only be an imitation.

Despite all this, though – despite the fights among gangsters, and trouble with the police – some nights made us forget it all. It was like London during the Blitz, or the band playing on the bridge of the *Titanic* as the ship sank. We partied to spite fate. No matter how badly some people behaved, they couldn't completely stop the great bits.

Even so, the comedian Keith Allen always said to me that you know you've got a drug problem when you feel like you're a god when you're not on it. And that was us: we had a problem. We were still off our heads. When the Haçienda celebrated its tenth anniversary, in May

233

1992, we built a bridge over the canal to a purpose-built Haçienda fair-ground. The event cost us £10,000. We'd intended to use that money to fund a Haçienda compilation CD, but Rob spent it on this fair-ground and renting rides, thinking we'd get the money back on the door. My mate Jan de Koning ran the fair, and Twinny (who'd quit being a roadie for Joy Division to work on fair rides all those years ago) helped to operate it. My mate Cormac ran the dodgems and handled the announcing: 'You want it to go faster? Put your arms up,' etc., etc.

At one point he boomed into the microphone: 'OK. All of you who are on an E, I want you off of these dodgems right now!'

Exodus. Nearly every car got vacated. Only Manchester's Lord Mayor and his deputy were left, sat right in the middle of the ride in a car of their own.

I missed the whole night because some prick spiked me with keta-mine. I came round only as the Haçienda closed. Apparently at one point in the evening I'd stood in front of the stage, nodding, telling anyone who'd listen, 'The guys in this fucking band are great. They're really, really good. You should get their name. They're gonna be big.'

There was nobody playing.

The Haçienda staff Christmas fancy-dress party that year was no better. In fact it was the worst party of my entire life. It was just horri-ble. I wore a Nazi military uniform, like an idiot, complete with Luger. Ang was dressed as Minnie Mouse. We started the party at Dry, then got a coach to the Haç.

Ridiculous amounts of drugs were passed around. It all went pear-shaped after serving the cake: tons of hallucinogens had been baked into it. If you bit into a slice it dribbled down your chin. That set us all off.

One of the bouncers (who'd never before touched drugs) and his girlfriend started fighting on the floor, over by the cigarette machine. They were pulling each other's hair and biting one another, locked together for what seemed like hours. I can still remember it, the lumps of hair flying around. All of the bar staff were freaking out, girls crying, the works. Complete pandemonium.

It did my head in. I went looking for Paul Carroll to stop the fight, walked out of the Haçienda and found him at Cheerleaders at a Cheetham Hill party. His costume was a Mexican poncho and som-brero, and he chomped down on a cigar. Kind of like Eli Wallach in *The Good, the Bad and the Ugly*.

I walked up and told him about the fighting. 'You're gonna have to fucking sort this out.'

Paul followed me back, separated the bouncer and the girl, then decked the guy so hard it broke his jaw and they had to take him to hospital . . . All while his girlfriend continued to attack him.

'Happy now?' said Paul, and fucked off again.

I went back in. That's when the Cheetham Hill gang arrived, having followed us looking for free drinks. The doormen had all long since fucked off. The gangsters walked straight up to me and asked, 'Why are you dressed like that, you bastard?'

They all gathered round, poking me. Thank God somebody – Ang, I think – came and saved me. I beat a hasty retreat, went home and locked the blessed deadbolt. Relief. I've never been so frightened in all my life – apart from all the other times in the Haçienda.

I gave Barney back his uniform the next day. Only joking.

Gang violence in the city continued. A gunfight at a Papa San gig at the International II in August 1991 had called a halt to reggae gigs at the venue. In June 1992, when members of a Salford gang were refused entry at Most Excellent held at Wiggly Worm (which was formerly the Millionaire, Peter Stringfellow's club) they returned in a stolen car and rammed the entrances, then set fire to the car; the club was closed for good. In October CS canisters were let off at the Funhouse at the PSV and the following week a gunfight resulted in a student being wounded in the leg.

Traditionally Friday nights pulled a wilder – and more violent – crowd than Saturday nights', which the gangsters thought of as being a bit soft. On Fridays we attracted people who loved music, wore T-shirts and baggy trousers and liked it a bit lairy. On Saturdays we got all the hairdressers, who drank brandy, took drugs occasionally and perhaps just showed up in the hope of copping off. I didn't usually go on Saturdays – they were Barney's territory.

Then, as we altered the schedule, the nights blurred together and so did the punters. Criminals showed up every night, fighting, preening and jockeying for position. Other clubs were safer because all the gang members were in ours.

There were four corners under the Haçienda balcony and each belonged to a gang: Salford young and Salford old, Wythenshawe,

Cheetham Hill and Gooch. They each took their own little section and if an opposing-gang member walked into the wrong corner it would really go off. Just about the only people allowed to move freely around the club were the musicians: me, Barney, the Mondays and the Roses. Even innocent punters would get a slap if they staggered in by mistake and this became one of our bugbears: some student would get a bit pissed, sit in the wrong corner, get a slap (if he was lucky), and then – quite rightly – complain. Whenever we asked Paul or Damien for an explanation, the pair of them invariably replied, 'Well, they shouldn't have fucking been in that corner anyway, should they?' To them, territorial rules explained it all away. I'd just think, 'Bleeding hell . . .' and we'd bribe the offended parties with free drinks.

That didn't always work. Some of our customers knew how to contact solicitors and were the kind of people cops listened to. In a funny way, the Haçienda brought working-class crime to a different segment of society. It spread out of our doors right around Manchester.

The cops insisted on making occasional night-time inspections, walk-throughs, knowing full well that them doing so would drive everyone mad. They'd arrive without warning. Ang would lead them in and our bouncers would have to escort them as they walked around the club. This wasn't one lone copper – I'm talking about as many as ten at a time.

People spat and threw drinks on the police but they didn't retaliate: they'd let our doormen wade in and chin whoever was responsible. Ang thought the cops took this approach because they had some kind of secret agenda, and I can see her point. It was like they were deliberately trying to wind up the gangs. A strange way of doing it.

A few of the big nights were recorded for broadcast by Terry Christian, a local DJ from Piccadilly Radio; he played me one of them, in which Mike Pickering stopped the music to tell everyone the police were outside about to storm the club. Scary.

Sometimes we'd have a snatch squad sent in to grab some kid who'd broken his bail conditions or whatever. An undercover cop working inside would give the tip-off and the snatch squad would run in and drag them out of the building. We never had any advance notice of such raids, so we couldn't protect innocent bystanders: punters would get trampled and battered as the cops moved in, and knocked out of the way as they left, getting injured when fights broke out because somebody had tried to escape.

Gangs terrorized everybody. The honeymoon period being by now well and truly over, there were non-stop full-on violent episodes and the mood of the club – and of the entire scene – went downhill.

And it wasn't just the gangsters to blame, either. There'd be complaint after complaint about the doormen slapping people. We'd been concerned about their treatment of women until we found out that the female punters were just as bad as the boys.

The Salford gangsters staked out separate sides of the alcove based on gender. They'd never sit together. The men were on one side, the women on the other – and God help anybody who crossed the girls. They were often worse than the men.

The funny thing is that, although we had trouble with Cheetham Hill outside the Haçienda, the ones who gave us the most trouble in the club were the Salford lot. Their affiliation with the Noonans ended once they passed through the doors and Damien couldn't seem to control them. Only the kitchen remained a gang-free zone. Suzanne was well protected because she got along with the older Salford lot who kept the younger ones in check; she was too much of a she-devil for them to rip her off – and anyway they were too busy elsewhere.

Bernard still socialized in the Haçienda a lot then. He met his wife Sarah in the Haçienda – 'the vision', we called her – and he had as many ecstasy buddies as I did. In addition to hanging out with the Mondays and A Certain Ratio, Barney was very well thought of in Moss Side and used to go to a lot of the house parties there. Afterwards he'd tell me about guys driving stolen cars into the cul-de-sacs, racing around and baiting the police all being part of the evening's fun.

I used to spend a lot of time at the Kitchen club in Hulme. It was in two flats knocked together, run by a guy called Tim, and was an after-hours club that opened once the big places had closed for the night. I'll never forget the first time I went. Entrance was £2 and in exchange you were given two cans of Harp lager. The Mondays were in the upstairs flat watching a band jam; there was this huge black guy playing bass and when I came in Bez got the bass off him and gave it to me. 'Here, give it to Hooky, Manchester's best bass player,' he was saying.

I played it for a while, all the time getting daggers off this geezer, then gave it back to him.

Bez turned and said: 'What you doin', man? Give it back to Hooky.'

The guy was still giving me daggers. I thought he was going to fill me in, so I played for seconds, gave it back to him and fled.

Shit. Can't have been an indie fan. Being in a couple of great bands meant I could usually get away with murder.

Amazingly, aside from one time when somebody threw a kid off the fourth-floor balcony (the kid survived the fall), there wasn't any trouble at the Kitchen, even though a lot of Gooch and Moss Side went there. Salford guys weren't welcome. As in the Haçienda, though, Barney and I could move about freely – I even parked my new company car right outside, a gunmetal XJS. We were allowed to do what most other people weren't allowed to do. So each of us continued to swan around, enjoying the assets of the city – free drinks, free drugs, perks like that – while the very criminals we'd fallen in with destroyed the Manchester club scene.

For instance, Mike Pickering left the Haçienda for good following an altercation with some kid who was banging on the door of the DJ booth. The kid was requesting a song: 'This music's shit; play this track for me.'

Mike said: 'I'll play it later.'

The kid came back: 'Are you gonna play that track or what?'

Mike: 'Oh, fuck off, you cunt, what do you fucking know?'

The guy pulled a gun out. 'Play the track.'

'Right. It's on next . . .'

He quit that night and never came back.

From that point on everyone was scared, even the DJs.

Over time, the heavy atmosphere had an impact on the music. When drum 'n' bass and hip hop became popular in 1995, we ended up being unable to hold so-called 'black-music' nights because there was so much trouble. Even the police encouraged us not to promote these shows and our bouncers eventually refused to work at them, too – and don't forget that our bouncers were lunatics themselves (in the nicest possible way). But even they said these nights couldn't be policed.

On his second-ever trip to the Haçienda, Peter Saville inadvertently went to a soul night and ended up getting accosted on his way to the bar by a huge aggressive black guy who said to him, 'What are you doing in here, you honky bastard?'

He beat a hasty retreat and never came back.

Rob really loved the music, though, and the black-music nights were financially successful so he looked for ways to deal with the issues. I must admit, the music sounded absolutely wonderful. Once inside I'd run to the DJ box and spend the night up there, just listening. I couldn't move about so I'd just stay put, relying on Anton to feed me drinks.

An independent black-music promoter told us, 'I can pack this place every night for you'; and the events were profitable, so Leroy didn't want us to pull them. But the nights continued to be miserable: the bouncers and the bar staff wouldn't work, and our usual customers wouldn't come in. Horrible. So, against Leroy's wishes, we finally stopped doing them. We were on our way down from the summit.

And then Factory went to the wall. Ultimately the company became unable to support the financial weight of its commitments. Dry had been opened; then there was a shop in Afflecks Palace, called FAC 281: The Area; then Factory moved offices from Alan Erasmus' flat on Palatine Road to a famously palatial building on Charles Street; plus there had been costly album projects, such as New Order's recording trip to Ibiza and the Happy Mondays' infamous recording trip to Barbados. Bankrolling all of the above soon brought the company to its knees. A deal had been mooted with London Records: Wilson had in 1988 struck up a relationship with the company's Roger Ames; the two had over the years kept in touch and gradually the idea of a London Factory began to take shape. But things moved too slowly to bail Factory out – it became apparent to London that Factory were in trouble and in fact they went into liquidation before anything was signed. Another deal was made, but this simply allowed London to acquire the aspects of Factory that made money.

The early 1990s was a tricky time for Factory. FAC 281: The Area was run by Fiona Allen and her sister Theresa. It specialized in overpriced, oversized T-shirts and posters. At one point someone even ordered a gross of one particular Haçienda shirt, yet most of them were still in the club when it eventually closed. The shop failed very quickly and very expensively. Its location didn't help, being right at the top of Afflecks, literally the last stall.

Meanwhile, we couldn't remortgage the Haçienda building because of the property crash in Manchester and the state of the company accounts. Nobody would lend us the money. When we bought the building the purchase was funded by New Order and Factory, who paid £700,000, while the remaining £500,000 came through a bridging loan. We were paying 14 per cent over the base rate on it. We just presumed someone would lend us the money afterwards but because of the crash there wasn't enough equity in it so nobody would give us a mortgage.

The same mistakes happened with the new Factory offices. Rather than take over some of the empty areas in the Haçienda building, Tony found a different spot to house the record company. This was a run-down building near the BBC on Charles Street that I was, ironically, also trying to buy to re-house my Rochdale recording studio, Suite 16. I wanted it but I was told there was another client who was bidding against me. These guys seemed to have pots of money and bid well over the asking price of £72,000; I finally dropped out at £110,000. Little did I know I'd been bidding against Alan Erasmus and Factory – who were using New Order's money, for fuck's sake.

Then they brought Ben Kelly in to renovate it. The project went over budget. At one point Manchester airport complained because the lights he'd fitted on the roof were so bright they were distracting pilots on their approach to land – never one to do things by half our Ben, eh? The building and offices looked wonderful, however. Beautiful, I must admit. It cost £695,000 pounds to build in 1990. They tried to remortgage that, too, but again the property crash meant they couldn't.

So that, plus overspending on Dry and on albums by Revenge (sorry, Tony),the Happy Mondays and New Order, saw Factory crumple.

Mismanagement lay at the heart of it all – but I'm bound to say that, aren't I? Admittedly, New Order's cost overruns on *Technique* had been everyone's fault, but none of us had wanted the party to end. Once we'd completed the tour that followed, and split up for the first time, the revenue that New Order traditionally brought to Factory via record sales had begun to dry up, while the label's debts continued to mount.

I'll accept the blame for Revenge: Tony gave us a more or less open budget for our album *One True Passion*, and nobody checked how much I was spending until it had escalated out of control. It was a hell of a learning curve.

In the meantime the Happy Mondays continued to destroy their reputation with drunken interviews and misconceived outbursts. This curbed their American record sales and again lost a lot of licensing revenue for Factory.

They had a complete and utter backlash. Their album *Yes, Please* flopped, with sales plummeting from 175,000 to 1,000, so there was no way to recoup the expenses. Factory fell into administrative receivership.

Around this time, New Order reconvened to record the album *Republic*. Tony and Rob hoped it would sell enough to bail them out and hurried us along. The pressure didn't help the band dynamic, which was at an all-time low (most of us being completely off our heads).

To my mind, the experience gave us our last great song of that period, 'Regret', and one of my favourite songs, 'Ruined In a Day' (remixed wonderfully by K-Klass). Both were well worth the process but recording under those circumstances was horrible. We made the record on sufferance; the problems of Factory and the Haçienda exacerbated the tensions within the band and to be honest things got so bad I'm surprised we ever made another record after that. It was a spiral that we were stuck in, and it needed to stop.

As it all fell apart, Rob and Tony fought like cat and dog. Tony resented the club because it sucked up Factory's money. I remember him saying to me, 'If it weren't for your club, I'd still have my record label.'

Once Factory went bump, Tony all but gave up on the Haçienda because he didn't have either the investment money or the heart to keep up with Rob and me; he turned his attentions instead to In the City, a series of music seminars he held in Manchester. He attended directors' meetings occasionally and was very verbal when it came to offering ideas – even towards the end, when he couldn't do anything about the Haçienda from a financial point of view – but I think his interest had waned.

Aside from the emotional fallout it caused, the collapse of Factory had direct impact on the Haçienda because the label stopped bailing it out. Ang once told me that at least £16 million passed through her hands during the time she worked there, but the Haçienda still required external funding on a regular basis. Profits on ticket and drink sales alone couldn't keep it open and pay the costs.

Where did it all go? Ang would open the doors at nine p.m. (the queues having started to form at seven fifteen), and after forty minutes she'd lock us in the building because she'd let in too many people. She oversaw eighteen staff and eight tills at the bar, three door staff and door takings, too. Her job for that first hour involved taking pound notes out of the tills and putting change back in. After that, she'd fill up cardboard boxes with money – with no time to count it – then dash to the offices and lock the money in the safe. It was mind-boggling.

We were surrounded by a fortune we couldn't keep and thugs we couldn't control. When a gangster from the Salford lot celebrated at the club one night Ang received a shock: he walked into her back area, a bottle of champagne in hand, looked around and told her, 'One day I'll be telling my son that this is his to inherit.'

It made her wonder how much power the gangs truly had over us, or at least how much they thought they had.

WHAT'S ON AT THE HAÇIENDA IN 1992

JANUARY

Friday 3rd	SHINE! Mike Pickering; Russ; plus guests
Saturday 4th	Graeme Park; Tom Wainwright
Thursday 9th	BEAUTIFUL 2000 Dave Haslam; Jason Boardman
Wednesday 29th	FLESH 'QUEERSEXY' Tim; Luke Howerd; PA by MC Kinky

FEBRUARY

Friday 7th	SHINE! Mike Pickering; Mr Fingers
Wednesday 12th	Sasha; Mike Pickering; PA by Joey Negro
Friday 14th	VALENTINE SHINE! Mike Pickering
Wednesday 19th	The Brand New Heavies; Ashley and Jackson Marco; Dean
Friday 21st	SHINE! Mike Pickering; Allister Whitehead
Wednesday 26th	FLESH Tim; Luke Howerd
Friday 28th	SHINE! Mike Pickering; PA by E-lustrious

MARCH

Wednesday 4th   ROBS RECORDS PARTY ACR; Anambi Jon DaSilva; Andy Robinson; Dave Rofe; Peter Robinson

Set-list (ACR): Manic – 'Good Together', Shack Up – 'Won't Stop Loving You', Spirit Dance – 'Teckno 4 An Answer', Wonder Y – 'Mello', 27 Forever – 'Be What You Wanna Be', Si Firmi – 'O Grido'

Set-list (Jon DaSilva): Sounds of Blackness – 'The Pressure', Tramaine – 'Fall Down', Gypsymen – 'Stoppin' Us', Lisa Lisa & Cult Jam – 'Let the Beat Hit 'Em' (The Paradise Garage Club Mix), Cookie Watkins – 'I'm Attracted to You', Photon Inc. – 'Generate Power', Blow – 'Cutter', New Grooves Vol. II – '2 A.M.', Joey Negro – 'Do What You Feel', The Emotions – 'I Don't Want to Lose Your Love', Korda – 'Move Your Body', Simone – 'My Family Depends on Me', Little Louie Vega and

Marc Anthony – 'Ride on the Rhythm', S.L.Y. – 'I Need a Freak', Clubhouse – 'Deep in My Heart' (Red Zone Mix), Jomanda |- 'Got a Love for You', D-Rail feat. Randy B – 'Bring it on Down' (Dub Mix), Cool House – 'Rock this Party Right', Julian 'Jumpin' Perez – 'Relight My Fire' (Mike Dunn's Mixx), K Klass – 'Rhythm is a Mystery', DSK – 'What Would We Do', Ralphi Rosario – 'You Used to Hold Me', Chris Cuevas – 'Hip Hop' (MAW Dub), DSK – 'What Would We Do' (Eight Minutes Of Madness Mix), Ralphi Rosario – 'You Used to Hold Me', The Bassheads – 'Who Can Make Me Feel Good', Kym Sims – 'Too Blind to See It', Ce Ce Peniston – 'Finally', First Choice – 'Let No Man Put Asunder', Members of the House – 'These Are My People' (Rainbow Mix), Rochelle Fleming – 'Love Itch' (Acapella), Band of Gypsies – 'Take Me Higher'

Friday 6th	SHINE! David Morales; Mike Pickering; Russ
Friday 13th	Sasha
Wednesday 18th	FUNK WITH A SHORT FUSE Dean; Peter
Thursday 19th	LAST OF BEAUTIFUL 2000
Friday 20th	Sasha
Wednesday 25th	FLESH Tim; Luke Howerd PA by Daryl Pandy; fashion show by Billy of Emporium
Friday 27th	Sasha
Saturday 28th	Graeme Park

Set-list: Bump – 'I'm Rushing' (Acapella), Shawn Christopher – 'Don't Lose the Magic' (Morales Mix), Little Louie Vega and Marc Anthony – 'Ride on the Rhythm', Sounds of Blackness – 'The Pressure', Frankie Knuckles – 'Workout' (Workin' Dub), Sinnamon – 'I Need You Now' (Disco Brothers 7" Remix), Todd Terry – 'I'll Do Anything', Partners Inc. – 'Hustle Ain't Over', Fire Island – 'In Your Bones', Double FM – 'Illusion', Queen Latifah – 'How Do I Love Thee' (Extended Club Mix), Daisy Dee – 'Pump it Up All the Way' (Pumped Up Mix), PM Dawn – 'Watcher's Point of View' (Todd Terry Melody Remix), Eleanore Mills – 'Mr. Right' (The Superb Parkside Mix), Kathy Sledge – 'Take Me Back to Love Again' (Shelter Me Mix), Bump – 'I'm Rushing' (Big Bump Mix)

APRIL

Wednesday 1st	APRIL FUSE DAY Dean; Peter; Norman Jay
Friday 3rd	SHINE! Sasha; Mike Pickering
Friday 10th	Mike Pickering; Sasha
Sunday 12th	Sasha; Altern 8
Friday 17th	Mike Pickering; Sasha

Monday 20th	BANK HOLIDAY FLESH Tim; Luke Howerd; Kinky Gerlinky
Friday 24th	Mike Pickering; Sasha
Wednesday 29th	FLESH WITH LOVE FROM LIVERPOOL PAs by Liverpool's '8' Records; Coloursex; Whole New Dream; Connie Lush; Jane Casey Tim; Luke Howerd; Princess Julia

MAY

Monday 4th	TEN: THE FASHION Tom Wainwright; fashion shows by Michiko Koshino; Vivienne Westwood; John Richmond; Body Map
Wednesday 6th	FUSE Don-E Dean; Peter
Friday 8th	SHINE! Sasha; Mike Pickering
Wednesday 13th	Pet Shop Boys; Derek Jarman; Cicero Sasha
Thursday 21st	TENTH BIRTHDAY PARTY Mike Pickering; Graeme Park; David Morales; Frankie Knuckles
Friday 22nd	BIRTHDAY SHINE! Mike Pickering; Russ; Frankie Knuckles
Saturday 23rd	Graeme Park; Tom Wainwright; David Morales
Wednesday 27th	Tom Wainwright

Set-list: Perception – 'Feed the Feeling' (Slam Mix), Black Sheep – 'Strobelight Honey', Little Louie Vega and Marc Anthony – 'Ride on the Rhythm' (MAW Dub), So Damn Tuff – 'Pleasure & Pain', Lil Louis – 'Club Lonely', Underground Mass – 'Music (Takes Control)' (Pucci Mix), Blake Baxter – 'One More Time' (Red Planet Mix), Soul II Soul – 'Move Me No Mountain' (Dum Dum Dub), Grace Under Pressure – 'Make My Day', Code Red – 'Deep Beats Vol. 1 Track B1', Urbanized – 'Helpless (I Don't Know What I'd Do)', Tito Puente – 'Para Los Rumberos (Kenlou Remix)', Frankie Knuckles – 'Workout' (1992 Vocal Mix), A Man Called Adam – 'Bread, Love and Dreams' (Parkside Mix), Virgo – 'Mechanically Replayed', Inner City – 'Pennies from Heaven' (Tony Humphries Norty Boy Mix), Joey Negro – 'Love Fantasy', Clubland – '(I'm Under) Love Strain' (Lost in the Jungle Mix), Pet Shop Boys – 'Where the Streets Have No Name' (Red Zone Mix), MK – 'Burning' (MK Extended Remix), Degrees of Motion – 'Shine On'

JUNE

| Friday 26th | SHINE! D-Influence, Sasha; Russ |

THE HAÇIENDA

AUGUST
Saturday 8th	Graeme Park
Saturday 22nd	Graeme Park

Set-list: Nightmares on Wax – 'Set Me Free', Kathy Sledge – 'Heart' (Hardubb Mix), Nightcrawlers – 'Push the Feelin' On' (MK's Dub of Doom), Double F.M. – 'Illusion', Planet X – 'Once Upon a Dancefloor', Sunscreem – 'Love U More' (Parkside Mix), Sheer Bronze – 'Walkin' On', Mombassa – 'Cry Freedom', the Reese Project – 'Colour of Love' (Deep Reese Mix), Mental Instrum – 'Bott-ee Rider' (Smack that Bott-ee Mix), Pamela Fernandez – 'Kickin' in the Beat' (Acapella), Pamela Fernandez – 'Kickin' in the Beat' (AIM Dub), Meli'sa Morgan – 'Still in Love With You' (Meli'sa in the House Mix), Malaika – 'So Much Love', Kathy Sledge – 'Heart' (Revival Mix), FPI Project – 'Feel It', TC 1992 – 'Funky Guitar', Urban Jungle – 'Bad Man', Solution – 'Feels So Right', Club Z – 'I Wanna Be Someone' (12" Vocal Mix)

Friday 28th	SHINE! Mike Pickering; Russ; David Morales

SEPTEMBER
Friday 11th	SHINE! Tyrrel Corporation; Mike Pickering; Russ
Monday 14th	FANTAZIA COMES TO THE HAÇIENDA *(part of the In the City music convention)*

NOVEMBER
Saturday 7th	Graeme Park

Set-list: Suzanne Vega – 'Blood Makes Noise' (MAW Mix), House of Gypsies – 'Samba', Lionrock – 'Lionrock', DV8 – 'C'Mon', Nightmares On Wax – 'Happiness!', KXP feat. Cybil Jeffries – 'Ain't No Mountain High Enough' (The Accapella), The S.O.U.L. S.Y.S.T.E.M. – 'It's Gonna Be a Lovely Day' (Palladium House Anthem I), Trilogy – 'Good Time' (Robi Robs House Anthem Mix), Bizarre Inc. – 'I'm Gonna Get You' (Todd Terry Rave Dub), East Side Beat – 'Alive & Kicking' (The Ken Wood Dub), Cynthia M – 'Everything I Do', Rapination feat. Kym Mazelle – 'Love Me The Right Way', Kathy Sledge – 'Heart' (Uplifting Dub Mix), MK – 'Always', UFI – 'Understand this Groove', Uncanny Alliance – 'I Got My Education'

Friday 13th	SHINE! Daniele Davoli; Mike Pickering; Russ
Monday 23rd	*Factory Communications Limited goes into receivership*

DECEMBER

Friday 4th	Sasha; Altern 8
Friday 18th	SHINE! CHRISTMAS PARTY Uncanny Alliance; Mike Pickering; Russ

EXCERPTS FROM THE COMPANY ACCOUNTS, 1992

FAC 51 Limited
Trading as: the Haçienda

ASSUMPTIONS FOR PROFIT AND LOSS (forecast for February to April 1992)

Trading Account

Gross profit for all three months has been assumed at 53 per cent based on average to date.

1. *February trading account is based on results for the first three weeks of the month, pro-rated to four weeks.*

   The actual results for the first three weeks include two Wednesday-night openings (Sasha and the Brand New Heavies).
   The estimated fourth-week result includes Tuesday-night hire, Flesh night with a four a.m. licence and estimated attendance of 1400 @ £6 and a fifth Saturday in the month with attendance of 1400 @ £8.

2. *March trading account is based on the following attendance figures:*

   Wednesdays: three nights open
   ACR/Robs Records Party (3 March): attendance of 950 people @ £7
   Sasha (18 March): attendance of 850 people @ £6
   Flesh night (25 March): attendance of 1400 people @ £6 with a four a.m. licence
   Thursdays: four nights open
   Assume average attendance of 550 people per night @ £2
   Fridays: four nights open
   Assume average attendance of 700 people per night @ £6

(From March, Sasha will be DJing)
Saturdays: four nights open
Assume average attendance of 1400 people per night @ £8

3. *April trading account is based on the following attendance figures:*

Easter Monday open: attendance 1200 @ £10 with a four a.m. licence
Wednesdays: three nights open
Fashion Cabaret night: attendance 900 people @ £6
Sasha: attendance 800 people @ £6
Flesh night: attendance 1400 people @ £6 with a four a.m. licence
Thursdays: four nights open
Assume average attendance of 560 people per night @ £2
Fridays: four nights open
Assume average attendance of 750 people per night @ £6
(Mike Pickering and Sasha will be DJing)
Saturdays: four nights open
Assume average attendance of 1400 people per night @ £8

Bar takings are based on attendance figures and average results for the previous three months. Saturday bar prices include an extra 20p on all drinks.

Expenses and Overheads

Expenses and overheads for the three months are based on:

1. Average results for the previous three months, pro-rated.
2. Number of nights open plus any expected special nights.

FAC 51 Limited
Trading as: the Haçienda

FROM THE REPORT AND ACCOUNTS (23 June 1992)

Following the balance-sheet date the company's nightclub outlet ceased operation due to operational problems. The closure was during January 1991 and is anticipated to be only temporary, such that no permanent curtailment of the company's activities is anticipated. The nightclub licence was also withdrawn shortly before the balance-sheet date. However, the withdrawal was appealed and a temporary extension was further extended on appeal for the first half of 1991, to provide a probationary period of trade.

If the nightclub should fail to reopen or should the licence be permanently revoked, then the company would cease to trade.

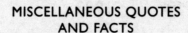

MISCELLANEOUS QUOTES
AND FACTS

This year marked a rare sighting of the Haçienda cat, which was pictured in an *NME* feature on Factory. Instead of a name the stray had been given its own Factory catalogue number, FAC 191, and was pictured with the caption 'Feline groovy at the Haçienda'.

'You don't pay me enough to bleed'

After a long wait the question of the basement was once again addressed.

The conversion was budgeted at £250,000 (comparatively cheap for a Haçienda project, but Ben Kelly was to put that right!).

I can't remember what we did to get the money. Did Rob/New Order put it in? Whatever happened, it went ahead, was built and the takings literally . . . didn't change.

The conversion did increase the club's capacity, though, which on big nights proved to be quite useful. The downside was that it made policing the Haçienda a lot more difficult, there being more dark nooks and crannies.

The club struggled on but attendance was tailing off. The crime was driving customers away.

It even scared off the hot-dog seller. He had been a Haçienda institution, a lovely old geezer, there for as long as I could remember. I never got one off him – my body is a temple – but everybody loved him. It happened one night when Damien threw one of the Salford lot out of the club and the hot-dog seller got in the way during the affray; ended up with a tipped-over cart and a bad beating. Completely unwarranted.

The doormen rushed up to save him but he left and never came back. 'It's over, Hooky,' they chorused. 'It's like the ravens leaving the tower of London.'

We'd entered a very sad phase, during which the club changed too much to ever return to its roots. Bit by bit we lost elements that we'd once cherished. The bonhomie, the friendliness, the specialness – they'd all gone.

It became a very nervy time. The staff came in one morning to find the safe – which must have weighed a ton – dragged halfway across the basement on its way out to the canal towpath. The thieves must have run out of steam midway through the job. They'd also downed a few too many drinks, judging by the empties we found nearby.

We reported it to the police. 'Know any big guys? Weightlifter types who might have the alarm code?'

'Er, no.'

'Oh well. Bye.'

So much for persistence.

In 1993 the boom in dance-music culture brought about two major openings in Manchester. Paradise Factory, initially a gay club, opened in Charles Street in the old Factory building in May that year; while September saw the launch of Home, which was owned by Tom Bloxham and run by none other than Paul Cons.

Ang's assistant, Anton Rozak – into the Smiths when she took him on, but we can't hold that against him – found the madness of it all unbearable. He's never mentioned in articles about the club because he wasn't a director, but he did a very good job: he was a nice bloke, just straight up and down the line. Rare for us. He'd been hired on his eighteenth birthday, in 1989, as a pot-washer and was subsequently promoted to assistant manager. He also DJed on the Stone Love night, on Tuesdays.

He and Ang did everything together and if she went on holiday he ran the place in her absence. He also ran things on Thursdays, when Ang went to the Paradise Factory with me on her night off – our busman's holiday.

Anton was always freaked out about guns. Once the police came into the building saying they were searching for a dead body. What had happened? Bear with me – it's a long one . . .

This guy had come to the door trying to get in. He was clearly off his face, so the doormen fucked him off. Now, for the sake of their own safety, the doormen always parked their cars right outside the front door. Obviously the more senior you were the nearer your car would be, so Damien's car was right outside. This jerk was mouthing off but they were ignoring him, so he decided to go one better: he jumped on the nearest car's bonnet and started leaping up and down to make his point.

Unfortunately for him the car he chose was Damien's brand-new

Ford Cosworth, the apple of his eye. Damien grabbed him and sparkled him in front of the queue. He didn't get up, so he lay there a few minutes in front of the murmuring queue. Then the bouncers thought they'd better do something. So they picked him up by his legs and dragged him into the club. Why they did that we'll never know. But obviously someone in the queue panicked and phoned the coppers, saying that the Haçienda doormen had just killed a guy then taken him inside the club so they could later dispose of the body, throw him in the canal, or something.

The police freaked and came down mob-handed to search for this guy. Damien kept them busy at the door while the guy got cleaned up and bandaged in the kitchen. With the help of one of the bar staff (a guy who we later discovered was there as a spy for the Salford lot, would you believe!), Ang put a hat and a big coat on him, then smuggled him past the police – pretending he was pissed and had passed out. They just shoved him in a cab, put £200 quid in his top pocket and told the taxi driver to drop him off in Swinton, where he lived. That got rid of the evidence and got the doormen off the hook.

Then Ang went to deal with the police, who didn't believe her when she told them he'd gone. They emptied the club, shut it down for the night, and proceeded to search the place from top to bottom. We knew what had happened but Anton looked around the basement, showing willing. Unfortunately he found a gun in there, which sent him absolutely hysterical. He garbled about it to Ang, who'd developed something of a blasé attitude to it all and told him, 'If you've not touched it, it's OK. Just relax, cover it back over and leave it there.'

He had to bluff the rest of the evening out, but the police eventually got bored and left with another dire warning ringing in our ears.

Anton had always wanted to go to the directors' meetings on Thursdays. When eventually he was given permission to attend one week, he came in full of serious suggestions about stock-takes and brimming with ideas about staff rotas and wastage, etc. Tony almost immediately stood up and screamed at him to leave – telling him to get the fuck out, that he had lost the ethos of what we were really about.

Anton was never allowed in again. He panicked – even more than when he'd found the gun – thinking he'd get sacked. In fact Tony later took him aside to reassure him that his job was secure: 'Don't worry, darling,' he said. 'It's just how we are.'

Nobody expected to hear sensible ideas at these meetings. They just wanted to talk football and birds, to argue and place bets on how many customers might show up based on our attendance projections, and to drink.

I called them Mad Hatter's Tea Parties. They were utter, utter nonsense that went on from two in the afternoon until early evening in the Round House section of the Haçienda building. The room became so hazy from everyone smoking draw, you'd lose track of time completely. The Round House (Shit House, I'd call it) was freezing during wintertime, impossible to heat. I'm sure we met there only so we'd feel like we'd got some use out of that half of the building. It always drove Alan Erasmus mad that we'd not rented it out; he made Paul Mason's life hell because of it. Office space like that in Central Manchester would be considered prime real estate today. It wasn't back then.

We'd start off sober. When we were sick of the latest tales of woe, Rob would order and pay for a crate of Sapporo. There'd be a dull middle bit spent sorting out a few practical things out – which burgers or toilet rolls to buy, for example – then things would degenerate as Rob simultaneously skinned up and slagged everyone off. Tony, always fashionably late, would leave first, usually followed by Ang and Paul Mason, leaving Rob and me to finish off the beer, befuddled.

This routinely meant the beginning of my weekend. I'd go to Dry afterwards, then to Paradise Factory, arriving home about midnight on Friday to recover before picking the kids up on Saturday.

At one Thursday meeting talk centred around how much VAT we owed. It seemed that our debts with the bank had become such a problem that any money we deposited was being swallowed by the overdraft on the current account. When the quarterly VAT payments were due there was no money put aside to pay them.

There I sat, a dumbo from Salford, looking at the management notes, trying to make sense of them. On paper everything appeared good. Profit from tickets? Yeah. Profits from bar sales? Yeah. Profit from the cloakroom? Yeah.

'Where's the VAT?' I asked.

'Oh, that figure includes the VAT,' somebody replied. They hadn't deducted the VAT from the figures.

'Surely it's not profit then?' I said.

'Oh, yeah. You're right, We'll have to change that.'

Fuck me. That had gone on for twelve years.

No one had thought to keep the VAT money separate so as to ensure that the sour-faced bastards at HM Customs & Excise remained paid off and happy (impossible, I know, but you have to try anyway). We slipped nine months (three payments) behind at one point, accruing late fees all the while: 17.5 per cent of three months' turnover at £300,000, which amounted to about £40,000 a quarter with penalties.

Meanwhile, we settled in as comfortably as anyone could with the gangsters. Indeed, some of the staff took interest-free loans from them rather than go through a bank. They'd borrow cash for a month at a time, sometimes as much as two grand, and be given a date on which they had to pay it back. Because of their connection to the Haçienda, the staff weren't charged interest – although by the same token neither were they able to welch. They might default on payments to a bank, but they'd never default with the gangs.

We saw unspeakable acts of wanton violence at the door. Horrible things were done to or by our doormen, then Damien would have to step up the next day to broker a deal – like a regular businessman – to smooth things out and save face.

For example, one night our doormen got attacked by a gang from Broughton. We had a hydraulically powered shutter door at the club, which shot down if you banged a button (God help anyone who got in its way). On this occasion they got the shutter down but the gang poked machetes and swords through the viewing slat. Our guys poked knives back. (Suzanne went mad; they used her best kitchen knives.)

Things died down, but honour needed to be satisfied so one of the doormen and his back-up went looking for revenge. (We later found out that the back-up was four armed guys in a car parked round the corner of the club every night it was open, in case of emergencies.)

The other gang were in Home by now, the doorman's spies told him, so an associate let him into the club via the back door. He went in alone to get his respect; the others were supposed to help if it went tits up. Inside, the other gang had been warned he was coming. They were ready and shot first. There was complete pandemonium, everyone screaming, panicking, trying to get out of the way. He tried to return fire but his gun jammed so he ran back outside and got shot in the thigh – just before he slid under a car to escape. His back-up were so busy listening to a Graeme Park mix tape in their car, they didn't hear the gunfire (Graeme's tapes were legendary). Our guy had to stay under there for a while, till things calmed down, in case he got killed. He went berserk when the others eventually came to find him. He had such an amazing capacity for pain, though. He actually went home, showered, burned his clothes, put clean clothes on, and then finally went to hospital – all with bullets still lodged in his leg.

Tony, Rob, Alan and I visited him in hospital in the middle of the night (there'd been another of those awful phone calls) and he told us what had happened. Apparently the coppers had come in to interview him just before we arrived; he'd got rid of them by picking up a chair and telling them he'd throw it out the window unless they fucked off. While he was recovering, a £30,000 compensation deal was brokered. If the shooters didn't pay, there would be retaliation. Thus the matter was resolved by the paying of a fine. Rough Justice.

Ang Matthews asked one of them how he could live this way.

He told her, 'What's the worst somebody can do? They can shoot me. If I'm shot dead, then it don't make any difference to me.'

He didn't give a fuck. I don't know if you call that courage. They were hard, hard men who acted decisively and took incredible risks. Amazingly, they had a soft side, though they let very, very few people see it. They could be incredibly nice and gentle, a weird contradiction. I suppose I was privy to that because I became friendly with them. They'd let their guard down occasionally but it would always go back up before too long. Honestly, hanging around with people like them felt cool. Like being an insider, dangerous but exciting. I remember one of them surprising his girlfriend with a weekend break in Greece. They duly arrived and he pulled out seven grams he'd secreted. All went well for a while, then some small argument escalated to the point where he smashed up the hotel room; she ran out screaming for help and brought the entire bar staff back upstairs. He leathered them, all seven of them. It took ten riot police with tear gas to overpower and arrest him. He was deported the next day. Who said romance was dead?

Our bouncers were so powerful and so bloody violent that anywhere we went we had the cachet of being associated with them. I remember one night going to the Paradise Factory (the club built in the Factory office building after it was sold when the company went bump) with a younger bouncer from the Haçienda – let's call him Jack – who was a bit like me: off it. We'd become friends, but hell he got me into some trouble.

The bouncers inside the Paradise Factory were fucking nasty, really obnoxious. After about ten minutes I asked, 'Are you getting the vibes? It's really heavy in here.'

'Oh, no, no, no. Don't worry about it. Everything will be fine.'

He went back to talking to some people he knew and I thought, 'I can't fucking bear this.' I finally talked him into leaving.

We went back to the Haçienda and I said, 'Fuck, the security were a bit unfriendly in there, mate.'

'Yeah, yeah. Well, I had one of those guys up against a wall with a machete last week. That's probably why.'

They'd refused entry to our flyer people and we had a reciprocal deal so the lads had gone down to sort it out.

'Oh, now you tell me.'

Visiting dangerous territory was a way of showing face. Things like that happened all the time when we hung out together. I came to understand his reputation through the sudden change in mood whenever we'd go someplace together. I'd think, 'God, it's really tense in here.' And leg it.

Another time, we met at the Corn Exchange in Manchester, which is now the Triangle, where he bought a knife off a stall – this big, fuck-off SAS survival thing with a serrated edge. I asked, 'What do you want that for, then?'

He went, 'Oh, it's for me collection at home. You want to come to the Conservatory for a drink?'

Like a mug, I said, 'Yeah.' In there we sat down and had a drink with another well-known gangster. The manager of the Conservatory came over so I thought I'd leave them to it and started to move off. Then I saw them brandishing Jack's brand-new knife. There's me, sitting there like I'm in on it with them. I went spare: 'Why didn't you tell me? I don't want anything to do with it . . .'

He just laughed.

I could do nothing but apologize profusely to the manager the next day. He said not to worry, he was used to it.

Fuck me. We were all in the same boat.

I suppose Jack saw me as his mate. He'd stand next to me at the Haçienda, minding me. One night two kids walked up, saying, 'Hi, Hooky, we're from Chicago. We've come all the way out here just to see New Order and their club.'

Jack started yelling, 'What are you fucking twats doing? Leave him alone?'

I said it was all right but he just kept screaming – 'You fucking cheeky bastards!' – and threw them straight out without listening to me at all. A bit over-protective. Like a dog with a bone.

Those incidents aside, we got along well and went to a lot of parties together. We knew all the same people, so there was common ground. If he sussed that I had something on me when I met him at the door, he'd leave his spot and stand beside me all night. It was like having my own private, uncontrollable, psychotic (but very friendly) bodyguard.

There are stories about bouncers you wouldn't believe. Like the fact that around Christmastime they'd 'ask' all the customers to each put £1 into a collection, which they'd duly take to a local children's hospital. Very thoughtful.

And say what you want about Damien Noonan, but he was devoted to his family. One night Ryan Giggs from United showed up. Damien told the doormen, 'Keep him here.'

Damien went home, roused his kids out of bed, dressed them in their Manchester United kits and drove them back to the club – this took an hour – then got their picture taken with Ryan and finally let him go in.

Whenever I came to leave the club and needed a taxi home, Damien had a habit of flagging down the nearest one and hauling out whoever was inside it regardless of what I or the driver said in protest. To my eternal shame I never refused to get in, though. (Do you know how hard it is to get a taxi at three a.m. on Whitworth Street on New Year's Day?) I once dragged my mate Ken out of the cocktail bar (off his head, talking to the wall) and Damien outside insisted on finding us a taxi.

'It's OK,' I told him. 'I'll walk down to the Ritz –' this being another club just down Whitworth Street West – 'he needs the air.'

Damien wouldn't hear of it. 'Stay there, mate.' You could never argue with him.

He called a taxi over, ejected the people inside by screaming, 'Fucking get out, you twats, this taxi's for Peter Hook.' Then he put Ken and me in it and closed the door.

As we drove off the driver asked, 'Was that Damien Noonan, then?'

'Yeah.'

Ken blurted out: 'Just drive, you bastard.'

I told him, 'Shut up, will you? Leave him alone.'

Ignoring Ken, the cabbie went on: 'Yeah, I was in the nick with Damien.'

Knowing even as the words came out that I shouldn't say anything, I nevertheless asked, 'Oh, what were you in for?'

'Murder.'

'Oh God,' I thought.

Ken yelled, 'Shut up, you bastard, and drive. Get me home; I want more!'

'Just *shut up*, Ken.'

In the end I had to slap him before he got us both killed.

'Yeah, I was in for murder,' the cabbie continued. 'I killed this guy. Ripped his fucking head off, I did. His wife thanked me. He was such a bastard. Come to think of it everyone thanked me'

All I could think was, 'How do I get in these situations?'

I looked outside. It was five in the morning and the sun was rising. What a life.

The club struggled on. Noonan's lot ran the door very well for a while but, as drug use increased, crime became more lucrative and the gangs started getting heavier and heavier. The violence increased.

Indeed. Dominic Noonan, who worked with his brother for the club, later told documentary-maker Donal MacIntyre that the Haçienda was a 'tough door'; that gangs from Moss Side, Cheetham Hill and Salford would turn up, all wanting to get in for free, 'so me and some of the lads who ran the door said enough was enough, let's take the trouble to them – and we did.'

He and another doorman paid a visit to a pub, his mate with a shotgun, Dominic wielding a machete. 'One of the gang lad's dogs was about [dog-lovers and vegetarians might want to look away now] so I just chopped its head off, carried the head inside the pub and put it on the pool table. I more or less told them, "Stay away from the Haçienda or the next time it'll be a human head," and they never came back.'

The club's eleventh birthday passed joylessly. Someone bottled David Morales (we had our suspicions who did it), managing to gash his back wide open.

'You don't pay me enough to bleed,' he told us.

It should have been a proud night. Instead, total anarchy. Gangsters fondled girls walking up and down the staircase into the basement. They felt untouchable. From that point on, things were awful. The gangs were ruling the roost and, try as they might, our doormen couldn't control them.

That night some of the Salford lot kidnapped a friend of mine. They told her they were taking her to a party, but instead they kept her at one of their houses high on acid for two days, during which they tried to persuade her to take her jeans off and whatever – just to mess with her mind, hopefully. She escaped when one of the gangster's mums came round. They also kidnapped a guy whom they'd discovered had dealt Es behind their backs. They took him to Ordsall, put him in a sack and kept him there for three days, giving him the occasional kicking. As with the girl, they fed him acid for the duration. Apparently this was a favourite trick of theirs, which they employed to ensure that nobody dealt without them getting a cut.

Meanwhile, the debts were piling up. Hidden away in the minutes of management meetings from the middle of the year is an anonymous report detailing 'the bailiff situation'. Also listed are sundry creditors:

without whom the running of the club becomes almost impossible. The involvement of bailiffs has become an issue towards the end of this week. Three in one week is hardly to be expected. The ones working for PRS are very aggressive (I know them from Factory days, and if payment is not made then they will take away whatever is required). The ones working for the rates people are less of a problem, but we obviously need to keep them happy each week. The third one works for the court, and is merely collecting small CCJs, but cannot be ignored.

For the next four years the Haçienda took up much of my time. At one point I nearly swapped music for full-time management of the club at Rob's request. New Order basically quit after we finished touring in 1993 – although we'd eventually get back together again, in 1998 – and we never socialized during the interim. Until the reunion I'd seen Bernard only twice in five years, and in all that time I didn't see Steve and Gillian even once. Without New Order to think about, Rob spent most of the time developing his record label, Robs Records, signing acts like Gabrielle's Wish and Sub Sub, who he'd showcase at the club. He'd spend most days in his office, tending to business or staring out of the window. The staff respected him for his reputation, his intelligence and his ability to spot great bands, but they learned not to disappoint him, either. If he noticed a spelling error on our flyers, he'd fly into a blind rage, insisting that they be reprinted or corrected by hand. He still genuinely cared about all the aesthetics.

In August New Order played what would turn out to be the band's last show for some time when they headlined the final day of the year's Reading festival.

In September an accountant's letter was sent to the members of New Order, who, as Gainwest, had put up financial guarantees for the future of the Haçienda and Dry. The message was bleak:

> the current situation of Haçienda and Dry Bar is now somewhat desperate in that, although the business have broken even over the summer months, they have not generated the profit (estimated at £15,000–£20,000 per month) that had been expected, largely due to a significant deterioration in the attendance at the Haçienda on Friday nights. Therefore whilst current trading is generating a small amount of cash and an upturn is expected as students return to Manchester in September and October, it is insufficient to meet current commitments to pay old debts . . .
>
> . . . If the companies are unsuccessful in raising further funds, the only option that may be left to FAC 51 and FACT 201 is to put them into liquidation or receivership.

The letter went on to say that this might mean the forced sale of the Whitworth Street building at well below its market value, plus New Order's guarantees – several as Gainwest, the parent limited company, and several personal – all being called in.

Gainwest Ltd and New Order personally were staring at a potential bill for hundreds of thousands of pounds.

Just days after this letter was sent the Haçienda's management team were once again gathered at the Round House, where plans were being made to shore up the creaky Friday night apparently responsible for the club's woes.

Out were resident DJs Buckley and Russ and in came Tim Lennox and Allister Whitehead. An optimistic Rob Gretton asked whether Tim Lennox would attract the gay crowd. Unfortunately not, offered Paul Mason in response. The team kicked around other ideas for more nights and money-raising opportunities. Bhangra Nights were discussed and then rejected – again thanks to their reputation for attracting violence between rival religious factions. Soul nights and Saturday matinees were discussed and viewed as possibilities to be investigated for another time, though there's no evidence that they ever were. More pressingly, a meeting with Whitbread had been arranged, the idea being to invite the brewery to contribute.

Before anything could take place, however, it was agreed that the deal with London Records should be completed, at which point, presumably, faces turned towards Tony Wilson. All outstanding points on the deal had now been agreed verbally, he replied, and it was 'just a question of the necessary paperwork being drawn up'. At which, notes the minutes, there were 'wry smiles all round'.

We couldn't file for bankruptcy because we were still afraid that the creditors would come after our personal guarantees as shareholders of the Haçienda.

We tried to sell the club many, many times. But nobody would ever buy it because when they looked at the accounts there were too many irregularities. For instance, director's loan accounts, huge investments that could never be repaid, and extraordinary items such as the security costs, which alone totalled £365,000 in one year, ten times higher than those of any other club in England.

Richard Branson of Virgin came to look at the Haçienda, as a possible addition to his club empire. He seemed very interested in buying it, and nearly reached the point of taking it over, but then realized there was no way to make a profit because the security costs were so high. Whenever prospective buyers looked into it, the truth about the gangsters would come out; and when they discovered how deep-seated the violence was – and the extent of it – they scurried off. They realized they couldn't keep the customers safe. They'd take a look at the accounts and think that the figure for our security costs was a mistake, a misprint. But once they'd walked around the club for a couple of nights, they knew better. Any sensible businessman would say, 'This is fucking madness.' It *was* madness. We'd just got used to it.

I would have thought that an investor with a big enough ego would decide, 'This club's rocking. I'm going to sort it out.' But most admitted that they could not. The guy who started Direct Line was very interested at one point, then got away as fast as his car could take him. Beep beep!

Meanwhile, the criminals even began shifting their focus from the night-time economy – clubs and bars – to the daytime economy – 'normal' businesses and businessmen and began setting themselves up in transport and, of course, security.

One interesting aside. We were invoiced by our security firm and always paid their invoice plus VAT. When we were asked during a special VAT inspection about those security invoices it transpired that our security firm weren't paying their VAT. What a surprise. In fact, they'd never paid any. The VAT number they'd provided us with belonged to B&Q, of all people. They just kept the money.

The tax office wanted us to pay the outstanding VAT (for the second time) so, not unreasonably, we suggested they get it off the security firm. Do you think they did? No. Even they were scared of the bouncers.

Meanwhile, Home had opened and was faced with the same problems . . .

I remember sitting in Home the night of the riot that shut the place down. This lot from Cheetham Hill just barged behind the bar, grabbed a whole shelf's worth of champagne and walked off. Just like in the Haçienda, nobody could do anything about it. They were fighting in the street outside for hours; no one could get out. Funny, I always thought Tom Bloxham's choice of name was much too close to ours. Haçienda – Spanish for 'homestead', geddit? Seemed to backfire on him, though.

When I watched some closed-circuit TV footage of the Haçienda's 1995 New Year's Eve party I saw that not a single person paid admission or showed a ticket from eleven p.m. onwards. The bouncers were religiously filling up their Lucozade bottles with champagne. That's how businesslike they were. It had been a really heavy night with loads of trouble. Ang had walked on to the cocktail bar landing, seen Damien arguing with some young kid and started kicking off, screaming, 'Just get him out.' There had been that much trouble, she just freaked. The next thing she knew she was picking herself up from the bottom of the stairs, very dazed and confused. Then Damien came up and said, 'You all right?'

What had happened was that as she started yelling the kid had pulled a gun and put it in her face. Damien had grabbed her by the collar and threw her down the stairs to get her out of harm's way. He beat the shit out of the gunman, came back, went downstairs and – like a gentleman – helped her back on to her feet.

Later, as she looked around the club, still in her dazed and confused state, she realized that she didn't recognize anyone in the crowd. Everyone who had partied at the Haçienda during the golden era had moved on, because of fear or age.

Happy New Year.

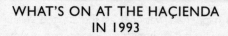

WHAT'S ON AT THE HAÇIENDA IN 1993

FEBRUARY

Tuesday 2nd — OPEN HOUSE Tom Wainwright; Russ; Miles Holloway

Tuesday 16th — OPEN HOUSE Tom Wainwright; Russ; Buckley

MAY

Wednesday 5th — BOY'S OWN PRODUCTIONS Andy Weatherall; Pete Heller; One Dove

Thursday 20th — A NIGHT IN THE LIFE OF . . . David Morales; Frankie Knuckles; Tony Humphries; Buckley; Angel; Danny Hussein; Allister Whitehead; Marshall; Tom Wainwright

JULY

Wednesday 21st — SOAK Allister Whitehead; Marshall; Danny Hussein; Andy Ward; Nightmares on Wax

AUGUST

Wednesday 5th — GRAEME PARK'S THIRTIETH BIRTHDAY PARTY

SEPTEMBER

Sunday 12th — HEAVENLY IN THE CITY St. Etienne; Espiritu; the Rockingbirds; White Out; Andy Weatherall *(part of the In the City music convention)*

Monday 13th — ROB'S PARTY Sub Sub; A Certain Ratio *(part of the In the City music convention)*

Tuesday 14th — MIXMAG/MINISTRY OF SOUND PARTY Tony Humphries; CJ Mackintosh; Justin Berkman; D:Ream; Juliette Roberts *(part of the In the City music convention)*

OCTOBER
Saturday 2nd   Graeme Park

NOVEMBER
Friday 5th   Todd Terry; Russ; Buckley; Dave Rofe

DECEMBER
Wednesday 1st   JAZZMATAZZ
Thursday 2nd   OPEN HOUSE Tom Wainwright; Danny Hussein
Friday 3rd   SHINE! Trannies with Attitude
Thursday 9th   OPEN HOUSE
Friday 10th   Laurent Garnier; Judy Cheeks
Thursday 16th   OPEN HOUSE
Friday 17th   DIY
Thursday 23rd   FLESH *(attendance 1380)*
Friday 24th   CHRISTMAS EVE PARTY Jon DaSilva; Jose;
                      Herbie; Buckley; John McCready; Mark Tabbener
                      (attendance 808)
Monday 27th   CHRISTMAS BANK HOLIDAY SHINE! Alex P;
                      Allister Whitehead; Tim Lennox; Dave Rofe;
                      Sam Mollinson *(attendance 978)*
Friday 31st   NEW YEAR'S EVE PARTY Tom Wainwright;
                      Roger Sanchez; Tim Lennox; Allister Whitehead;
                      Buckley; Herbie; Jose; Mark Tabbener

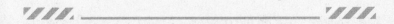

EXCERPTS FROM COMPANY ACCOUNTS, 1993

FACT 51 Limited
Trading as: The Haçienda

NOTES

Sundry creditors include Swivel, Sandypress, Clean-Machine, etc., without whom running the club becomes almost impossible.

The involvement of bailiffs has only become an issue towards the end of this week. Three in one week is hardly to be expected. The ones working for PRS are very aggressive (I know them from Factory days and if payment is not made then they will take away whatever they feel is required). The ones working for the rates people are less of a problem, but we obviously need to keep them happy each week.

The third one works for the court and is merely collecting various small CCJs but cannot be ignored.

We can always pass on the contents insurance as before, despite the obvious drawbacks and dangers. There is no way that the buildings insurance cannot be paid.

This cash-flow makes no provision for saving towards the next VAT return – due on 31 October 1993.

Bar and door sales figures are estimated on the performance of the previous five weeks with increases for the late openings during September.

The PAYE people are running out of patience with us. If we were not involved with the bailiffs I feel that we could have dealt with them satisfactorily but obviously this is now not the case.

There is a chance we could get away with not reducing the bank overdraft each week but we risk losing their support.

As I write I do not know when we will receive the Stella Dry or whether there will be VAT of £700 on top of it.

No provision has been made for any further payments to PLT (the building bridging loan company).

Saturday door has been increased to £12.00 per person for September. No adjustments have been made for Friday nights.

RTL fee has been calculated on the basis of recent bills and has been adjusted for the later opening during September.

I would like to think that this is very much a 'worst case' scenario, but if we are asking people to inject yet more money into the club then they should be made aware.

In conclusion, if there had not been a sudden influx of bailiffs I still feel that the situation was manageable until the autumn when we come into our busiest period and the ownership issue will (hopefully) have been resolved. Unfortunately this is now not the case.

(Uncredited)

FAC 51 Limited
Trading as: the Haçienda

CASH FLOW TO THE END OF SEPTEMBER

	29/08 (£)	04/09 (£)	11/09 (£)	18/09 (£)	25/09 (£)
Bar					
Sunday				4000.00	
Monday	1500.00			2000.00	
Tuesday				4000.00	
Wednesday	5000.00		2000.00	2000.00	
Thursday		750.00			
Friday (prev)	2250.00	2750.00	2750.00	2750.00	2750.00
Saturday (prev)	7500.00	8500.00	8500.00	8500.00	8500.00
Door					
Sunday				2000.00	
Monday	1500.00			0	
Tuesday				1500.00	
Wednesday	2750.00		2500.00	1000.00	
Thursday					
Friday (prev)	2250.00	2250.00	2250.00	2250.00	2250.00
Saturday (prev)	11,000.00	13,200.00	13,200.00	13,200.00	13,200.00
	33,750.00	27,450.00	31,200.00	43,200.00	26,700.00
Stella Dry				4000.00	
Outgoings					
Staff wages – net	2750.00	3350.00	3250.00	5000.00	2750.00
DJs	600.00	1125.00	2225.00	1125.00	1125.00
*Sundry creditors	5000.00	5000.00	5000.00	5000.00	5000.00

1993

Whitbread, etc.	7133.00	4545.00	5108.00	8708.00	4208.00
RTL	4300.00	6250.00	4750.00	6250.00	11,250.00
*VAT	2500.00	2500.00	2500.00	2500.00	2500.00
*PRS (bailiff)	3500.00	3500.00	3500.00	3500.00	3500.00
*Rates (bailiff)	1000.00	1000.00	1000.00	1000.00	1000.00
*Sundry (bailiff)	1000.00	1000.00			
*Contents insurance	5500.00				
*Buildings insurance		4100.00			
Bank decrease in o/draft	1000.00	1000.00	1000.00	1000.00	1000.00
	41,783.00	36,370.00	31,333.00	37,083.00	35,333.00
Deficit	-8033.00	-8920.00	-133.00	6118.00	-4633.00
Accumulated deficit	-8033.00	-16,953.00	-17,085.00	-10,968.00	-15,600.00

* These cash payments include/or consist of arrears and therefore do not reflect in September profit and loss account.

TALES OF THE MAD HATTER'S TEA PARTIES

Extract from the minutes of a weekly management meeting held in the Round House on Thursday 23 September 1993:

The Haçienda

The opening of Home has not made any impact on Saturday-night attendances. There was currently no Friday night in terms of a club night but the bar was open late. At the last Flesh night Paul Cons was handing out promotional material for their Saturday, which he is promoting. This was put a stop to as soon as it was discovered.

The police had requested to see plans of the club in order to inspect the fire exits and potential means of entry. As a result PM [Paul Mason] had not allowed as many people in the previous Saturday as he was worried that the police could have been filming.

RG [Rob Gretton] asked if the metal detector was working properly. PM explained that it either worked too well or not at all. It was suggested and agreed that it should be set off occasionally by the door staff to give the impression to customers that it did work, and that it should be done on known potential troublemakers and their friends.

Any other business

PM had £5 bet with RG that Manchester would get the Olympics. [Paul Mason won: the Olympics went to Sydney].

Extract from the minutes of a weekly management meeting held in the Round House on Thursday 30 September 1993:

Other potential investors

There was a discussion as to who might consider investing in the business in the event of there being no assistance forthcoming from Whitbread or other breweries.

The following list of potential investors who could be approached was put together (in no particular order of sanity):

Elliot Rashman/Andy Dodd
Messrs Jabez & Clegg
Tom Bloxham
Pete Waterman
Gareth Hopkins
Jim Ramsbottom
Richard Branson
Ed Bicknell
Quincy Jones
Carol Ainscow
Peter Gabriel
Chris Blackwell

It was felt that AHW [Tony Wilson] was the best person to approach these people if it came to this.

Extract from the minutes of a weekly management meeting held in the Round House on Friday 28 October 1993:

Haçienda Album
AM said that a friend of hers had heard a tape of the album and was keen to release it if we were no longer interested.

RG pointed out that it wasn't the fact that we were no longer interested. When the album was first due to be released there were not sufficient funds to finance the project. He had hoped to put it out to his own label, but has had to put all his spare cash into the Haçienda to keep it going. There was also the problem that several of the tracks needed to be licensed from Polygram. We do not want to alert Polygram about the album so there [can be] no chance of it falling under 'the deal', and so there could be no progress with the project until 'the deal' was completed.

With regards to financing the project, AW said that Vini Reilly had recently received some money, and maybe this could be put into the album project.

RG asked AW why the money could not go into the Haçienda instead to help with various cash problems. AW felt that he could not recommend this to Vini as he thought it was too risky.

RG stressed his amazement at the statement as he and PH had put in considerable sums of their own money to keep the club going, thereby risking their own financial position.

It was agreed that the album would eventually come out on our own label but not until the Factory/Polygram deal had finally been completed.

Any other business

RG had a £5 bet with AE [Alan Erasmus] that Manchester United would be knocked out of the European Cup.

Extracts from minutes of a weekly management meeting held in the Round House on Thursday 18 November 1993:

New Year's Eve

AM said that there was potentially a problem with Roger Sanchez as we might have to pay for a flight, but he was also playing at Hard Times so we might be able to split the cost with them.

RG said he was very surprised if he was playing at another club on the same night. PM said that apart from Tom Wainwright all of the New Year's Eve DJs were also performing at other clubs on that night.

On-U-Sound night

This had been cancelled on Monday as only forty tickets had been sold. The only cost to the club was the flyering and this was being refunded by the promoter.

Flesh

No progress had been made as Paul Cons had been away. PH [Peter Hook] asked if it was felt that Cons might take the huff and maybe move the night to Home, but it was felt that as long as it was handled properly there would be no problem; and anyway it was already agreed that Haçienda owns the name.

Extract from the minutes of a weekly management meeting held in the Round House on Friday 17 December 1993:

Thursday nights

It was agreed that the current Thursday was dead and that it will need to be re-launched in the new year. It was agreed that by the next meeting people would have come up with some new ideas, but there was also discussion at the time.

RG had attended the trance night at the Airdri and reported that it seems to have been a very successful night, although most of the people there were openly smoking dope, something it was felt that could not be allowed to happen in the Haçienda.

AM and LR had been to the trance night at Heaven and said that it was the same there as well.

RG had been in touch with the Trance Europe Express people but they were not available until late February, which would be too late to use them to launch a new regular trance night in the New Year.

It was noted that on Thursdays other clubs were organized by outside promoters.

MISCELLANEOUS QUOTES AND FACTS

'Fundamental Uncertainty:

The company is dependent on continued finance being made available and the ongoing support of its shareholders in respect of the amounts owed to it. Continuing financing is required both to enable the company to meet its liabilities as they fall due and to operate without the immediate realization of its assets. The directors believe that continuing finance will be made available and that it is therefore appropriate to prepare the accounts on a going concern basis.'

From Ernst & Young's 'Fac 51 Limited Report and Abbreviated Accounts' for the year ending 30 June 1993

1994–1996

'Albert's an eight-foot boa constrictor. He's probably down the settee'

Clubland had moved on. It was the beginning of the era of trance and the superstar DJ. The era of Cream, Renaissance and Ministry of Sound. The Haçienda, however, had history on its side and therefore retained a powerful allure and, for about three years, operated as much like a 'normal' nightclub as it ever had or ever would. It 'ticked over'.

Our worst promotions of all were the Jolly Roger nights in 1994. They featured two DJs called Luvdup. As part of the deal they asked us to build them a pirate ship in the club; this ended up costing a fortune, plus we'd signed a contract to do six performances. It turned into the biggest loss-maker of any night in the Haçienda: about £30,000 altogether. I went mad. It was a complete balls-up. Literally about six people turned up for each show. The whole sorry saga was relayed to us each week at the Director's meetings.

Attendances at the club were down. Not only was the Jolly Roger night a flop, but also Transform, the Haçienda's shot at keeping up with the trance phenomenon, attracted just 452 clubbers, few of whom had paid.

It's funny but, because I took so many drugs, the actual situations I found myself in were far removed from anything I would have gone near sober. I think a lot of us associated with the Haçienda were desensitized. We adapted to the strangeness; insanity just seemed like the norm. I'd spend hours in the Salford corner, holding the fire doors closed to stop people coming in for nothing. I'd be screaming, 'Get a bouncer! Get a bouncer!' and everyone around me would just laugh. It was surreal, hallucinatory.

One night on our way to a party Cormac said he wanted to pop home and get his stash. When we arrived at his place he said, 'I wonder where Albert is?'

I sat on the settee – twatted – while he kept going on about looking for Albert. I thought that must be his mate.

'That's weird,' he said. 'I've not seen him for weeks. I really don't know where he is.'

Finally asked, 'I've never heard of him. Who is he?'

'Oh, he's my snake. Albert's an eight-foot boa constrictor. He's probably down the settee.'

I jumped up from the settee, terrified. We looked and there he was, hibernating. Like I said, strange things happened to us while we were high.

Even stranger still, I got married that year – marking the beginning of an eighteen-month period when I literally didn't set foot in the Haçienda. Still went to the management meetings, which, sober, weren't any better but . . .

Christ, what was I thinking? There I was, having the time of my life: a different girl every night; all the drugs I wanted; my own nightclub, one of the hippest places in the world. And I turned my back on it for what I thought was love.

Listen, if you learn anything from reading this book the first thing (obviously) should be: never open a nightclub with your mates. The second thing: never marry an actress.

Marry in haste, repent at leisure, my mum always said and bloody hell she was right.

Things were fine at first. Of course they were; we wouldn't have got married otherwise. But things soon changed. It wasn't long before she found she'd had enough of clubs and drugs and gangsters, and dropped the lot. And, because I was married to her, I had to drop them too. No matter that I owned the bloody nightclub. That was it. It was either her or the Haç, and I did what I thought was the right thing at the time.

The downside of this was that I dutifully stopped going to the club and obediently dropped all my mates. Mad nights out became a thing of the past and comedy clubs replaced nightclubs.

The upside – at least there was *one* – was that I got off class As. She absolutely hated drugs and never took them. If I did, she physically stopped me. If she knew I'd taken them she'd go nuts, absolutely berserk, and it was a terrifying sight. To be honest, I was too scared not to stop.

Of course the downside to the upside was that I swapped them for booze and together we became heavy drinkers – something that would take a heavy toll on us both.

Tell you what, music is a doddle compared to TV. In TV they're all arse kissers. I was all right, because everybody was terrified of me. No idea why, they were just scared of my reputation (ha ha). Being in a band, you can just tell people to fuck off all the time and get away with it; it's expected of you. But comedians? They have to kiss some major arse or they can wave their careers goodbye. In TV comedy if you cross anyone you're fucked and you'll never work again. I saw up-and-coming comics say one wrong word to the wrong person and then disappear, never to be seen again. It's an awful industry to work in: there's no loyalty and no allegiance. It makes rock 'n' roll look secure, I'm telling you.

Eventually my wife and I split, and began divorce proceedings. The split seemed to drag on forever; it was really tough and this became a very, very bad time for me. There was a ruckus at Bill Wyman's Sticky Fingers restaurant when I ran into her and her new boyfriend – the less said about that, the better. It was a setup that backfired. Another tip: if you plan to try and assault a club owner make sure he is not with one of his head doormen at the time. Turned out the photographers had been tipped off about the action to come and the trap duly sprung. But as they struck good old Leroy leathered the lot of them. I couldn't get a punch in; I couldn't get near anyone. They got thrown out and the manager looked after me every time I went in after that. ('You can't buy publicity like that – thanks!') Wonder what Bill thought? I suppose us bass players should stick together.

My friends rallied round me, God bless them, but when I went back to the Haçienda things had changed. Eighteen months away and everything was different. The atmosphere wasn't like it used to be – gone was the heaving, sweating mass, hands in the air. Worse, I didn't recognize anyone again. A whole new crowd had moved in . . .

The violence of Gunchester continued. In April 1995 Terry Farrimond, a doorman at the Haçienda, was shot and killed near his home in Swinton. That summer, the trend for letting guns off during drum 'n' bass club nights reached a climax when a clubber fired a pump-action shotgun at the PSV. So many bullets were taken from the ceiling that the club flooded the next time it rained. The following month three girls were injured by ricochets, forcing the cancellation of future events.

In June, police mounted raids on the clubs Equinox, Cheerleaders and Home, during which clubbers were searched for drugs and the music stopped. Home continued to be plagued by violence and, after a skirmish between around forty Salford gang members wearing balaclavas and police that took place on the dance floor and elsewhere in the club, owner Tom Bloxham shut up shop for good in September. For the Haçienda the news was almost as grim. Stringent security measures were off-putting for the average law-abiding clubber, yet didn't seem to prevent the violence. Attendance figures continued to fall as the club struggled to keep up with shifting musical trends. Having missed the trance boat and voluntarily opted out of drum 'n' bass, neither was it able to capitalize on the emergence of trip hop, a musical genre not suited to the Haçienda's cavernous space.

Rob, God bless him, always held out hope. He visited the Haçienda almost every night. Being an optimistic, glass-half-full type of person, he was always convinced that the next week would be the one to turn it around. He was always dreaming up some scheme for making it work.

He found the element of risk exciting. A true gambler, he believed that you cured a losing streak by finding enough money to take another stab at it. The Haçienda was his ultimate game of chance.

His enthusiasm was infectious. Well, I thought so, anyway. Which was why I found myself going along with a lot of what he suggested. By now, it was really just us two on the deck of this sinking ship. Tony seemed to lose interest after Factory folded; he was busy trying to get Factory Too off the ground. The other members of New Order had long since turned their backs on the club, and Alan Erasmus was being Alan Erasmus: enigmatic and difficult to pin down.

Just me and Rob, then. It felt like the future of Manchester and the Haçienda completely rested on our shoulders.

Casting about for ideas to help save the club, we began to think again about how it had benefited the city. Think about it: during that post-1989 period further education in Manchester was permanently over-subscribed, we were bringing so much money into the city – millions – yet seeing precious little recognition or support for what we were doing. In those days, of course, the idea of getting council or government support for a club was unheard of, whereas now they're chucking money at the Manchester International Festival, for example. But back then, if you weren't a ballet you were fucked.

Even so, we were adamant that the club should be recognized for what it was – a vital local asset, a boost to the economy, an important tourist attraction. So we applied to the Manchester City Council for a grant to pay for renovations. Ben Kelly was brought in, this time against Tony's wishes, submitted a design and the 100 per cent grant was finalized. And then the council changed its mind, for some reason and our £150,000 grant got cut in half. By now the deposits had been paid and materials ordered; the scaffolding had even gone up. Somehow, though, we'd made yet another mistake. Our grant, which we'd thought had gone from £150,000 to £75,000, now actually turned out to be £37,500. They weren't giving us half the original sum – they were giving us quarter.

Guess who had to make up the shortfall?

As if that wasn't bad enough, our attendance had been virtually cut in half as well. Legally we'd been getting 1600 in each Friday and Saturday (capacity having gone up since we built the basement club), on top of which we'd been sneaking in as many as we could get away with before the place groaned. That lasted until the week that the scaffolding went up.

After that, attendance fell to below 600 and never ever picked back up, though we tried everything to claw it back. Whether people thought we were closing down, or things were changing too much – the death of acid house, perhaps? – I don't know. We'd spend hours, weeks, at meetings, trying to figure out what had gone wrong.

In the end it was decided that another shake-up might help. Rob was concerned that Ang had lost her edge, so brought Paul Cons back in to book the nights for us. For a while it seemed to be working – Paul got numbers up – but then we discovered that he was allowing a lot of people in for free (though they were at least buying drinks).

Ang, meanwhile, being convinced that she'd done everything possible to combat the violence and keep the club open, was so annoyed about being sidelined by Paul that she tendered her resignation. We refused to accept it.

Rob was most adamant: to him, Ang represented the most important link to the club's past. She was the longest-serving member of staff and he valued her knowledge and experience; he liked the fact that he was able to show her a flyer for a gig and she'd know in what year it had taken place. She was a demon at the Haçienda pub quiz, Ang was. The younger employees just didn't have that – they knew fuck all compared to her.

'Don't over-react,' Rob said. 'If you're fed up, what about doing days and we'll find somebody else to work nights?'

So Ang took on the daytime shift but soon got bored. She needed more, so we reached a compromise: she'd work at Dry and Leroy would come back to run the Haçienda. She hated Dry, though. She didn't love bars the way she did clubs. They're two very different animals.

In the meantime the renovations continued: we added coloured bricks to the exterior, plus beautiful customized stained-glass windows. The windows were about twenty-five feet high and came in twelve sections. They cost £32,000, and they were beautiful. Trouble was, they were only visible only if you climbed down the derelict canal towpath at the back of the building and looked up; you couldn't view them from inside the club – they weren't even lit. Also, because they were placed above the kitchen, they soon gained a disgusting coating of fat that completely obscured them. I had them removed and put into storage by Peter Burke, the guy who installed them, when the building was sold.

When I went to the club nowadays – which was much more rarely than I did previously – I found it had changed too much. The world had moved on.

I'd go alone there alone before, knowing there'd be loads of mates there; I'd be at home as soon as I arrived. But now I felt distanced from the punters – they were strangers. It was rare to run into someone I knew. Ang, Leroy and I would stand in our corner, look around and realize that between us we didn't know anybody. I missed the old camaraderie. We'd lost so many mates to drug overdoses, police activity or simply burnout; a fair few had wised up and were enjoying family life; the violence scared many away, too. You can't blame them for that – we'd have legged it too if we hadn't owned the gaff.

It was the same at Dry. Whereas I'd once loved the sense of community, really I now connected only with the older members of the staff, like Andy and Amanda, who had been there for years. I'd still be there seven nights a week, though. You can't own a pub and not go, can you?

Many of us who'd spent the late 1980s and early 1990s off our faces now came crashing down to Earth. I'd behaved like a pig in shit, lording it up at the Haç, treating it like party central. Not any more.

Luckily I met my wife, Becky, around this time. We were introduced by a friend of mine, Francis, who ran the Brassiere Saint Pierre, and his girlfriend, Victoria. We hit it off and we've been together ever since.

She'd been to the Haçienda a few times herself, but we didn't spend much time there as a couple. On the odd occasion we did go there were so many problems it was ridiculous – there was no chance of having a good time. Also, she cottoned on pretty quickly that Rob took advantage of my good nature (or stupidity, whichever you fancy).

Rob was at our wedding party, on 5 December 1996, and once he was pissed dragged me round and round the garden, trying to persuade me to give him more cash for the Haçienda, while Becky (inside the house, watching us through the window) shouted to Ang, 'I've got to get out there! I've got to get out there before he gives all our money away.'

The missus was kicking off; I knew the end was near.

The club had tried to raise money but couldn't. The economy was still weak and property prices were low, so we still didn't have the equity to remortgage the place. We couldn't borrow anything and we couldn't earn enough to pay off all the debts.

We were at the limit of our overdraft. Not a good position to be in. I was funding the Haçienda and had been for the last two years; it was costing me seven grand a month because Rob was skint. He had tax problems, too; he'd put everything into the club. He kept moaning to me: 'If only New Order would tour . . .' but I was the only one who would even consider it.

It was at around this time that my accountant asked me a loaded question: 'What are you doing the Haçienda for, your wallet or your ego?'

He'd hit the nail on the head. When I thought about it I realized it was my ego: I liked the power that having the club gave me. I'm sure everybody would have, even though it had never turned a profit since the day it opened. Heaven or hell, it was my own private playground.

We just sank deeper into debt. Although there were customers who remained loyal to the club, and many more who were drawn by its reputation, the culture had shifted. People were going to bars instead of clubs. There was no admission charge and they had those late-night licences we had fought so hard for.

Everything special about the Haçienda was in the past, buried under years of violence.

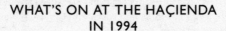

WHAT'S ON AT THE HAÇIENDA IN 1994

JANUARY

Friday 7th	A Man Called Adam *(attendance 600)*
Saturday 8th	*(attendance 797)*
Friday 14th	Derrick May *(attendance 1145; 44 tickets sold at Dry)*
Saturday 15th	ROB'S FORTY-FIRST BIRTHDAY PARTY Prime Time DJs – Andy Robinson & Nadine Andrews
Friday 21st	*(attendance 977; 29 tickets sold at Dry)*
Saturday 22nd	*(attendance 1576; 71 tickets sold at Dry)*
Wednesday 26th	FLESH *(attendance 1277)*
Friday 28th	Kevin Saunderson *(attendance 857; 24 tickets sold at Dry)*
Saturday 29th	*(attendance 1633; 112 tickets sold at Dry)*

FEBRUARY

Friday 4th	NORTHERN EXPOSURE Sasha, John Digweed *(attendance 1794)*
Saturday 5th	*(attendance 1458; 138 tickets sold at Dry)*
Friday 11th	INDIA *(attendance 620)*
Saturday 12th	*(attendance 1404; 147 tickets sold at Dry)*
Monday 14th	PASSION *(private party) (attendance 1170)*
Wednesday 16th	TRANSFORM *(attendance 452)*
Friday 18th	Daniele Davoli; DJ Power *(attendance 801)*
Saturday 19th	*(attendance 1636; 163 tickets sold at Dry)*

MARCH

Wednesday 2nd	LUVDUP PRESENTS JOLLY ROGERING AT THE HAÇIENDA Adrian & Mark; Terry Farley & Pete Heller; Those Salty Sea Dogs; Moonboots; McCready; 6 Golden Nuggets *('swashbuckling fun')*
Friday 4th	Robert Owens; Allister Whitehead; Tim Lennox

THE HAÇIENDA

Friday 11th	CREAMY SHINE! Dave Seaman; Paul Bleasdale; James Barton; Allister Whitehead; Tim Lennox
Friday 18th	CHICAGO SHINE! Farley 'Jackmaster' Funk; Felix Da Housecat; Allister Whitehead; Tim Lennox
Thursday 24th	FOUNDATION
Friday 25th	Derrick May; Allister Whitehead; Tim Lennox

MAY

Tuesday 10th	PRIVATE PARTY
Wednesday 11th	PRIVATE PARTY
Wednesday 18th	TRANSFORM
Friday 20th	THE TWELFTH BIRTHDAY PARTY, PART I John Digweed; Sasha

Set-list (John Digweed): Nush – 'U Girls', Hed Boys – 'Girls + Boys', Rebound – 'Make It Funky', Memphisto – 'State of Mind', Bump – 'House Stompin'' (Ramp Stompin' Mix), E-Lustrious – 'In Your Dance' (Bivouac Mix), Praxis feat. Kathy Brown – 'Turn Me Out' (Delormes UK Club Mix), Anna Din – 'Angel', Taiko – 'Echo Drop' (Original Hard Mix), Ascension – 'Move to the Music', Sound of One – 'As I Am', Positive Science – 'Soul Feel Free', Liberty City – 'If You Really Love Someone' (Original Mix)

Set-list (Sasha): Sasha – 'Higher Ground' (Brothers in Rhythm Mix), Paz Pooba – 'Hold Me Tight', Sandee – 'Notice Me' (Afro Morning Mix), SLP – 'Supernova' (Trance Mix), Underworld – 'Dark & Long', Funtopia feat. Jimi Polo – 'Do You Wanna Know', Asli Tanriverdi – 'Eastern Lover', Jody Watley – 'Ecstasy' (Morales Nocturnal Mix), Techno Bert – 'Neue Dimensionen', F Machine – 'Lost in America', Jump – 'No Rich Fat Daddy', Fly Baby – 'Fiesta' (Way Out West Mix)

Saturday 21st	THE TWELFTH BIRTHDAY PARTY, PART II Joe Roberts
Monday 30th	BANK HOLIDAY SPECIAL DJ Pierre

JUNE

Wednesday 1st	JOLLY ROGER John DaSilva
Thursday 2nd	The Charlatans
Friday 3rd	SHINE! Ce Ce Rogers
Tuesday 7th	AMBIDEXTROUS
Friday 10th	IBIZA SHINE! Alex P; Paul Hudson
Tuesday 14th	AMBIDEXTROUS
Wednesday 15th	TRANSFORM Pollen

Friday 17th	SHINE! Angel
Tuesday 21st	AMBIDEXTROUS Cygnus Loop
Wednesday 22nd	Graham
Thursday 23rd	Fred the Cellar Man
Friday 24th	SHINE!
Tuesday 28th	AMBIDEXTROUS
Wednesday 29th	FLESH
Thursday 30th	HOTTER

JULY

Friday 1st	SHINE!
Saturday 2nd	Paul Hudson
Monday 4th	STUDENT NIGHT
Tuesday 5th	AMBIDEXTROUS the Grind
Thursday 7th	Carleen Anderson; Corduroy; Freak Power
Friday 8th	SHINE! Cream; John DaSilva
Tuesday 12th	AMBIDEXTROUS
Thursday 14th	COCKTAIL BAR PARTY
Friday 15th	SHINE! Marshall Jefferson
Tuesday 19th	AMBIDEXTROUS Strange Brew *(sponsored by Robs Records)*
Thursday 21st	TRANSFORM Richie Hawtin
Friday 22nd	SHINE!
Saturday 23rd	LOVE 2 INFINITY Paul Hudson
Monday 25th	COCKTAIL BAR PARTY
Tuesday 26th	AMBIDEXTROUS
Wednesday 27th	FLESH
Thursday 28th	HOTTER
Friday 29th	SHINE!

AUGUST

Tuesday 2nd	AMBIDEXTROUS
Friday 5th	SHINE!
Tuesday 9th	AMBIDEXTROUS
Friday 12th	SHINE! Paul 'Trouble' Anderson
Tuesday 16th	AMBIDEXTROUS
Thursday 18th	TRANSFORM
Friday 19th	SHINE!

Tuesday 23rd   AMBIDEXTROUS
Thursday 25th   HAÇIENDA CLASSICS: THE LAST FROM THE
                         PAST Jon DaSilva; John McCready
Friday 26th   SHINE!
Sunday 28th   FLESH
Monday 29th   SHINE! BANK HOLIDAY Michael Watford;
                         DJ Disciple
Tuesday 30th   AMBIDEXTROUS

SEPTEMBER

Friday 2nd   SHINE!
Monday 5th   Oasis; the Creation
Friday 9th   SHINE!
Friday 16th   SHINE!
Sunday 18th   IN THE CITY *(music convention tie-in)*
Monday 19th   IN THE CITY *(music convention tie-in)*
Tuesday 20th   IN THE CITY *(music convention tie-in)*
Wednesday 21st   IN THE CITY *(music convention tie-in)*
Thursday 22nd   MC Teabag; Punishment Farm
Friday 23rd   SHINE! Kenny Carpenter
Wednesday 28th   FLESH
Thursday 29th   POLLEN
Friday 30th   SHINE!

DECEMBER

Saturday 17th   Sasha

Set-list: Duke – 'So in Love With You' (Pizzaman 5 a.m. Dub),
Sharon Nelson – 'Down that Road', Sade – 'Pearls' (Remix),
Prince – 'Most Beautiful Girl in the World' (Marvin & Hornbostel
Remix), BT – 'Nocturnal Transmission', SLP – 'Supernova'
(Aquarius Mix), Buzzin' Cuzzins & Romanthony – 'Let Me Show
You Love' (Bad Yard Club Mix), Histerya – 'Love Nation' (Joy &
Kaya Remix), Tenth Chapter – 'Prologue' (Atlas 1st Addition Mix)

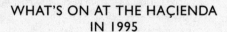

WHAT'S ON AT THE HAÇIENDA IN 1995

FEBRUARY

Monday 20th   Hopper; Flinch

JUNE

Tuesday 20th   *Raymond & Martha (a play: 'a world of pulp serial-killer literature')* Pete Robinson; Dave Rofe

JULY

Saturday 1st   Graeme Park
Tuesday 4th   Str8-Up
Saturday 8th   Graeme Park
Saturday 15th   Graeme Park
Tuesday 18th   Leaky Fresh; Semtex; Hewan Clarke
Friday 21st   SUNSHINE! Todd Terry; Jon DaSilva
Monday 24th   FACTORY TOO SHOWCASE East West Coast; the Orch; Italian Love Party; K-Track
Friday 28th   SUNSHINE! Farley 'Jackmaster' Funk; Barbara Tucker
Monday 31st   Tom Wainwright; Bobby Langley (plus Carry On Down the Canal: a boat trip)

AUGUST

Friday 4th   Digit; Max Mistry
Friday 11th   SUNSHINE! Dave Seaman
Thursday 17th   DOMINA Andrew Weatherall; Matt Thompson; Pete Robinson
Friday 25th   SUNSHINE! Victor Simonelli; CeCe Rogers
Monday 28th   HAÇIENDA CLASSICS Jon DaSilva; Nipper & Roy Baxter; Guru Josh

THE HAÇIENDA

SEPTEMBER

Friday 1st
ULTIMATUM RECORDS RELEASE PARTY Carl Cox; Laurent Garnier; Eric Powell; Daz Sound; Trevor Rockcliffe

Sunday 3rd
DODGY: 'The National Band Register Throws a Chocolate Grenade' Arch Stanton; FTV; J. Fisher; Defacto; the Colour Wheel; the Free Agents

Monday 4th
THE IMMORTAL SHOWCASE: 5th Man Manchester Records Launch Party Toni DiBart; Love to Infinity; Sam Mollinson; Up Yer Ronson; New Industries; Gabrielle's Wish; Bad Man Wagon; Kill Laura; Pete Mitchell

Tuesday 5th
Danny Rampling; Graeme Park; Dave Clarke; Nick Warren; James Lavelle; Paul Bleasdale; Kris Needs; Richard Fearless; James Barton

Friday 8th
DIGIT DJ Buck; Ra Soul; Max Mistry; Neon Leon

Saturday 9th
Bobby Langley

Thursday 14th
Jean Daniel; Eric Powell

OCTOBER

Wednesday 11th
Marion; Northern Uproar; Gabrielle's Wish; Hopper; Disobey; Chris Carter; Gilbertpossstenger

Sunday 29th
The Durutti Column

Set-list: 'Collette', 'What is it to Me (Woman)', 'The Next Time', 'War Torn', 'Tangled', 'Jacqueline', 'Otis', 'Organ Donor', 'Guitar for Mother', 'The Missing Boy', 'The Beggar'

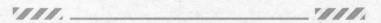

WHAT'S ON AT THE HAÇIENDA IN 1996

FEBRUARY
Tuesday 6th   Gabrielle's Wish

APRIL
Saturday 6th   Armand van Helden
Friday 26th   Manic Street Preachers

MAY
Monday 20th   Dub Syndicate; Freedom Masses; Joey J; DJ
                     Manners
Tuesday 21st   Marion
Thursday 30th   The Fall; Gabrielle's Wish

JUNE
Sunday 30th   Gabrielle's Wish

JULY
Friday 5th   PLEASURE Steve Cobby
Friday 12th   PLEASURE DJ Krust
Friday 19th   PLEASURE Richard Moonboots
Friday 26th   PLEASURE Hidden Agenda
Tuesday 30th   Gabrielle's Wish

SEPTEMBER
Wednesday 25th   A Certain Ratio

NOVEMBER
Tuesday 5th   Gabrielle's Wish
Wednesday 13th   FEVER Sister Sledge; John McCready
Monday 18th   Jesus Loves You; Justin Robertson

THE HAÇIENDA

Wednesday 20th   PLEASURE CHRISTMAS PARTY DJ Gusto;
Nelson & McKinney; Pete Robinson; DJ Rofe;
Jay Brown

DECEMBER
Tuesday 31st   Bobby Langley

MORE TALES OF THE
MAD HATTER'S TEA PARTIES

Extract from the minutes for weekly management meeting held in the Round House on Thursday 6 January 1994:

New nights

PM [Paul Mason] and AM [Angela Matthews] had put together a calendar of events planned over the first two months of 1994.

Apart from two private parties in the cocktail bar, there were no other special events planned in January and CS [Chris Smith] expressed his disappointment at this fact as it had been stressed at the last meeting that we should be arranging as many events as possible to make sure we have enough money to pay the VAT at the end of January.

PM explained that three weeks' lead time was required to properly arrange and promote a night and a Christmas break meant that it had been impossible to get anything arranged in time for January, and hopefully the Jazz night through SJM on 27 January will be confirmed.

Three new Wednesday nights had been arranged for February, with a monthly Luvdup Jolly Roger reunion night, the first retro night and the first trance night.

PM and AM were meeting Luvdup later that day to finalize matters.

Extract from the minutes of the meeting held in the Round House on Thursday 13 January 1994:

New nights

The first Jolly Roger night had been postponed until the first week in March due to technical problems.

No suitable DJ had yet been found to front the first Retro night, and there was a discussion as to who might be suitable but no one could come up with anybody. It was suggested that we ask a DJ to programme the night and get someone else to play the actual records but it was felt that no DJs would be prepared to do this.

The trance night was still scheduled to go ahead on 16 February. RG [Rob Gretton] requested that a late licence be obtained for this night.

Extracts from the minutes of the weekly management meeting held in the Round House on Thursday 27 January 1994

Trance night
AM had prepared a budget of the first trance night. It was agreed that the entrance price should be £5 in advance and £6 on the door and that the night was to be called TRANSFORM.

Jolly Rogering
The Luvdup monthly Jolly Roger night was still going ahead, and it was still planned to link up with Dry on these nights.

Extract from the minutes of the weekly management meeting held in the Round House on Thursday 10 February 1994:

Transform
Preparations for the first Transform had not gone well. The name and date on the flyers were both incorrect and another Herbal Tea Party was being held at the Airdri on the same night, with Charlie Hall from the Drum Club DJing

PM suggested that we put back the first night until March, as we create negativity towards the night if the first one is not a success. RG felt very strongly that the night should go ahead as we had to face up to the competition at some stage and we had a very strong line-up from March in the shape of the Trance Europe Express.

It was agreed to proceed with the night.

Basement improvements
A meeting had been arranged for Friday 11 February with the archi-tect. Those attending would report back to the next meeting. AHW

[Tony Wilson] asked to go on record that we would be making a mistake if we did not involve Ben Kelly in the project. Following lengthy discussions regarding the cost involved and BK's track record of constantly going way over budget, AHW also asked to go on record to say that we would be making a mistake if we did use BK.

Extract from the minutes of the weekly management meeting held in the Round House on Thursday 17 February 1994:

Transform

While the night had not been a success in financial terms, those who had attended the night agreed that there was a good atmosphere and that the club had looked excellent there was also no problem with drugs.

About 450 had attended, nearly all free, but apparently there was only about 300 at the Herbal Tea Party, and Herbal Tea Party had already contacted us with regard to making sure that we don't clash again in the future. The Trance Europe Express night in March had been cancelled, but AM felt that using Justin Robertson as the resident, and bringing in guest DJs and acts such as Andy Weatherall and Aphex Twin, should be a successful formula for a regular monthly night.

Extract from the minutes of the weekly management meeting held in the Round House on Thursday 24 February 1994:

Gigs and fashion shows

RG felt that we were not exploiting the club's full potential as a live venue. Our two main club competitors, Home and Paradise Factory, did not have the ability to put on shows and he felt that we were the ideal venue for acts attracting crowds between the capacity of the Academy and the Boardwalk, although he admitted that there were problems with the size of the stage and the lighting.

PM said that he was constantly trying to book gigs but could only try to get what was available and we have the problem of not being available for Fridays and Saturdays, which is why we lost the Incognito gig.

Extracts from the minutes of the weekly management meeting held in the Round House on Thursday 3 March 1994:

Jolly Roger

Only 190 had attended the first Jolly Roger night.

Flesh

There was a general feeling that Flesh was going stale and that Paul Cons, being aware of this, was not spending as much as in the past, thus creating a downward spiral. AHW suggested that if this was the case we should look to promote the night ourselves in the future, but the general feeling was that this would not work.

It was decided to arrange a meeting with Paul Cons to discuss the matter further.

Extract from the minutes of the weekly management meeting held in the Round House on Thursday 10 March 1994:

Jolly Roger

AHW felt that one of the biggest problems was that the advertising to the first night did not push the Luvdup aspect of Jolly Roger hard enough, but the artwork and printing for April had already been done on the same lines.

PM said that we were going to hire a lorry and parade around the city centre with a sodding pirate on the back and also have it suspended from outside the club.

It was agreed to distribute 1000 free tickets for April, subject to agreement from Luvdup.

Extract from the minutes of the weekly management meeting held in the Round House on Thursday 24 March 1994:

Transform

AM had prepared a budget for the April Transform. It was agreed that the DJ line-up of Alex Patterson, David Holmes and Fabio Paras was more than was necessary for the night and that we should look to drop one of them from the line-up. It was agreed that the security was too much and that we should be looking to drop one regular doorman and one supervisor if possible.

Classics 88
PM asked if he could spend a total of £750 on props for the night and in particular buy a new swimming pool. He was asked to wait until after the weekend to see whether or not we could afford it or not.

Extract from the minutes of a Haçienda/Dry meeting held in April 1994:

Haçienda matters
Classics 89 – 196 tickets sold. £1000 for June, July, August.

The accounts will be ready week on Thursday.

Charlatans confirmed.

Oasis might get moved to Haçienda from University. AM to chase up. [The gig wasn't changed. Oasis played the University that June and the Haçienda in September.]

AHW explained CD ROM to A Matthews.

RG has put AHW in charge of the Haçienda CD-ROM.

Ministry of Sound tour has sold badly. Keep price at £8 on the door, £6 for students.

Extracts from the 'brief' minutes of a weekly management meeting held in the Round House on 28 April 1994:

AM reported that the doormen felt that too many people were being knocked back on Flesh nights due to their alleged heterosexuality.

RG bet both PH and AK £20 that there would be more than 500 customers on Friday night.

There was to be one last shot at getting Jolly Roger up and running in June.

It was decided that this was not the best time for Dry to invest in a computer.

THE HAÇIENDA

From the Haçienda monthly newsletter, 1995

In 1995 the Haçienda was brought to you by:

Rob Gretton: Managing Director
Paul Mason: Operations Manager
Ang Matthews: General Manager, Club Diva, Friend of the Stars
Andy King: The Trendy Accountant
John Reid a.k.a. Fred: Maintenance, Health & Vinyl Flooring
Anton Razak [*sic*]: Assistant Manager (Mr Lover Lover)
Jon Drape: Production, Man about Town
Andy Jackson: PR Princess
PC: Creative Director (Graphic Design)
Mel Dymott: Office Manager & Merchandise
Bobby Langley: DJ & Tours
Little John: Publicity
Gavin Richardson: Cellar Dweller
Stephen Page: Lighting, Tour Production & *Guardian* Crossword
Thomas Piper: Sound
Catrina Bill: Cashier
John Nowinski: Maintenance & Paint

1997

'The calculator is mightier than the gun'

There was another setback in June 1997. Our licence had come up for renewal, so the licensing committee decided to have a look round the infamous Haçienda and see if it was worthy. The committee of seven magistrates turned up in a minibus and Rob and Leroy were waiting to greet them. Unfortunately we'd already had trouble, a minor skirmish, and at that precise moment the four Salford lot who had been thrown out earlier did a drive-by. They rode their car on to the pavement, leaned out of the window and hit the offending bouncer with a wheel brace, smashing his head open and sending his blood raining all over the licensing committee.

It didn't help much, let's put it that way.

That spelt another closure order from Great Great Greater Manchester Police,' wrote Tony Wilson in 24 Hour Party People. *'One that even George Carman couldn't save [us] from.'*

Things got even worse. We owed Whitbread a lot of money and because we hadn't paid them they stopped supplying us with beer. So we closed the doors one Saturday night. We didn't know it then, but that would be the last night of the Haçienda. There was no farewell party, no final goodbye. We just closed.

A couple of days later Rob called a meeting of possible investors – as many as he could muster – who had been invited via New Order's financial planner. There were some big investors there: about eight of the city's biggest money men. Politely they listened to what we had to say and it was obvious they loved the romance of the place – its history, the whole rock 'n' rollness of it. But, at the end of the day, they were businessmen, and rock 'n' rollness doesn't pay the bills. None of them would invest.

Now Rob was desperate. So, when Paul Carroll approached him with an offer of cash, he saw a way out. Paul stood to lose a lot from the Haçienda closing: the doormen were out of pocket by thousands every week it was shut.

Paul could lend Rob the money needed in order to get Whitbread off our backs and pay off some other outstanding debts: this amounted to £40,000.

Rob and Ang met Paul outside the club, where he delivered the cash in a bin bag. (Ang stuck her head inside and stared at all the money, incredulous.) Rob went to the bank straight away, having already made an arrangement with the bank manager whereby we could deposit the money and use it to get the club up and running again, without it going towards our debt with the bank. This was supposed to be bail-out money, used to reopen the club. But the bank panicked because the club was shut and illegally took the money to pay off our overdraft with them; our overdraft facility was simultaneously shut down.

Rob had got the money he'd needed then lost it all – in the same day! Now we weren't even back to square one; we were deeper in trouble than we had been before, because suddenly we owed money to the creditors, to the breweries and to the fucking gangsters . . . And we couldn't reopen the club.

Paul went berserk. Rob told him: 'I can't open the club. They've taken the money and used it.'

Paul's immediate response was the same as anyone else's would be: 'I want the money back.'

'I haven't got it now. It's gone.'

At that point Rob was given several options, none of them suitable for family reading.

Rob phoned to tell me what had happened.

'Oh my fucking good God,' was all I could say.

I ended up giving him the cash to pay Paul back. Ironic, really, since Paul had already phoned me to let me know what a bastard Rob was, how he'd disrespected him, etc.. And to advise me not to lend him the money because he needed to be taught a lesson.

Well, at least it was over.

At the same time, we were having problems with Companies House.

We had three years of accounts outstanding with them, which were accruing late fees every month. Companies House threatened to wind up the Haçienda and Dry if we didn't file them immediately.

All we needed was our accountants to tidy up and submit them. And they chose that moment to announce that they wanted upfront the £10,000 it would cost to do the job, the bastards. They knew we were on our way out, didn't they – they'd seen the accounts.

It was a tiny amount compared to what we had paid them over the years. They'd earned hundreds of thousands of pounds off the Haçienda, New Order, Joy Division and Factory, but ultimately pulled out over ten grand. Thanks, Mr Ernst and Mr Young.

By now the situation was hopeless. The club was shut, we couldn't pay our debts or reopen and Companies House planned to make us bankrupt.

It was jumped or be pushed. So we jumped.

We agreed to go into voluntary administration; in other words, voluntary bankruptcy.

The liquidator told us everything would be easy. We would be able to reopen the club under another trading name and start again, with the lease reverting back to the building owners: us. Please don't anybody ever believe a word a liquidator says to them.

I thought it was a bad idea. As far as I was concerned it was definitely time to bail out. But Rob as always wanted to carry on, his sense of honour still to the fore. He thought we would be able to reopen, lose the debts and then earn enough money to pay back the creditors.

I still loved the club but I was sick of throwing good money after bad into Martin Hannett's 'hole in ground called the Haçienda' with not a cat in hell's chance of seeing any of it ever again.

I was still paying the Haçienda mortgage – seven grand a month – to keep the building. At that point in my career I wasn't even working, New Order being in hiatus. Try as I might, it was all slipping through my fingers. I was staring personal bankruptcy in the face.

My accountant told me, 'You cannot sort this out. There is no way.'

*

So in the end it wasn't the gangs, the drugs or the violence that brought down the Haçienda; it was a bunch of people doing sums – they were the biggest fuckheads of the lot. There you go: the calculator is mightier than the gun.

Heartbreaking or not, it was my escape route and I took it. Rob and I spoke over the phone.

'Shut the fucking thing down,' I told him. 'I can't handle it any more. I'm finished. I'm not putting any more money in. This has gone far enough and it's not going anywhere.'

He was bitterly upset. '*Judas*. You betrayed me.' He yelled. He screamed. 'You stabbed me in the back.'

Afterwards it was very difficult, especially in the meetings about the building being sold. We banged heads many times but I suppose he had to talk to me because he was still managing New Order/Joy Division. His livelihood came from us, whether he liked it or not.

For many, the last 'proper' night of the Haçienda was the club's Fifteenth Birthday Party on 15 May. The place was packed and it was difficult to move, with more than 2500 clubbers gathered to see Sasha and Digweed play the main room, with Jon DaSilva and Laurent Garnier downstairs.

The night also marked the launch of a long-awaited three-CD compilation, released through Deconstruction and mixed by Dave Rofe, Jon DaSilva and Pete Robinson. Fittingly, it was beautifully packaged yet exorbitantly expensive: its £27 price-tag proved to be off-putting to most (though the CD is now a much sought-after collectors' item).

It was released on 26 May and was called Viva Haçienda! *The irony was terrible.*

Just a month later, the club closed for good.

Essentially we were too idealistic. We didn't want to run the Haçienda as a business – we wanted a playground for ourselves and our friends. You need a different philosophy to operate a club as a business, especially if you want to make a success of it. We couldn't bring ourselves to stop the staff from having a great time. We wanted everyone to enjoy it with us, so we treated it like a big party. The best Manchester has ever seen.

The last night of the Haçienda was Saturday 28 June 1997. Dave Haslam was DJing, and had no idea it was to be the last-ever night. The club was full and there was, for once, no violence.

I remember that after we'd closed one of the gangsters stopped me on Market Street in Manchester to lament: 'We've got fucking nowhere to go now, man. It's all downhill for Manchester.'

What a joke. All I could think was, 'It was the likes of you who shut it, you fucker.'

Couldn't say it, of course. And anyway it wasn't quite true. When the Haçienda shut down the Salford lot who had taken up residence there went out and caused mayhem in every other club in town. They just charged right in, straight past the doormen, and took over.

I for one was delighted, to be honest, because we'd had to put up with them while all the other clubs in Manchester stayed quite safe and nobody had ever given us any credit for that. Now the other clubs shat themselves as the Salford lot ran riot all around town.

It quietened down after a while because none of the other clubs had the same allure as the Haçienda. Also cocaine use had spread like an epidemic. A lot of the gangsters stayed at home to get high and didn't want to go out as much. That's the difference between ecstasy and coke: you don't want music when you're on coke; you want to sit and talk shit.

The staff couldn't quite believe we'd gone bankrupt. Some were uncommonly loyal. We'd seen a very low turnover of staff compared to that in other clubs, not because of great wages but because they loved the Haçienda/Factory ethos and Rob and Tony. With the building locked up, and the staff not allowed back inside, they gathered at Dry and we all sat together, in shock.

I remember that when we sold Dry, to Hale Leisure in October, Ang handed me the keys then burst out crying. I asked her what was wrong.

'What do you think is wrong? That's it for us. We're done now. It's over.'

Then Anton showed up, having been hired by Hale Leisure to run the place. He'd been poached, much to his embarrassment – although nobody minded; in fact many of the staff stayed on. Mind you, I think they felt shocked at finally being treated as employees, not as friends, by the new owners: they'd be calling Ang up all the time, crying because they weren't allowed more than one glass of orange squash per shift; they'd been used to getting pissed for nothing when they worked for us.

Hale Leisure also solved the problem of polishing that brass handrail by painting it black. Why didn't we think of that? Because it looked shit, that's why.

Even with the Haçienda gone we still had to tie up the loose ends. We got £1.2 million for the property minus costs, having bought it for £1.2 million plus costs in 1992 and been forced to sell it during a slump in the property market. Two years later it would be resold for £5 million, and then sold again at double that to the company that turned it into flats.

The sale of the building paid off the ridiculous bridging loan that had crippled us since we first bought it and also paid back Rob's directors' loans.

At the end, me and my mates grabbed whatever we could from the Haçienda. The only thing Rob took was the 'FAC 51' sign from beside the front door.

I took the six-foot mirror-ball, the doors, the mats, the bar-tops, the banisters, the bollards and the front-door plate that everyone walked over to get in (under which I found the hidden CCTV tapes of New Year's Eve 1995: we'd had a lot of trouble that night so the bouncers must have hidden them where the police couldn't find them. I'm going to put them out on DVD).

I felt I was losing something dear – very bloody dear – and wanted to keep any part of it I could. I don't know what I'd thought I could to do with a bloody dance floor, but luckily I didn't have the problem because Tony's builders took it out (it ended up being thrown away).

Below the stage at the back was a closed-off section that had been used as a Factory storage area and later for the barrels. The barrels were on a platform and to keep the platform level someone had shoved a quarter-inch tape box underneath it.

I pulled it out. Covered in old beer and sweat and condensation, it was one of the master tapes of Joy Division's debut album, *Unknown Pleasures*.

It made me smile. It was an absolutely perfect metaphor for the Haçienda.

Joy Division had held the whole fucking thing up.

WHAT'S ON AT THE HAÇIENDA IN 1997

MARCH
Tuesday 4th   Gabrielle's Wish
Wednesday 5th   Gabrielle's Wish; High Society
Tuesday 18th   Hopper

JUNE
Tuesday 24th   Dave Haslam
Saturday 28th   Dave Haslam

UNDER THE HAMMER

The Haçienda Auction was hosted at Manchester's Richard Conrad Building on Saturday 25 November 1997. An official website was created, www.hacauction.com, on which were featured the pieces of Haçienda history up for sale. Proceeds went to Manchester youth charities. The complete list of auctioned items was as follows:

1 × disc-jockey booth
8 × central supporting steel columns (RSJs), hazard-stripe design
10 × 1m^2 pieces of dance floor, cleaned, sanded, varnished and
    mounted on 18mm timber
5 × pieces of stage floor, cleaned and mounted on 18mm timber
1 × changing room
1 × sound-engineer/light-operator booth
1 × Kim Philby Bar
1 × first-floor Can Bar
1 × section of banquette seating
1 × 'ruined' arch (entrance to upstairs Can Bar)
1 × arch to dance-floor area
2 × feature columns adjacent to arch (sold as one lot)
various sections of stage
various sections of stage surround in black and white hazard stripes
various sections of banquette seating from Mondays' Corner
    (Salford's, actually)
1 × handprint and signature set in concrete – signed 'Tony '94'
1 × handprint and signature set in concrete – signed 'Hooky 94'
various bundles of fluorescent wall-light fittings
various bundles of electrical components and light fittings
3 × blue and red external perimeter light
5 × black and yellow acoustic baffles
3 × pallets of 200 mixed green-, blue- and red-glazed exterior bricks
3 × pallets of 200 plain bricks

THE HAÇIENDA

4 × section of balcony balustrade
various stainless-steel sanitary ware from lavatories
various lavatory doors
kitchenware
freezers
4 × TV monitors
1 × cash register
1 × drinks-purchase book
6 × Victorian radiators in Haçienda and Round House
various lavatory mirrors, bar fixtures and fittings
notice boards
1 × pay telephone
various speaker supports
sale items
loose strips of dance-floor
loose green-, blue- and red-glazed exterior bricks

Epilogue: The Fifteen-Year Party People

How did it last for fifteen years?

Tenacity. Rob's mainly. Like a pit-bull terrier, even when everyone beat him with sticks he just wouldn't let go.

I sometimes wonder how the club affected his family. He was so single-minded in the way he looked after it, which must have had a terrible impact on them; they had to live with the Haçienda and with him.

We never even considered that at the time – we were so up our own arses we never thought about the people who put up with us. Now I think about it, and all that they went through. Sorry.

Looking back on those years feels like narrowly missing a fatal traffic accident and marvelling that you weren't among the casualties. My greatest times at the Haçienda were at the end of a night, after we'd closed and got all the stragglers out. The adrenaline would be flowing (everything was flowing) because it was all so dangerous and edgy and it felt nice to relax as a group, because we'd be down to the amenable drug-heads: the staff and some key punters. We'd all sit together to share a drink, savouring the fact that we'd got through it one more night. Phew.

After the building was sold we auctioned off souvenirs. The place was rammed with fans and collectors – all sorts of people. One guy bought the door to a toilet cubicle because he'd had sex against it and he wanted to remember the event. Another item was a lump of concrete from outside the door, into which Ang and I had carved our names. The auctioneers put it inside a frame; it looked quite nice. I bid on it and the price kept rising. Then Ang herself ran up to the podium, grabbed the microphone off me: 'Stop bidding, Hooky, it's me.' She was the other person trying to buy it. Together we'd accidentally driven the price up. Typical.

Bobby Langley, an ex-Haçienda DJ, bought the DJ box. He'd heard a rumour that Cream was going buy it, and told me beforehand that his bosses at Bench had set a limit of £8000 to keep it in Manchester ('Don't let the Scousers get it!'). I was the auctioneer for that particular lot.

I remember Bobby's first bid: £100. Then a mystery bidder on the other side: £200.

Everyone looked but couldn't see the other interested party. The bidding went on until the other guy dropped out, at £7900; Bobby got it for £8000.

When I told him years later that there'd been no other bidder he went effing mad. Turned out his boss had been joking and he nearly got sacked.

Ah well, it was a good cause. Tony had wondered aloud: 'What's he going to do? Run a burger bar out of it?' (Actually Bobby brought it out for a Tribal Gathering event in Southport during 2002, where it was promoted as the main attraction. It was last seen rotting in a car park somewhere in the Northern Quarter.)

I bought two of the huge beams that held up the ceiling and loads of other stuff that I couldn't store. They went missing. It is amazing nowadays how much gear I get offered from the Haçienda – stuff that people have stolen. Great that I get to pay for it twice.

Even before it closed people said how important the club had been in their lives. I usually just said, 'Oh, right. OK. Excuse me.' Then I'd run off, embarrassed but smiling.

Time's a great healer. You get on with things. And now I find it easier to talk about the club. It was Eric Barker, 808 State's dancer, who said to me at Glastonbury one year, 'It's time to let it go, Hooky.'

He was right.

Rob died of a heart attack on 15 May 1999 (just a week short of what would have been the Haçienda's seventeenth anniversary).

Rob Gretton, the ideas man, is the one to blame and to thank for everything that the Haçienda accomplished, good or bad. It truly was his baby.

Tony Wilson might have presented himself as the father of the club, but really he functioned as Rob's enabler; left to our own devices, New Order never would have attempted to open the place. It was Rob's goodwill and love of Manchester that sparked it all. He was the sort of person who wanted everyone to party with him. He always loved company and was generous to a fault. Once he'd discovered at that first Factory Records Christmas party that it's easier to give something away than to sell it, he never looked back.

He thought about things constantly, whether it was the club or the band. He stuffed his notebooks with plans and strategies, page after page of things to do or not to do, of problems to sort out. He wrote it all down. He was very positive – a doer, which to me is the mark of a good businessman. He hated networking in a formal manner. He couldn't bear to mix with record companies. He thought it was all bullshit. You'd never hear him say, 'Hi, I'm Rob Gretton, New Order's manager.' If somebody wanted him for business reasons they'd have to find him; and, if they did, as likely as not he'd tell them, 'Oh, fuck off, leave me alone.'

If you've got a great band you can do anything. Rob was very lucky. He had two.

Today there are flats on the site of the club. I like that. If it had carried on as a club it would have been like seeing your girlfriend out with someone else. It's a shrine. Everyone moaned at me for allowing them to use the Haçienda name, but I think it's given the city a great focal point. In ten years' time people may ask, 'Why is it called the Haçienda Apartments?' They'll get to hear our story and will be stunned.

The builders, Crosby Homes, paid a fortune for the building only to knock it down. Tony and I started the bulldozer. Then, blow me down, three weeks later the film company decided to rebuild the club as a set for the film *24 Hour Party People*. It cost £280,000.

Seeing the Haçienda reconstructed for the film ticked a few boxes, if you like. The movie may have been a distorted account of the rise and fall of the place, but it gave us a proper way to say goodbye – the closing party we never had, as Barney says.

And it was mind-boggling. To go back to the Haçienda, rebuilt down to the last detail – only the edges were different – was both a dream and a nightmare. It was the strangest experience of my life.

Paul Mason was there, everyone was there. That evening, while they were filming, I walked up to Barney and said, 'Fucking hell, all that's missing is Rob Gretton.'

He turned and went, 'Look.'

There stood the actor Paddy Considine dressed as Rob.

I wanted to get drunk. I wanted to cry. It was so confusing, a weird and total head-fuck, too difficult to deal with.

But there was one terrific, hilarious postscript.

Apparently the Manto Group bought the movie set for £100,000 with the intention of moving it into a warehouse and running it as a club to cash in on our fans' nostalgia. Had the bastards pulled this off I would have been devastated. They had no right to exploit the Haçienda's memory.

And they didn't.

While we all lay soundly asleep in our beds the morning after we'd all been to the Haçienda set to film the party scene, the film crew's carpenter got on a walkie-talkie and asked the head of production, 'Are we saving this? Yes or no?'

The head of production said, 'No, it's been sold,' but the carpenter never heard anything after the word 'No'.

He ripped the whole place apart, destroyed it.

I was absolutely delighted.

The Haçienda remains a part of the lives of everyone who went or worked there. Some of the employees still benefit from their connection to it to this day. Leroy can go to New York or Amsterdam and be treated like a king because he's the ex-manager.

Tony Wilson always said that Factory was more about art than money. I wonder whether we'd still have gone in with him if he'd told us that at the start? I'll never know, but I can't say that I regret one moment of the whole mad mess.

Tony contracted kidney cancer. When the National Health Service refused to cover the costs of the medicine he wanted, friends banded together to collect the money for him; he was inundated.

We remained great friends to the end. We'd been so entwined in each other's lives, I felt very close to him. He died in 2007. It was so sudden. In February he introduced us on stage and he was perfectly well. By August he was dead.

I miss him.

Ang has ended up in Salford. She works managing the Vivienne Westwood store in Manchester. She's a great fan, so it's her dream come true.

Suzanne ended up living in Salford too. She's a mate of Twinny's so I see her a lot. She was married to Tim, one of the guys who filmed bands at the Haçienda for us, and is a mother of twins. Those kids are the maddest pair of little fuckers I've ever met in my life – wonder where they get that from? Suzanne went into outside catering and landscape gardening, and now works for Salford Reds.

Twinny is still my best mate – him and his brother Paul. In fact all of the Bellinghams have been a huge part of my life.

Paul Carroll disappeared.

Damien and Dessie Noonan are dead – and a few other doormen are too, I'm afraid. I still see a few of the lads who worked for us. I went to the opening of a new club in Cheshire last week and was welcomed in by one of them. Lovely.

Slim, always a big character around Manchester, works at the Academy and the Apollo. He's a mainstay in our city, just like Sarge.

Cormac became a barber, after serving time in prison. I also bumped into Gordon the Chef for the first time in years during the summer of 2007. He's still around. Works at the Trafford Centre.

Debbie and Bowser still cook. They own Little Red Courgette and provided catering for the crew making *24 Hour Party People*. Tommo also stuck with cooking. He served up food for Amy Winehouse until she entered rehab.

Jasmine, who worked the door, found God and became something of a religious fanatic.

Jack moved to Sheffield. He now does re-enactments of the Cromwell war. He plays one of the Roundheads.

Anton Rozak left Manchester, entirely out of touch with everybody but Ang. He now runs a baby-clothes shop in Leeds.

Hindsight being 20/20, I now see that the invulnerability we felt during those years was stupidity. Some people – myself included – became alcoholics and drug addicts. When I eventually entered rehab, a kid came up to me right away and said, 'Hello, remember me?'

'No, who are you?'

'Don't you remember? I used to serve you up with Es in the Haçienda.'

Turns out he would be my rehab counsellor. I met loads of people like that. Another guy I spent time with in rehab had been a big friend of Bowser's. He formerly ran a hotel in Withington where people would come for a few days to sniff coke around the pool in the basement. There's no telling how many of us crashed and burned, but I don't know anybody who's doing drugs the way we used to.

Now that I'm straight I suspect that a lot of the employees survived the acid-house era unscathed because they stayed straight. When you're wasted you automatically assume everyone else is off their heads, too. Now I know differently. I'd been suckered into thinking we needed drugs for the scene; that we couldn't live without them. That's the primary component of an addictive personality: you mistake the things that cause trouble for the things that cure them.

Clichés build up around rock 'n' roll. The drug aspect to the Happy Mondays, New Order and other bands have been built up beyond reality. The truth is that most people in the Haçienda were not on drugs. They just loved it as meeting place in which they could get pissed, listen to great songs and have a good time.

Would I run a club again? No. Too much responsibility – plus the wife would kill me.

Other clubs and bars picked up on aspects of the Haçienda, its tendency to place art above common sense.

You come across places sporting brass doors, candle chandeliers and pink marble that you only even notice if someone smacks your head against it. Interior designers like Bernard Carroll, who worked on the Manchester restaurants Reform and Panacea, make a living from creating places that offer customers that same sort of visual experience. Ultimately, though, you incorporate things like that to please yourself. I remember Ross McKenzie, who opened One Central Street in 2002 with Leroy Richardson, talking to me about the kind of slate he installed. I told him, 'No one's going to fucking notice. Just paint it black, mate.'

No one cares. They only come to get off their heads. Did anybody notice the projections on the walls of the Haçienda? Or the spear jutting out of Dry towards Spear Street? Those elements were so subtle they were overlooked by most people. Whenever Barney sees Ben Kelly he rips into him for overdoing things. Rightly so.

Manchester's a difficult city to run a club in. I look through my membership cards and am reminded of how many failed. The fact that the Haçienda lasted from 1982 to 1997 is quite an achievement. To my knowledge, no other place succeeded so well for so long.

It's taken years for me to come to terms with the club, what it cost me and what it meant to me. Whenever I'd get drunk or off it, I'd complain to anyone about how pissed off I was. It consumed me for a long time: I suppose I became something of a Haçienda bore.

As for my own work as a musician, Revenge and Monaco – my bands with Pottsy – proved to be successful on their own terms. We released three albums, which I'm very proud of.

After the Haçienda closed New Order reunited and recorded two more albums (*Get Ready* in 2001 and *Waiting for the Siren's Call* in 2005) but the fun of it only lasted a short time.

I don't blame my band-mates for New Order's demise. I'm adult enough to realize that the problem was mine. I'd had enough of the bullshit.

Although my first love is playing music live, I love DJing. Travelling and playing is still something I enjoy.

The Urbis Centre, a museum in Manchester, had a Haçienda Twenty-Fifth Anniversary exhibition in the summer of 2007, which simultaneously pleased me and lodged a bone in my craw because when I looked at the collections of memorabilia that people donated, I thought, 'Where did they get that from?'

Opening night was great because of all the old familiar faces. Ben Kelly and Peter Saville turned up. I'd not seen Ben for ages. I don't hold a grudge – in fairness, he'd been handed the reins and allowed to run off in any direction, which pleased him – but I love taking the piss.

My favourite moment occurred while Sasha DJed and his computer crashed. The music immediately stopped.

After about two minutes of silence, which confused everybody, I walked up to him to ask, 'Are you all right, mate?'

'Oh, fuck no, Hooky,' he panicked. 'No. All my stuff's on the computer.'

'Haven't you got any CDs?'

'No,' he said, 'you'll have to go on.'

My dream come true! I went on instead of Sasha. Fuck me. The weirdness of the whole thing just made me laugh. I'd come to the rescue of the world's top DJ. In the right place at the right time. Because, let's face it, after all is said and done, anybody can play records.

I heard that Sasha later walked around the exhibition and cried because of all the memories it conjured up.

It felt like a family reunion. I took my son and daughters and it felt nice to walk around the exhibition with them. I enjoyed it. I said, 'There's your inheritance, kids. Rob spent it.'

A cottage industry has sprung up around the Haçienda legend. The twenty-fifth anniversary in 2007 opened the floodgates as people reflected on what it all meant to them. Adidas produced a limited-edition pair of Haçienda trainers, designed by Yohji Yamamoto (Saville has worked with Yohji since the late 1980s, creating his catalogues and advertisements).

They retailed for £345 but people queued up from midnight just to be first through the doors to buy a pair. The shoes disappeared in twenty minutes – all soled out.

The Haçienda doesn't exist physically any more but it will always be with me, coming up in conversations and in my dreams and nightmares. The public and media interest in it means I'll be asked about it forever.

The people and the nights will always stay with me too. The fans will make sure I'm reminded about it always.

Bernard always takes the piss out of me, saying I'm melancholy. 'You like to live in the past,' he told me, and it's true. I dwell on it. I can't just forget it and move on. I've seen 24 Hour Party People three or four times. It's bollocks, but it's enjoyable bollocks. You couldn't make a boring film about the Haçienda if you tried.

Tony Wilson's son Oliver is mystified by how we fucked it up. He can't believe that anyone could have wasted the opportunity.

EPILOGUE: THE FIFTEEN-YEAR PARTY PEOPLE

Wasted the opportunity? I suppose we did. There was more than one. We were pretty good at it. But if you're going to waste an opportunity, there are a few important things to remember. Do it in style. Do it in public. And, above all, do it in Manchester.

Postscript: The Factory, FAC 251

One of the most popular questions on my Unknown Pleasures speaking tour was something along the lines of: 'You have just published a book called *How Not to Run a Club*, detailing the stress, angst, frustration, danger and the risks involved, financial and otherwise, in running a club in Manchester. Why the hell have you opened another?'

Answer: 'Phew! Well, believe me, it was as much of a shock to me as it is to you!' But to do the question justice we're going to have to take a trip back in time, so cue falling calendar dates and the swirling mists of time to a summer's day six years ago . . .

RING RING!

'Hello?'

'Hooky! I need yah!'

'Oh, hello, Mani – how's it going?'

'Never mind that! I need you! So-an'-so's let me down and I need a celebrity DJ for a gig at Razzamatazz in Barca, Espana!'

Now, I had resisted valiantly all efforts by anyone to get me to DJ. A lot of people had tried, especially in the early nineties; they would always say how easy it was. I always said no. I thought DJs were egotistical, self-obsessed, talentless, bigmouthed arseholes, with a hugely overblown sense of their own importance. This is probably why I fitted in so well when I did become one, but for the moment I wasn't yet involved, so . . . When I'd recovered from the shock and gleaned a few more details, it seemed we'd be getting 500 Euros each, return flights and two nights, all meals and drinks included, in a five-star hotel in Barcelona.

'What do I have to do, though, Mani? You know I can't DJ.'

'Just stand there, look pretty, and tell them why New Order won't tour!' he cackled. 'It's the best way to get pissed and off your head for nothing in the world! Let's have it!'

*

So fast-forward to the night in Barcelona. Mani and Imelda, Becky and I, suitably refreshed, inhabiting Razzamatazz's DJ booth in the big room no less, watching 800 to 1000 people, I reckon, all grooving away. Over dinner, with the help of a couple of bottles of wine, Mani had been explaining the role of the 'celebrity DJ' to me.

'No one expects too much – they just come to see the old bastard who used to be in a band!'

Well, so far I'd been having a great time, completely off it, signing a few autographs, explaining why New Order won't gig, etc., etc. At one point I'd felt so *UP!* I'd demanded a microphone so I could rap like Bez: 'MANCHESTER IN YOUR AREA!' Luckily by the time it turned up the moment was gone – as was I! But a little later I'm dancing on a podium (carefully, because Imelda had already fallen off one and been rescued by the bouncers) and I look down and see Mani scratching away on a record but it's not switched on. No scratching noise, you see, so I slap him, screaming over the noise . . .

'That record's not switched on!'

Mani is confused. He screams something back at me, trying to get what's going on. Unfortunately, while he's screaming at me the other record finishes, leaving the dance floor in complete silence. It isn't long before the crowd start making some noise – a resounding bunch of cat-calls and booings, with plastic glasses, empty and full, being flung at the DJ booth.

Mani yells, 'You garlic-crunching fuckers!'

Wrong country, surely, I think. Then he reaches down, picks the records carefully off the decks and throws them at the crowd, Frisbee-style. Next he starts emptying his record box. It's mayhem! The crowd are all screaming, ducking and running for their lives (no one wants to get decapitated by an 'I Am the Resurrection' 12-inch, do they?), but I look at him with love in my eyes and have a 'Eureka!' moment . . .

I could do that! I could be a DJ!

So, then and there, I become a fully fledged celebrity DJ – my career just beginning, the whole world my oyster. But for now the bouncers arrive again, calm things down, and we manage to get another tune on before a proper DJ turfs us out. A great night. Thanks, José.

*

Cue mists of time again, and a couple of weeks later I'm off to my second gig, this time arranged by Clint Boon (Inspiral Carpets/XFM) who is over the moon that I'm now a DJ.

'You're one of us at last!'

The venue is the Castle in Oldham, an old pub that has been turned into a new music venue. I'm playing for a mate of his, Aaron, who newly owns the club. Now, the last time I performed in Oldham was in 1977, when Joy Division played the Tower Club. We'd been booked because Sad Cafe had sold out the week before so the owner thought any punk band would sell out. Unfortunately we didn't and we got the princely sum of thirty quid and no one came. So I'm a little apprehensive and nervous tonight, but full of my celebrity-DJ self. I arrive and it's pretty rocking. Another old mate is here: Gilly, who DJs at South in Manchester and is also the Inspiral Carpets drummer.

He introduces me to Aaron and I say, 'Who's putting my records on?' (They're CDs, actually.)

'What?'

'Who's putting my tunes on? I'm a celebrity DJ – I can't actually do it,' I scream over the music.

'Fookin' hell!' he retorts.

By this time Gilly – who, it turns out, is also the resident DJ here – has disappeared, so Aaron reluctantly agrees to do it. We go in to the DJ box, I hand him the first CD and he cues it up. It goes down well and the next one is duly handed over.

'This is shit! You should do it yourself. You've got two minutes thirty-four seconds!'

'What! Don't be daft, I'm a . . .'

Before I can finish he's gone. I'm on my own. I look down at the CD player's time display: two minutes twenty-eight seconds, twenty-seven seconds . . . SHIT! I start panicking, spinning round like a headless chicken, but somehow I manage it. I learn to bloody DJ! After a fashion. I put the next one on and get away with it. Phew! So far so good, but I kiss goodbye to my newfound celebrity-DJ status and have a pretty good night.

Over the next few years I DJed for Aaron many times: Newcastle, Brighton, Manchester, Huddersfield, Oldham. He had quite an empire and turned out to be a big Joy Division/New Order fan too. We became friends – cue violins and falling hearts.

During that time, he was always asking me if I would like to open a club again. He'd heard how I had gotten involved with Bar Cuba in Macclesfield, so maybe that spurred him on. We even got to the point of nearly looking at a property in the Northern Quarter, but my heart wasn't really in it. My ego was, but that's another story.

So, cue those pesky mists of time again and I am doing a book signing in Newcastle and who should turn up but Aaron.

He gets his book signed and says, 'Are we going to do that club, or what? I've got a great idea for us. You'll love it! I'll phone you next week!' And then he disappears.

RING RING!

'It's Aaron. I've got a property! I know you're going to love it. Come to town now and I'll show it to you!'

Very soon after that I'm walking around a dilapidated but very familiar building, on Charles Street in Manchester, that I once tried to buy then ended up paying for anyway.

The old Factory headquarters. Bloody Hell! I said before that the wife'd kill me if I bought another club; now I know she will. Turns out the building had become a victim of the credit crunch. It had been sold to a developer to be turned into apartments (just what Manchester needs, more apartments) but before it was finalized the developer had gone bust. It was now on the market for rent, but it was also back on for sale at the princely sum of £3.5 million – a slight improvement on what Factory paid for it: £103,000 pre-build, £674,000 post-build. (Factory went bust on the Friday, Rob Gretton and I went to see the liquidator on the following Monday morning to buy it for New Order but were told it had already been sold. Very puzzling. It had cost us £674,000 to build and was sold for £225,000. Can't resist a moan!) Caroline Ainscow, who became the owner after Factory went bust, very successfully ran it as the Paradise Factory from 1993 to 1996 with her partner, Peter Dalton. My favourite Thursday night out. Heady days.

This time ego and heart were in sync. I won't bore you with the business details but I am now the proud partner/shareholder with my friend

Aaron in our new venture, the Factory, FAC 251. My former boss's office. I can't quite believe it myself. We had agonized over the use of the name and it became the source of much debate . . .

Reasons for	Reasons against
History	Ditto
Heritage	Ditto
Hard work	Ditto

It rages on still. Surely we were using the past as a platform for the future? Using our bad experiences, our mistakes, so we could get it right this time? Here would be a new venue, run by old hands, experienced old hands. Let's face it, with all our mistakes we couldn't be more experienced, could we? Here to help New Musicians, New Promoters, New Bands, etc., I was spurred on in other ways, too. I'd been hearing a lot about bands being made to pay to play in Manchester, in the guise of selling tickets for their gig – the upshot being that if they didn't sell enough tickets there was *no gig*. This was even spreading to new DJs: if they sold twenty, thirty tickets for the venue/night, they could play; if not, they couldn't. I thought this was disgusting. Not good for Manchester at all. I mean, with an attitude like that we're going nowhere. So, weighing up all the odds, and with a few delicate lawyer's meetings and *almost* everyone's blessing, we went ahead.

The new Factory headquarters were born – reborn even.

We immediately approached Ben Kelly with a view to restoring it to its former glory, with a close eye on the costs this time, of course, and a much more businesslike attitude right to the fore. Ben was delighted and here is what he wanted to do . . .

The Ben Kelly approach to the redesign of the former Factory HQ

The client wanted to make subtle references to the legacy of Factory. It was agreed that we would attempt to produce a design which referenced Factory but also looked very much to the future. We attempted to achieve this through the use of materials, colours and graphic references. The first and most important thing was to put the main fabric of the building back to its original form. Over the years the building had been hacked about and treated without any respect. The first move was to infill the opening which had been cut out of the first-floor level. This helped to create the max-imum floor area for the new club. Secondly we wanted to allow views from the ground-floor entrance up to the new DJ booth at first-floor level. This was achieved by designing a part-glazed cantilevered DJ 'box' which hangs out over the double-height entrance space.

All three floors were required to have bars and DJ booths. This gave us the opportunity to make a new statement on each floor of the building. We aimed to layer and thread a new language through-out the building. We referenced the blue-glazed bricks, which were originally used at either side of the double-height entrance slot. These have been used to build low walls at the reception and around each DJ booth and also around the ground-floor sound desk. The glazed bricks offer a robust protection to these areas. We also developed a powder-coated steel structural-support system that is common to all three bars. All the bar tops are made from a dark blue/grey slate which matches the original slate window sills throughout the building. For the ground-floor bar we introduced a back-illuminated orange translucent material called AIR-board. The first-floor bar has an adhesive striped yellow and white prismatic material applied in stripes on to the front bar panels. When this material is illuminated it has an amazing reflective glowing effect. This is the same material that is applied to the sides of police cars and ambulances. For the third-floor bar we referenced an Orchestral Manoeuvres in the Dark album cover designed by Ben Kelly and Peter Saville. This is a perforated album sleeve. The bar front is a hugely scaled-up version created from mirror which has angled laser-cut lozenge shapes cut out.

All columns have been painted with coloured striped sections. A Haçienda-style yellow neon-striped chevron wraps around the silver-painted first ground-floor column and greets all the customers. The stairwell housing the main accommodation staircase is decorated in International Orange. The main body of the club is painted Pigeon Blue to match the original Haçienda colour scheme.

Aaron thought that we should use as many people as possible from the past to work with us towards the future. Kevin Cummins to document the rebuild, Peter Saville as a design consultant, Leroy Richardson as bar manager, same accountants . . . Only joking on that last one! Some could help and some couldn't. It was very exciting and when we announced it the reaction was fantastic. There were a few keyboard terrorists but we were too busy to get involved in that. Internet criticism, the new deadly disease, frightening people to death worldwide. It has been very hard work but seeing it develop and grow, watching the business come together, a delicate blend of idealism and realism. I'll leave you to guess who was responsible for which. And on 5 February 2010 it triumphantly opened – a little rushed, but isn't everything? There's an old suspicion in club circles that if you're not screwing the toilet-roll holders on the wall five minutes before the doors open you're not doing it right. I'm glad to say we stuck to it. Another week and it would have been perfect. (I'm thinking of putting that on my bloody gravestone. It seems to apply to everything I do these days.)

Ben Kelly has done a great job and is involved in a lot of aspects of the club even as it runs, improving it all the time. The next big project is an outdoor smoking area over the canal, to go with that Victorian overhanging toilet next door. (We've had to leave in place the plumber's merchants next door because the aforesaid toilet is Grade 1 listed.)

I'm very proud of the club. Bringing the building back to life has been a labour of love for us all, and we are building up a great team. Many of the management and staff are regulars who have worked for Aaron for many years, a great testament to the organization, which also includes a few of the original owners/artists' kids. I feel very blessed at my time of life to have been handed an opportunity like this, dealing with this club in our new Manchester of 2010, which is an absolute pleasure compared to how it used to be. We now liaise with the police on all aspects of security, at last making sure that staff and customers are totally safe. One interesting and positive aspect of our European immigration rules is that we now have a team of Polish doormen. The great thing here is that, if any of our local villains do appear at the door, these wonderful men, each built like a brick shithouse, have no idea where Gorton, Moss Side, Gooch, Longsight or even Salford is so there is no discrimination, respect-wise, as the bouncers don't have a clue who's who or where's where – so one aspect of the gang problem has been solved at a stroke. The day-to-day running I leave to the experts, but do like to stick my oar in regularly with ideas for improvements that I'm sure seem more of a hindrance than an asset. In fact it makes me wonder if I could bring the whole of his empire down with a little more effort. We have had a healthy list of DJs and bands already, with the Haçienda Saturday Night in the Board room being responsible for quite a few old and new faces. For opening night, Aaron suggested I 'do something'. I thought he meant DJ but he had something else in mind.

'How about playing? Like that Monaco night you did at the Ritz for Oxfam? A retrospective of your long and illustrious career?'

I literally froze, this had not crossed my mind.

The thought was intriguing. At the Ritz in Manchester, David Potts and I had done some Monaco tunes with a smattering of Joy Division and New Order – well why not? So I duly rang him. No reply. I rang his mum and she informed me he was in Argentina, backpacking, off to find himself. Shit! So I was on my own, phoned round a few compatriots and recruited the following:

Paul (Leadfoot) Kehoe, drums, Monaco
Andy Poole, keyboards, Monaco
Nat Wason, guitar, Haven/Freebass
. . . and me!

If I was going to sing we'd need someone to play bass. This was tricky. Mani? Too busy. Rourky? Now living in New York. So who? Then I had it. Another 'Eureka!' moment. Jack, my son: he was a pretty good player already – though he had shattered me with some news the year before.

'Dad? I've got some bad news for you.'

'What, son?' My mind was boggling.

'I'm giving up my group to concentrate on my studies.'

Where did I go wrong?

So, keeping it in the family, he was duly enlisted/press-ganged and the Light were born and rehearsals began. Now, there is always a feeling of guilt about playing these songs outside of Joy Division/New Order; I can't quite put my finger on why, but it does feel like I am doing something wrong. Obviously there is an entitlement to play them, as I was part of the writing process, but it's like a weird kind of protocol has been implanted in my brain that says I shouldn't be playing them without the others. We even had this in New Order with Joy Division songs. But I soldiered on. I wanted the opening-night performance to feature all my incarnations, including my new one, Freebass, so a set-list was duly drawn up:

'Dark Starr' (Howard Marks vocal/Mani bass); 'Dark Starr' (Gary Briggs vocal/Mani bass); 'You Don't Know This About Me'; 'Dreams Never End'; 'Ceremony'; 'Sister and Brother'; 'Shine'; 'What Do You Want from Me'; 'Atmosphere' (Rowetta vocal); 'Insight' (Rowetta vocal); 'Shadowplay'; 'Pictures in My Mind'; 'Interzone'; 'Warsaw'; 'Transmission'; 'Sunrise'; 'Love Will Tear Us Apart'; 'Blue Monday'

Around this time I was approached by a cartel of superfans. These boys, the Closed Order, were specialists in the collecting of rare and obscure gig/rehearsal tapes. Their collection is mighty and an outsider had got hold of something, so the cartel asked me to try and stop its widespread release. This was timed quite handily because I had been involved in a few meetings – quite positive ones, I might add – with the rest of New Order/Joy Division about creating our own specialist web-site, at last selling our own rarities, remixes and merchandise, and this was just what we needed to start the official site. It actually transpired that the gentleman in America who had the 'rare' tape was very nice and just handed it back to its rightful owners. He did, however, point out to me one Joy Division song on the tape that I swear I had never heard before – I suppose by that I mean I had no recollection of the song at all. 'Pictures in My Mind' was an almost-finished track that we must have shelved: we were very prolific then and, though we only practised for a couple of hours a week, would easily write a song a session if not more. Ian Curtis used to say that you should always finish every song you do because there'll always be someone who likes it, so I don't understand how this one had slipped the net. Although wary of the dreaded internet criticism, and of dwelling on the past, I thought I'd finish it off for the gig; and, while I was at it, thought why not feature one of my favourite unreleased New Order songs from *Waiting for the Siren's Call*, 'Brother and Sister', which to my eternal frustration has still not been released. The rehearsals went very well and with the help of my co-producer/programmer Philip Murphy it all started to sound very good indeed.

I must admit I was terrified both before and on the opening night, but very happy with the support shown by the most discerning people on the planet . . . you! So thank you again for all your support. The night was a great success and bodes very well for the future of the Factory. Here's to the future. (We have already been criticized for being too full too often, which just goes to show – the Haçienda having been empty for the first six years – that you cannot please everyone.) If FAC 251 can earn a place in people's hearts and the history of musical culture the way the FAC 51 Haçienda did, I will be very happy indeed. The heritage will live forever.

I'd like to thank Aaron Matt Mellor for his inspiration and support; and Nigel Myles, Kirk, Rob and Caroline, Denise, Steve, Jase@A2, James and Joanna, Tony Andrews and all at Funktion One, Martin at Pioneer, Dave, Steve and all at FullSpec and, of course, Ben Kelly.

One last thing: we stocked the club with what we thought was enough for the first ten days – the amount worked out by experience from all Aaron's other establishments' drinking histories. The whole lot went on the first night. We stocked the same again, and it went on the second night too. We have created a monster . . .

Peter Hook
July 2010

Acknowledgements

I would like to thank ... my mother Irene, her sister Jean, my wife Becky, for her constant love, support and guidance, my children Heather, Jack and Jessica for everything.

Michael and Carole Jones.

Claude Flowers, who started the whole bloody thing in the first place, hopefully, mate, the Joy Division one will be easier?

Andrew Holmes for doing a fantastic job shaping the raw material and bringing it to fruition.

Lesley Thorne for handling that messy business of business.

Angela Herlihy of Simon & Schuster for deciding to publish the thing!

Diane Bourne of the *Manchester Evening News* for the initial push and inspiration for the title.

Eric Barker for letting me know what a bore I had become.

Twinny and Carlo for being the best mates a man can have.

Phil Murphy for being a great sounding post.

Andrew Liddle for his great pictures.

Ang Mathews for her great help, patience and knowledge.

Leroy Richardson for his support, when I needed it most.

Paul Fletcher and Natalie Plumridge at One Love Music for their sterling efforts in putting The Haçienda back where it belongs.

Paul Chadwick for his great musical knowledge.

Terry Mason.

Stephen Lea for his legals.

Claire at Lea & Co.

Wendy Fonarow from one author to another.

Anthony Addis for his common sense.

Stephen Jones at Addis & Co.

All at Addis & Co for putting up with my little quirks.

Tim and Tom at New State for the success of *The Haçienda Classics*.

Paul Brown for suggesting it in the first place.

Phil Beckett for his great help in compiling it.

James Masters for being a fountain of knowledge.

Many thanks to David Sultan, a great friend and colleague.

Graeme Park, Mike Pickering, Jon DaSilva, Sasha, Justin Robertson, Arthur Baker, Allister Whitehead, Dave Haslam, The Whip, David Morales, Tom Wainwright, Derrick May, Todd Terry, Andrew Weatherall, John Digweed, Kevin Saunderson, Jon Carter, Frankie Knuckles, A Guy Called Gerald, Danny Rampling.

Sasha and all at the Warehouse Project.

John Drape at Ear To The Ground.

David Vincent and all at Sankeys.

Ricky at Colours.

Oliver Wilson.

Ken Niblock and David Potts for our wild nights at the Hac.

Clint Boon for teaching me to DJ.

Mani for refining it.

Imelda for the gigs.

Andy Fisher.

Gary Aspden at Adidas.

Bobby Langley and Slipstream.

Kickers.

Sam Findlay.

Taka Motomura.

808 State and The Happy Mondays.

Terry Christian for the tapes.

Alan Erasmus, man of mystery.

Peter Saville, it's great working with you again.

Trevor Johnson.

Ben Kelly, a great man despite what I say, and for the plans and the pictures too.

Bill and Ben at Morph.

Dave (Dee) Harman R.I.P.

Gill Smith R.I.P.

All at Urbis Museum Manchester.

All the bootleggers, it's a compliment . . . but.

Finally, all the customers of the Haçienda past and present and future and the wonderful people of Salford and Manchester, without you we'd be nothing!

Bibliography

The following were invaluable sources of reference and/or are recommended background reading.

Books

24 Hour Party People, Tony Wilson (Channel 4 Books)

Adventures on the Wheels of Steel: the Rise of the Superstar DJs, Dave Haslam (Fourth Estate)

Bernard Sumner: Confusion, David Nolan (Independent Music Press)

Energy Flash, Simon Reynolds (Picador)

From Joy Division to New Order, the True Story of Anthony H. Wilson and Factory Records, Mick Middles (Virgin)

Gang War: the Inside Story of the Manchester Gangs, Peter Walsh (Milo)

The Haçienda Must be Built, Jon Savage (ed.) (Independent Music Press)

High Life 'n' Low Down Dirty, the Thrills and Spills of Shaun Ryder, Lisa Verrico (Ebury)

I Swear I Was There, David Nolan (Independent Music Press)

Joy Division Piece by Piece, Paul Morley (Plexus)

Manchester, England, Dave Haslam (Fourth Estate)

My Magpie Eyes Have Seen the Prize, David Cavanagh (Virgin)

Plans and Elevations: Ben Kelly Design, Catherine McDermott (ed.) (ADT Designfile)

Rip it Up and Start Again, Simon Reynolds (Faber and Faber)

Shake, Rattle and Rain, C. P. Lee (Harding Simpole)

Touching from a Distance, Deborah Curtis (Faber and Faber)

Who Killed Martin Hannett? The Story of Factory Records' Musical Magician, Colin Sharp (Aurum)

Websites

Ben Kelly Design (www.benkellydesign.com)

Cerysmatic (www.cerysmaticfactory.info)

DJ History (www.djhistory.com)

Manchester District Music Archive (www.mdmarchive.co.uk)
New Order Online (www.neworderonline.com)
Pride of Manchester (www.prideofmanchester.com)

Sleeve-notes

Discotheque Volume 1: The Haçienda (a bootleg, the bastards), sleeve-notes by Tim Lawrence (Gut Records)
Chicago Acid and Experimental House 1985–1995, sleeve-notes by Tim Lawrence (Soul Jazz Records)

Stuff on the telly

24 Hour Party People (Dir. Michael Winterbottom)
A Very British Gangster (Dir. Donal MacIntyre)
New Order Play at Home (Dir. Don Coutts, Peter Orton, Dom Shaw)
Celebration: Madchester – The Sound of the North (Granada Television)
The Alcohol Years (Dir. Carol Morley)
Joy Division (Dir. Grant Gee)
Control (Dir. Anton Corbijn)

Index

INDEX

INDEX

INDEX

Enhanced Ebook of *The Haçienda* is now available for iPhone, iPad & iPod:

- full book you can carry in your pocket!

- includes full audiobook synchronised to the text

- plus exclusive material only found in the app!

- customisable fonts, unlimited bookmarks, full book-search and many more features

Go to http://bit.ly/Hacienda-app for more information

Created in partnership with Enhanced Editions Ltd.
http://www.enhanced-editions.com

Enhanced Editions